INDIVIDUAL AND GROUP THERAPY AND WORK WITH PARENTS IN ADOLESCENT PSYCHOTHERAPY

OTHER BOOKS BY RICHARD A. GARDNER

The Boys and Girls Book About Divorce

Therapeutic Communication with Children: The Mutual Storytelling Technique

Dr. Gardner's Stories About the Real World, Volume I

Dr. Gardner's Stories About the Real World, Volume II

Dr. Gardner's Fairy Tales for Today's Children

Understanding Children: A Parents Guide to Child Rearing

MBD: The Family Book About Minimal Brain Dysfunction

Psychotherapeutic Approaches to the Resistant Child

Psychotherapy with Children of Divorce

Dr. Gardner's Modern Fairy Tales

The Parents Book About Divorce

The Boys and Girls Book About One-Parent Families

The Objective Diagnosis of Minimal Brain Dysfunction

Dorothy and the Lizard of Oz

Dr. Gardner's Fables for Our Times

The Boys and Girls Book About Stepfamilies

Family Evaluation in Child Custody Litigation

Separation Anxiety Disorder: Psychodynamics and Psychotherapy

Child Custody Litigation: A Guide for Parents and Mental Health Professionals

The Psychotherapeutic Techniques of Richard A. Gardner

Hyperactivity, the So-Called Attention-Deficit Disorder, and the Group of MBD Syndromes

The Parental Alienation Syndrome and the Differentiation Between Fabricated and Genuine Child Sex Abuse

Psychotherapy with Adolescents

Family Evaluation in Child Custody Mediation, Arbitration, and Litigation

The Girls and Boys Book About Good and Bad Behavior

Sex Abuse Hysteria: Salem Witch Trials Revisited

The Parents Book About Divorce–Second Edition

The Parental Alienation Syndrome: A Guide for Mental Health and Legal Professionals

The Psychotherapeutic Techniques of Richard A. Gardner–Revised

Self-Esteem Problems of Children: Psychodynamics and Psychotherapy

True and False Accusations of Child Sex Abuse

Protocols for the Sex-Abuse Evaluation

Testifying in Court

Conduct Disorders of Childhood: Psychodynamics and Psychotherapy

Psychogenic Learning Disabilities: Psychodynamics and Psychotherapy

Psychotherapy with Sex-Abuse Victims: True, False, and Hysterical Dream Analysis in Psychotherapy

The Parental-Alienation Syndrome: A Guide for Mental Health and Legal Professionals–Second Edition

The Utilization of the Gardner Children's Projective Battery

INDIVIDUAL AND GROUP THERAPY AND WORK WITH PARENTS IN ADOLESCENT PSYCHOTHERAPY

RICHARD A. GARDNER, M.D.

JASON ARONSON INC.
Northvale, New Jersey
London

This book was printed and bound by Book-mart Press, Inc. of North Bergen, NJ.

The hardcover edition was entitled *Psychotherapy with Adolescents*

10 9 8 7 6 5 4 3 2 1

Library of Congress Cataloging-in-Publication Data

Gardner, Richard A.
Individual and group therapy and work with parents in adolescent psychotherapy / Richard A. Gardner.
p. cm.
Includes bibliographical references and index.
ISBN 0-7657-0207-X
1. Adolescent psychotherapy. 2. Group psychotherapy for teenagers. 3. Group psychotherapy. 4. Family psychotherapy.
I. Title.
RJ503.G377 1999
616.89'14'0835—dc21 98-53682

Printed in the United States of America on acid-free paper. For information and catalog write to Jason Aronson Inc., 230 Livingston Street, Northvale, NJ 07647-1726, or visit our website: www.aronson.com

I dedicate this book to

My teachers at The Bronx High School of Science and Columbia College.

Their formidable influence on me during my own adolescence—as teachers, models, and mentors—has served me well throughout the course of my life.

This book represents only one small derivative of their influence.

PSYCHOTHERAPY WITH ADOLESCENTS

A Series of Books by

Richard A. Gardner

VOLUME I:

Developmental Conflicts and Diagnostic Evaluation in Adolescent Psychotherapy

VOLUME II:

Individual and Group Therapy and Work with Parents in Adolescent Psychotherapy

VOLUME III:

Psychotherapy of Antisocial Behavior and Depression in Adolescence

CONTENTS

ACKNOWLEDGMENTS xiii

INTRODUCTION xv

1. CENTRAL ELEMENTS IN THE DEVELOPMENT OF PSYCHOGENIC SYMPTOMS AND PRIMARY FACTORS IN THE PSYCHOTHERAPEUTIC PROCESS 1

THE ORIGINS OF SYMPTOMS 2
THE THERAPY AS A WAY OF OPENING UP NEW OPTIONS 8
COMMENTS ON TIME-LIMITED THERAPY 10
THE THERAPIST–PATIENT RELATIONSHIP 13
Genuine Respect vs. Idealization and/or Idolization of the Therapist 14
Receptivity to the Therapist's Messages 15
Identification with and Emulation of the Therapist 15
Trying to Help Patients vs. Helping Patients 21
Therapy — An Educational Experience 28

The Therapist as Teacher 29
The Levels of Therapeutic Learning 29
WALT DISNEY'S PINOCCHIO AS A METAPHOR FOR THE PSYCHOTHERAPEUTIC PROCESS 34
CONCLUDING COMMENTS 40

2. THE THERAPIST–PATIENT RELATIONSHIP AND THE PSYCHOTHERAPEUTIC PROCESS 43

THE ADOLESCENT PATIENT'S PERSONALITY 44
Insight and Motivation 44
Dealing with the Adolescent Who Refuses to Attend the Initial Visit 46
Using Anger as a Vehicle for Self-Revelation 47
Final Comments on the Adolescent's Personality 47
THE THERAPIST'S PERSONALITY 48
Liking Children and Adolescents 49
Projection of Oneself into the Patient's Position 49
Frustration Tolerance 50
The Therapist as Parent 52
Memory of One's Own Childhood 52
Comfort with Patients' Anger 53
Comfort with Therapeutic Failure 54
The Therapist's Sex 54
Therapists Who Are Still Adolescents Themselves 55
Concluding Comments 56
FACTORS IN THE THERAPIST–PATIENT RELATIONSHIP CONDUCIVE TO BRINGING ABOUT THERAPEUTIC CHANGE 56
The Therapist's Affection for the Patient 57
"Unconditional Positive Regard" 60
Treatment of the Projected Self 63
Taking the Patient's Side in His or Her Conflict with the Parents 65
The Resolution of the Transference Neurosis 67
The Transference Cure 69
The Corrective Emotional Experience 71
The Patient's Identification with the Therapist 72

The Therapist as Educator 74
Intimacy and Self-Revelation 82

3. CONFIDENTIALITY 85

CONFIDENTIALITY IN ADULT THERAPY 86
CONFIDENTIALITY IN ADOLESCENT THERAPY 90
CONFIDENTIALITY IN CHILD PSYCHOTHERAPY 92
FURTHER COMMENTS ON CONFIDENTIALITY IN ADOLESCENT PSYCHOTHERAPY 95

4. INDIVIDUAL TREATMENT 99

ADOLESCENCE AS A PERIOD OF THERAPEUTIC RECEPTIVITY 100
BASIC TECHNICAL CONSIDERATIONS 102
Beginning the Therapeutic Session 102
The Therapist Bringing Up a Subject 103
Dealing with Silences 104
Dealing with Preoccupations of Parental Blame 107
Asking the Patient to Repeat What I Have Said 108
Asking to See My Notes and/or Chart 109
The Use of Contracts 111
Soda, Pretzels, and Candy 112
The Value of Philosophical Discussions 112
Learning from the Patient 114
Relating One's Own Personal Experiences to the Patient 116
Discouraging Pathological Use of the Treatment 116
"If You're Going to Take Something Away from Someone, You Should Give Him (Her) Something Back in Return" 119
The Comparison of the Therapist's Statements with the Parents' Statements 121
SEXUAL AND DATING PROBLEMS 122
The Therapist's Values Regarding Adolescent Sexual Activities 123
Helping Reluctant Boys Make Their Initial Dating Overtures 128
Helping Sexually Inhibited Boys 133
Helping Girls Who Feel Unattractive 136

Helping Promiscuous Girls 138
CLINICAL EXAMPLE OF A THERAPEUTIC REPORT 139

5. THE TALKING, FEELING, AND DOING GAME 149

THE BASIC FORMAT OF THE TALKING, FEELING, AND DOING GAME 149
EXAMPLES OF CARD RESPONSES 155
Talking Cards 155
Feeling Cards 163
Doing Cards 173
CONCLUDING COMMENTS 178

6. PSYCHOANALYTIC INQUIRY AND DREAM PSYCHOANALYSIS 181

THE USE OF THE TALKING, FEELING, AND DOING GAME IN FACILITATING PSYCHOANALYTIC INQUIRY 182
DREAM PSYCHOANALYSIS 186
The Purposes of Dreams 186
Teaching Adolescents How to Psychoanalyze Dreams 203
CLINICAL EXAMPLE OF DREAM PSYCHOANALYSIS 213

7. GROUP THERAPY 231

TYPES OF GROUP THERAPY 231
PRIMARY BENEFITS OF GROUP THERAPY 233
GROUP STRUCTURE AND TECHNICAL CONSIDERATIONS 234
The Question of Optimum Group Size 235
Homogeneous vs. Heterogeneous Groups 236
The Optimum Duration of the Group Meeting 237
After-Group Meeting Without the Therapist 238
A Comparison of the Three Levels of Child and Adolescent Group Therapy 238
Sibling Involvement 241
THE GROUP THERAPY EXPERIENCE 243
Preparing Newcomers for the Group 243

The First Meeting 245
Corrective Emotional Experiences 246
Peer Influences 249
Self-Esteem Enhancement 251
Encouraging Desensitization 254
Dealing with a Breach of Confidentiality 256

8. WORK WITH PARENTS 259

THE VALUE OF THE THERAPIST–PARENT BOND IN ENHANCING AN ADOLESCENT'S TREATMENT 260
PARENTAL COUNSELING REGARDING THE PATIENT 261
Counseling Parents of the Adolescent Who Tries to Preclude Their Involvement in Treatment 262
Parental Ambivalence about the Adolescent's Treatment 263
COMMON ADVICE GIVEN PARENTS OF ADOLESCENT PATIENTS 267
Differentiating between the Controllable and the Uncontrollable 267
Differentiating between Normal and Abnormal Behavior and Dealing with Noxious Normal Behavior 270
Discipline and Punishment 272
The College Disease 274
WAYS IN WHICH PARENTS (USUALLY THE MOTHER) CAN BY USEFUL IN AN ADOLESCENT'S INDIVIDUAL SESSIONS 277
SITUATIONS IN WHICH THE PARENT'S INVOLVEMENT IN THE TREATMENT IS CONTRAINDICATED 281
Excessively Punitive and Sadistic Parents
Psychologically Fragile Parents 281
Parents Who Exhibit Formidable Hostility Toward the Therapist 282
Overbearing, Intrusive Parents 283
The Parent with an Incurable Illness 284

CLINICAL EXAMPLE OF PARENTAL AND STEPPARENTAL INVOLVEMENT IN AN ADOLESCENT'S TREATMENT 285
DIRECT TREATMENT OF PARENTS 290

REFERENCES **293**

AUTHOR INDEX **297**

SUBJECT INDEX **299**

ACKNOWLEDGMENTS

I wish to express my gratitude to my secretaries, Linda Gould, Carol Gibbon, and Donna La Tourette for their dedication to the typing of the manuscript of this book in its various renditions. I am indeed fortunate to have such committed assistants. I am grateful, as well, to Robert Mulholland for his astute editing of the manuscript. He did more than edit; he gave good reasons for his changes and taught me some useful grammatical principles in the course of our work together. I appreciate the contributions of Jo-Nell Long and Elizabeth Quackenbush for their careful reading of the page proofs.

My greatest debt, however, is to my adolescent patients who have taught me much over the years about the kinds of problems they can have. From their parents, as well, I have learned much that is included here. Although their names and other identifying data have been disguised, their experiences have been recorded herein. My hope is that what I have learned from them will be put to good use through this series and will contribute to the prevention and alleviation of grief and stress in others.

INTRODUCTION

This volume begins with a statement of what I consider to be the central factors operative in the development of psychogenic symptoms and the therapeutic process that is designed to alleviate them. It is a statement of what I consider these factors to be at this point, after doing psychotherapy for over 40 years. It is crucial that therapists read this chapter if they are to understand optimally my psychotherapeutic approaches.

Chapter Two is devoted to a discussion of the factors that contribute to the development of a good therapist–patient relationship, without which there can be no meaningful psychotherapy. Although there can be productive electroconvulsive therapy, drug therapy, and even behavior modification without a good relationship between the therapist and patient, psychotherapy is not likely to be successful unless the relationship is a good one. When the therapist–patient relationship is impaired, there is no receptivity to what the therapist has to say, no emulation of him or her, and thereby no identification with the therapist's personality traits and values. And all of these processes are necessary if there is to be any therapeutic change.

Chapter Three deals with the topic of confidentiality. This is important to discuss because my therapeutic approach is one in which I work significantly with parents and other members of the youngster's family, both individually and in joint interviews. On the one hand, the adolescent needs work alone with the therapist as a step toward separation from the family and the development of autonomy. On the other hand, one still wants to have close relationships with family members because of the important therapeutic benefits to be derived from such involvement. There is a trade-off here and at times a dilemma. In this chapter I describe the position I take with regard to this issue.

Chapter Four is devoted to the technical details of conducting individual, face-to-face psychotherapy with adolescents. Although theoretical material is provided, the emphasis is on technical considerations. Numerous clinical vignettes complement the text and provide the examiner with clinical examples that demonstrate my theoretical principles. In Chapter Five I discuss in detail the utilization of *The Talking, Feeling, and Doing Game* in the treatment of adolescents, especially younger adolescents. Younger adolescents present a problem for the therapist. They are generally too old to involve themselves in projective play, especially doll play. Accordingly, these rich sources of information about the patient's underlying psychodynamics are not available to the therapist. Yet, the younger ones are not comfortable sitting in a room with a therapist, for 45 or 50 minutes, with his or her beady eyes staring and asking what they want to talk about. Older adolescents are much more receptive to such direct inquiries. *The Talking, Feeling, and Doing Game* provides younger adolescents with a vehicle that facilitates self-expression and revelation. My experience has been that many patients in this age bracket will ask to play the game and openly state that they play it because it "gives me ideas about things to talk about."

As mentioned, adolescents, because of their narcissism and introspective tendencies, may be excellent candidates for introspective psychotherapy. And some of them (especially those who are very bright) may be excellent candidates for psychoanalytic inquiry. Chapter Six focuses on this technique, with special emphasis on dream psychoanalysis. I present here what I consider to be an excellent statement of the different kinds of dreams and the functions they serve. Freud's contribution, in which he emphasized the wish-fulfillment function of dreams, cannot be underestimated. However, I believe that his view was a somewhat narrow one and he did not give enough attention to other functions that dreams serve — especially their function of alerting the dreamer to danger.

Of the three age groups, adolescents are the best candidates for group psychotherapy. Group therapy for younger children is most often a disaster because of their rambunctiousness, distractibility, and disinclination to sit around in a circle and talk about their problems. Adults are generally receptive to this sort of thing, but they are not as dependent on the opinions of their peers as is the adolescent. Adolescents are very much group enthusiasts. Their antennae are continually out searching for the signals emanating from their peers. They may distrust their therapists because they equate them with parents and others of that ilk, but they trust their peers who know what's "in" and what's "the latest." They join in with their peers in believing that adolescents are the incarnation of all the wisdom that has ever existed in the history of the human race. Accordingly, they are receptive to availing themselves of the sage advice that their fellow teenagers can provide them.

Chapter Seven is devoted to group therapy, the supreme form of therapy for the adolescent. These youngsters travel in groups and thrive in groups. Their dependency on their peers is a step up from their dependency on their parents and a step toward their ultimate autonomy and independence. Group therapy derives therapeutic mileage from this phenomenon. Therapists who do not utilize group therapy with adolescents are depriving themselves of a valuable therapeutic modality for youngsters in this age bracket. Of the three ages (childhood, adolescence, and adulthood), I consider group therapy to be most efficacious for the adolescent group. When one combines group therapy with individual therapy one has a valuable combination indeed, a combination that is certainly more than the sum of its parts.

Chapter Eight presents a description of the kinds of work I do with parents and the kinds of advice I provide them when working with their adolescents. The therapist who excludes close work with parents is making a serious mistake. One can still provide the adolescent with separate individual sessions, confidentiality, and other experiences necessary to develop autonomy, yet still have ongoing contact with the parents.

ONE

CENTRAL ELEMENTS IN THE DEVELOPMENT OF PSYCHOGENIC SYMPTOMS AND PRIMARY FACTORS IN THE PSYCHOTHERAPEUTIC PROCESS

The theoretical principles presented here regarding the origins of symptoms and the central elements in the psychotherapeutic process are applicable to children, adolescents, and adults. Although the general principles presented here apply to all three age categories, there are differences in the therapeutic application of these principles regarding the degree to which the therapist relies on the patient to make active contributions to the treatment. The younger the child, the more it behooves the therapist to actively elicit, encourage, and even suggest the ways in which the child should respond to particular life situations that are causing difficulties. The older the patient the more the therapist should encourage (and at times require) the patient to contribute the solutions to these life problems. But even with the most mature and healthy patient, an occasional suggestion and the judicious introduction of recommended solutions are warranted. Here I will focus on the ways in which these principles apply to the adolescent.

THE ORIGINS OF SYMPTOMS

I view symptoms to represent maladaptive and inappropriate ways of dealing with the problems of life which confront all of us. The patient's selections of solutions to these problems have originally been devised because they appeared to be the most judicious. What we refer to as psychodynamics are basically the pathways and processes by which these problems produce symptoms. Symptoms then can be viewed as the "tip of the iceberg"—the most superficial manifestations of the disease process. At the base of the iceberg are the fundamental problems of life for which the symptom represents an injudicious solution. Between the base and the tip of the iceberg are the processes by which the symptomatic solution is created. These processes are called psychodynamics.

The iceberg analogy holds because most of the etiological processes operative in symptom formation are not apparent to conscious awareness; it is as if they were submerged. (In the case of the iceberg, six-sevenths is under water.) What is above the surface is well viewed to be the conscious material (what is readily observable), and what is below the surface is well considered to be subconscious (not immediately in conscious awareness, but readily available to such scrutiny) and unconscious (not readily available to conscious awareness, but potentially so via such procedures as psychoanalytic therapy, especially dream psychoanalysis).

As an example of the above let us take Bob's situation. Bob is 14 years old and in the ninth grade. His social studies teacher has informed the class that there will be a big test the next day. Bob is quite upset about this because he was looking forward to watching his favorite television program. The problem then for Bob is whether he should watch his program or study for the test. If he indulges himself and watches the TV program he may get a low grade on the next day's examination. A good grade might only be obtained by his depriving himself of the television program. Bob is being confronted here with one of the common dilemmas of just about all school children. Bob is facing one of the fundamental problems of life which, like all such problems, lends itself well to the utilization of maladaptive solutions.

Bob decides to watch the program in the hope that he will be lucky enough to know the answers to the questions his teacher selects to give on the test (already we sense trouble, that is, a maladaptive solution). The next day, as luck would have it, Bob finds that he doesn't know the answers to most of the questions. In order to protect himself from the embarrassment and discomfort of getting a poor grade, he decides to copy from the paper of the girl sitting next to him. Such behavior is called *cheating,* a symptom. Like all symptoms, it is an inappropriate adaptation and may result in more trouble and discomfort for Bob than that which he would have suffered had he studied for the test and deprived himself of the gratifications of watching his favorite television program.

Now let us consider the possible outcomes of Bob's symptomatic resolution of this conflict. One outcome is that the teacher will catch him cheating, reprimand him, give him a failing grade, and possibly report the event to his parents. He may then suffer further disapprobation at home. Perhaps the teacher won't catch him but his classmates observe what he is doing. He may suffer from them a certain amount of criticism and alienation. Or, the girl from whom he is cheating may get angry at him, cover her paper, and then may reject him subsequently as a "cheater." Perhaps none of these occur and he appears to be "successful." However, when the grades come back, and Bob sees that he has gotten a high one, if he has anything approaching healthy superego development, he is likely to feel less proud of his high grade than he would have had he come by it honestly. In his heart he knows that it was not deserved and so he cannot enjoy the gratification he otherwise would have had he achieved his high grade by honest effort.

The possibility still remains, however, that Bob could have cheated and *not* suffered any of the above difficulties. Let us suppose there was no negative feedback from any of the aforementioned individuals (that is, "he got away with it") and his superego development was so limited that he suffered no guilt or remorse over his behavior—behavior that would generally be considered unacceptable in the classroom. But even then there would be the untoward effect of his not having gained the optimum benefit from his educational process. His failure to study would have deprived him of the information learned by those who had studied. Although this outcome might not have caused Bob any immediate discomfort, in the long run, especially if this pattern were repeated, Bob's education would suffer. Thus, the aforementioned principle still holds.

All of these outcomes are examples of the principle that the selection of the symptomatic solution generally results in the individual's suffering with more difficulties than he or she would have if the more judicious and healthy solution had been utilized. In this case it would have been Bob's deciding to forego the pleasures of television and appreciating that such deprivation would ultimately be less painful than the discomforts and embarrassments associated with the consequences of his cheating.

Another example: An adolescent boy doesn't have friends because of personality problems. However, he learns that he need not suffer loneliness very long if he provides peers with cash and other presents. His utilization of *bribery* (the name of the symptom) is seemingly successful in that he now finds himself more popular. He enjoys thereby an alleviation of his painful feelings of loneliness. However, his pleasure is compromised by the inner knowledge that his friends are being bought and that they would not be there if he did not have the wherewithal to pay them off. In addition, his position is a precarious one because he does not have a steady supply of bribes to insure that he will not once again be lonely. And this unstable feeling also compromises his pleasure. At some level he probably senses that his "friends" do not basically respect him, and this cannot but lower his feelings of self-worth. Last, if and when he does run out of bribes (the usual case), he cannot but feel "used." Bribing, the psychopathological symptom, was devised in an attempt to deal with the common human problem of loneliness. Ostensibly, it served its purpose of providing friends; however, it was an injudicious selection. As is usually the case when psychopathological symptoms are used to resolve a problem, the individual usually ends up being worse off than he or she was before.

Jim is afraid to try out for his high school's basketball team. He fantasizes public humiliation if he misses a basket or drops a ball in the course of the game's action. Jim is a well-coordinated boy, and there is no reason to believe that he would humiliate himself. He chooses to take the safe course, doesn't try out for the team, and thereby protects himself from his anticipated humiliations. The solution that Jim has chosen does "work" in that he doesn't suffer the tensions he would have experienced had he joined. However, he suffers even worse repercussions as a result of his withdrawal. He becomes somewhat lonely in that when his friends are playing basketball he has little to do. But more important, he has deprived himself of the ego-enhancing gratifications that he would have gained as the result of his participation. He has deprived himself of the joys of playing well in an area in which he has every reason to believe he would have been competent.

There is an extremely important principle demonstrated here that pervades many aspects of living. Most new things are anxiety provoking. The healthy person tolerates such fear with the knowledge that it is usually transient and that the benefits to be derived outweigh the loss of joy and ego-enhancement to be suffered from failure to act. The philosophy is epitomized in the aphorism: *Nothing ventured, nothing gained.* All individuals can choose the safe course and avoid risk and anxiety. In the extreme, the individual psychologically digs a hole in the ground, hides therein, thereby protecting him- or herself from the vast majority of life's inevitable rejections, disappointments, indignities, and traumas. However, a heavy price is paid for such "safety." One leads an extremely boring existence, and one is deprived of the ego-enhancement that comes from accomplishment. Again, the psychopathological solution to this problem causes the individual more difficulty than he or she would have suffered had the healthier course been pursued.

Another example: While playing alone with a ball, Jane, age 13, accidentally breaks a neighbor's window. To the best of her knowledge, no one has observed the incident. A conflict is immediately set up. On the one hand, she would like to run away as fast as she can and thereby avoid any responsibility or repercussions for the damage. On the other hand, part of her appreciates that such flight would be "wrong" and that she would not respect herself for doing so. Furthermore, she might be observed and then would suffer punishment for having "run from the scene of the crime." Jane decides to take her chances and run as fast as she can. She gets home and breathes a sigh of relief. To the best of her knowledge she was unobserved, and she feels that she has "gotten away with it." However, there is some lingering guilt as well as fear that she might have been seen and that word of her misdeed will ultimately get to her parents. So even at this stage the pathological course is not without its negative repercussions. She is enjoying the pleasure of not having to own up to her responsibility for her transgression, but her pleasure is compromised by her guilt and fear of disclosure. Of course, if her superego development has been impaired, she will not suffer this guilt and she truly will have "gotten away with it." Last, if she were observed, and the incident is reported to her parents, then she is likely to suffer repercussions for her flight.

Had she gone to the neighbor and reported the incident, she would probably have been respected and even praised for her honesty, even though the neighbor might have been angry as well. If she offered to pay for the window, she would have to suffer the privations attendant to such payment. However, this negative element would have been more than offset by the ego-enhancement that comes with the knowledge that one is doing the "right" thing. In addition, she might have been praised by others for her honesty, and this could further enhance feelings of self-worth. She would have avoided the guilt and fear of detection that she might have suffered following the commission of her "crime." The ancient aphorism *honesty is the best policy* is not trite. There is great wisdom in it. The honest course usually (though certainly not always) is the best course because its advantages usually outweigh its disadvantages. People who utilize psychopathological mechanisms for resolving disputes may not be aware of this ancient truth.

Mary, at 15, finds herself quite lonely. Because of shyness and passivity, she has few friends and has not developed the repertoire of information about her adolescent world that makes her an interesting person to be with. She learns that providing boys with sexual gratifications enhances her popularity immensely. Whereas prior to her "liberalization" she got little attention from them, afterwards the telephone hardly stopped ringing. Although she obtained little if any gratification from sexual intercourse, she did enjoy somewhat the carressing and even more the enhanced popularity she was now experiencing. Mary's promiscuity (the name given to this symptom), like all symptoms, has many drawbacks which she may not wish to recognize. She may not appreciate that the boys are attracted to her primarily, if not exclusively, because of the ease with which they can obtain sexual gratifications and basically have little or no respect for any other aspect of her personality. This cannot but be humiliating. And, when she allows herself to appreciate the basic reasons for her popularity, she cannot but feel "used." Furthermore, she has to come to recognize the fact that once she starts to preserve her sense of pride and withholds the sexual favors, she may find herself lonely as she is depriving her so-called boyfriends of the one and only thing they want from her. And, not incidentally, she may pick up a sexually transmitted disease or become pregnant as a result of her pathological utilization of sexual behavior.

Jim, an 18-year-old, is very dissatisfied with his boss at the fast-food restaurant where he is employed. The situation has reached the point where he often dreads going to work because of the indignities he suffers while on the job. Jim is a somewhat timid person who fears expressing resentment. He feels that if he were to assert himself with his employer he might lose his job. In addition, even if he were not to lose his job, he is afraid of his boss's anger. These fears contribute significantly to his failure to assert himself and to discuss in a civilized manner the problems he has with his employer. Most often (but not always) such failure to assert oneself is pathological. It is a heavy price to pay for job security and protection from the possible resentment of the person to whom a complaint is directed.

A healthier course for this boy would be to assert himself and make reasonable attempts to resolve the conflict with his boss. If he is successful in this regard, he will have accomplished his goal of a better work relationship with his boss. In addition, he will have reduced, if not eliminated, his loathing of work as well as the self-loathing that comes with repression and suppression of pent-up resentment. He will enjoy the sense of well-being that comes with successful resolution of a problem. However, such assertion could conceivably result in his being fired. This repercussion will have to be taken into consideration before he decides to assert himself. Having made the decision to act, he must bear this risk. He might even have to suffer the discomforts of trying to find another job, and he might not even be able to find one. He has to consider the discomforts and loss of self-worth that come with unemployment. Although these are certainly formidable negative repercussions of self-assertion, he would at least be free from the self-loathing and the painful effects of not expressing his resentments.

Ruth, a 19-year-old teller in a bank, makes an error. Although some discrepancy will ultimately be detected in the accounting process, the person who caused the error may not readily be identified. Ruth knows that if she reveals the error, there might be some criticism and reprimand. However, her position is such that it is extremely unlikely that she would lose her job. Moreover, if she says nothing, there may be no repercussions because the process of detecting the person who made the error is so cumbersome that the company accountants may not wish to go to the trouble. Or, another person might be falsely implicated. She decides to say nothing. During the ensuing days she hears talk about the repercussions of her mistake and the resentment felt by her superiors toward the individual (still unknown) who could have been so careless. Although "innocent," she suffers with the fear of disclosure and some guilt. Had she admitted the error, there would have been criticism, but no job loss and no ongoing fear of being caught. The pathological way seemed easier at first but ended up being the more difficult course.

I do not claim that the examples given above explore in great depth all the ramifications of a psychopathological act. They focus on the symptom as a manifestation of the individual's attempt to find the solution to a common, if not universal, life problem. They demonstrate how the pathological solution causes the person more trouble than the healthy one. The examples have not focused on the complex psychodynamic factors that play a role in determining whether the individual chooses the healthy or pathological adaptations to the conflict. Nor have I elucidated the psychodynamic pattern by which the fundamental conflict brings about symptomatic solution.

THERAPY AS A WAY OF OPENING UP NEW OPTIONS

Therapy involves helping people learn better ways of dealing with life's inevitable conflicts and problems. Therapy must open up new options—options that may not have been considered by the patient previously, options that may not have been part of his or her repertoire. The utilization of these more adaptive solutions *over time* lessens the likelihood that the patient will have to resort to the maladaptive, symptomatic solutions. Let us take Bob's case, for example, the previously discussed boy who cheated on tests. If Bob were in therapy, it would be important for the therapist to help Bob appreciate the various consequences that might result from his cheating. He would do well to help Bob figure out *himself* the variety of discomforts and inconveniences he would suffer as a result of the symptom. We would do well to ask Bob first to try to predict what these would be and then, after Bob could not provide any more, the therapist would suggest others for his consideration. Between the two of them, they should be able to come up with a list of the various consequences previously mentioned, such as alienation of the child from whom Bob was copying, alienation of those who observed the cheating, actions taken by the principal, measures possibly taken by his parents, the loss of the opportunity to enjoy the esteem-enhancing experience of a high grade, and the compromise of his education. Furthermore, if Bob were exhibiting psychopathic tendencies, then the therapist would do well to make attempts to fan any sparks of superego development that might nevertheless be present. Here the attempt would be to help Bob appreciate *in advance* how short-sighted was his decision to indulge himself in television viewing without giving serious consideration to the potential consequences of his utilizing the cheating solution. The hope here would be that the next time he is confronted with such a conflict, his knowledge of the consequences might play a role in his choosing the more judicious course.

In the course of such a discussion, the therapist might have asked Bob if he could think of any other solution to his dilemma. If Bob's family owned a video cassette recorder, then the option of making a videotape of the program and studying at the same time could have been discussed. Then, he could watch the program on the weekend and so both television watching and studying would have been accomplished. Or, if Bob himself doesn't own a videocassette recorder, he could be asked if he had a friend who might be prevailed upon to tape the program for him. The video tape recorder resolution, then, becomes a new option—an option that may not have previously been considered by Bob. Once utilized, this solution might become an automatic consideration for Bob when confronted in the future with this conflict. Although this new option originated in treatment, it can now become a part of Bob's repertoire.

In each of the other examples, the therapist could have helped the patient consider healthier options. The boy who used bribes to gain "friendships" could have been helped to appreciate the precariousness of his situation and the lowered feeling of self-worth that comes from being so utilized. Jim, the boy who was afraid to join the basketball team, could have been helped to appreciate the wisdom of "nothing ventured, nothing gained"—that those who do not venture forth will often lead very lonely and unrewarding lives. Jane, the girl who accidentally broke a neighbor's window, could have been helped to appreciate that it was ultimately to her benefit to take the initially painful but more courageous course of admitting her guilt. And the youngster who was dissatisfied with his boss could be helped to appreciate that the security and ego-enhancement potentially derived from healthy and civilized self-assertion are much more likely to outweigh the risks and disadvantages associated with passive submission. Ruth, the teller in the bank, could have been helped to appreciate the wisdom of the "honesty is the best policy" aphorism.

COMMENTS ON TIME-LIMITED THERAPY

I do not believe that one can tell in advance how long therapy will take. One cannot know whether or not the patient will be receptive to the therapeutic messages and experiences, and, even if so, how long it will take until they become incorporated into the psychic structure. Therapy is best viewed as just another life experience, having much in common with the kinds of experiences one has outside the therapeutic situation. Although there are some differences, there are more similarities. The main difference is that the therapist (it is hoped) is sensitive to psychological processes that the average person is not appreciative of. If the therapy does indeed turn out to be short, then I am quite pleased. But one cannot know in advance how long it will take. Anyone who claims to know is, in my opinion, simple-minded and/or grandiose. There are certain things in life that cannot be quantified in advance, and therapy is one of them.

Furthermore, the imposed time limits are likely to compromise significantly the nature of the work accomplished in each of the sessions. If the patient is watching the clock, is pressured into working quickly, and is trying to figure out a solution to a particular problem within time limitations, it is likely that the solutions so derived will be injudiciously selected. The patient who is involved in time-limited therapy is likely to be watching his or her watch during the course of each session and counting the number of sessions until "cure." This counting process is inevitably going to reduce the likelihood that the therapy will be successful. While preoccupied with the ticking clock, the patient is being distracted from focussing on the problems for which he or she is being treated. And the therapist, too, may also be involved in the same process.

If a boy were to call up a girl and ask her in advance to go out with him for ten dates and then break up, he would be considered strange. If a man asked a woman to marry him for 12 days, weeks, months, or even years – and then to divorce – he would probably be considered by the woman to be insane. Yet the same kind of arrangement is frequently made between therapists and patients, and there are many who do not consider this absurd. Sometimes the figure regarding the number of allotted treatment sessions is derived from some statistical analysis of the number of sessions that patients in the same clinic received for the treatment of that particular disorder. To me, this is like saying that the average marriage in a given community lasts 12.5 years; therefore, it is recommended that people commit themselves to a marital union of exactly that duration.

It is not that I do not do brief psychotherapy. I do it all the time, but I only do it in situations where happily it takes place. It occurs in situations where I cannot know beforehand how long the treatment will take, and in some cases it does indeed turn out to be brief. But I have never promised it would be brief at the outset because I could not know the degree to which the parties would cooperate, whether or not a relationship would be established, whether there would be receptivity to what I had to say, and what things would come up in the course of the treatment.

Psychotherapy in which a patient is told at the outset that a specific number of sessions is all that will be required is basically a "rip off" by clinical administrators on a gullible public. Such therapy is an administrative maneuver that satisfies those who are funding the clinic and who are often quite naive regarding what therapy is all about. It is one way of rationalizing giving a little therapy to a lot of people rather than a lot of therapy to a select few. If one is going to do this, then one should at least be honest and let people know that they are getting a watered-down form of treatment. Time-limited therapy is mainly for the poor, who often have little choice. People who are in better financial positions most often get as much treatment as they need. And those rich people who do opt for brief psychotherapy are often the naive and gullible ones, those who, despite their financial positions, are still simple-minded enough to be attracted to this absurd form of treatment.

Unfortunately, there are therapists who recognize the validity of what I have said here, but appreciate that their job security rests on their adherence to the time-limited therapy concept. Even worse, there are others who actually believe that such therapy is as good as long-term treatment because of their desire to bring about quick cures or to satisfy other pathological needs. Last, and most important, the main flaw in time-limited therapy is that it loses sight of the importance of the development of a good therapist-patient relationship as the foundation upon which treatment is built. Relationships must evolve *over time;* they cannot be expected to develop in accordance with a fixed schedule.

The reader may have noticed that in the above discussion on therapy as a way of opening up new options, the words *over time* are italicized. My purpose here is to emphasize the point that meaningful therapeutic changes are not likely to take place quickly. Although there are rare occasions when a brief encounter with the therapist can bring about long-term therapeutic results, such situations are unusual. Therapy first requires the establishment of a meaningful therapist-patient relationship. In the context of such a relationship, therapeutic messages are received by the patient with receptivity and therapeutic experiences take place that, when repeated over time, bring about personality change. Freud feared that psychoanalysis would degenerate in the United States because of the lack of patience that Americans had for solutions that might require a long-term investment of time and energy. He feared that the method would be bastardized by a wide variety of quick and seemingly attractive short cures. And he was right. Short-term methods of treatment have sprung up everywhere and promise better, more rapid, and less expensive results than long-term psychoanalytic therapy or psychoanalysis. I consider this to be a deplorable development. It is not that I do not have criticisms of psychoanalytic treatment (many have been and will continue to be presented in this book); it is only that I am critical of quick methods of treatment, especially those that promise results in a prescribed period of time, even before the patient's problems are known.

Short-term and brief psychotherapies are very much in vogue. Often a specific time limit is imposed upon the patient from the outset. Ten to 15 sessions is a common figure. The selection of such a number demonstrates complete ignorance of what I consider to be a crucial requirement of meaningful psychotherapy. One cannot possibly know how long it will take to develop the kind of relationship in which meaningful therapy is most likely to be productive.

THE THERAPIST-PATIENT RELATIONSHIP

If patients are to experience an alleviation (the reader should note that I did not use the word *cure* here) of the presenting symptomatology, it is highly desirable that both the therapist and the patient possess certain qualities. The importance of the therapist-patient relationship in therapy is often spoken of. However, the specific personality qualities that are important for each to possess and the ways in which these bring about symptomatic alleviation and therapeutic change are not often elaborated upon. The main reason for this, I believe, is that these issues have not been studied to the degree that is warranted. I present here a few of the important elements that I consider necessary to be present in each party if therapy is to be meaningful. Only basic principles will be presented here. In Chapter Two I will discuss these in greater detail.

Genuine Respect vs. Idealization and/or Idolization of the Therapist

The patient should be reasonably respectful of the therapist because of *actual* qualities that the therapist has that engender such respect. Idealization (viewing the therapist as perfect) and idolizing (viewing as God-like, worthy of worship) of the therapist is anti-therapeutic in that it creates unfavorable comparisons with the therapist that are ego-debasing to the patient. Such a view of the therapist reduces the likelihood that the patient will relate realistically to other human beings who will inevitably reveal qualities that will be considered deficiencies by the patient. The classical analytic model, especially, is likely to result in such distortions of the therapist. One might argue that the kind of "blank screen" created by the analyst sitting behind the couch will provide him or her with the "purest" kinds of free associations, which are less likely to be contaminated by input from the analyst. However, whatever benefits there are to be derived from this approach (and I do not deny that they exist), there is a heavy price to be paid for them—a price that far outweighs the benefits. As stated, one of the prices is that the patient, having been studiously deprived of vital information about the therapist, is likely to view him or her as being perfect or close to it. This is intrinsically ego-debasing because it produces unfavorable comparisons between the patient and the therapist. Feelings of low self-worth are intrinsically associated with most (if not all) forms of psychogenic psychopathology. Idealizing and idolizing the therapist only adds to this disparity. Furthermore, this unreal atmosphere interferes with the patient's relating to others in the world who will inevitably reveal their deficits (real or so-viewed by the patient) and who will not provide the patient with the same kind of accepting and tolerant environment that the therapist provides.

We live in a world where certain conspiracies of silence are prevalent. When speaking with someone in a social situation it is generally considered inappropriate to criticize directly the individual's spouse or analyst. A woman, for example, may meet someone at a cocktail party who tells her that she has marital problems and that she is in treatment with Dr. X. The listener may know that Dr. X's general reputation at the hospital is that every one of his five wives despised him. In addition, two of them might have been personal friends of hers so she knows first-hand that this is the case. Yet, she may not reveal any of this information to Dr. X's patient, lest she "rock the boat" and/or compromise the treatment. I believe that it would be far better for the listener to present the information that she has about Dr. X, even at the risk of its being somewhat distorted. The information would certainly serve as "grist for the mill" during the next session. As a result of the patient's confronting her therapist with this information, there could be one of two outcomes. The patient might decide to leave the therapist, from the recognition that his personality deficiencies are so grave that it is not likely he can be of help to her—especially in the treatment of her marital problems. Or, she might decide to stay in treatment because of the appreciation that Dr. X still has enough on the positive side to warrant his remaining an effective therapist. ("No one is perfect.") In either case she is less likely to view him as a perfect person, and this cannot but be therapeutic.

Receptivity to the Therapist's Messages

The patient should be receptive to the therapist's comments, but not to the point of gullibility. If there has been no idealization or idolizing of the therapist, then there is less likely to be gullibility. If there is a good relationship and genuine respect, that is, respect based on genuine qualities that the therapist actually possesses and exhibits (as opposed to fantasized ones), then there is a greater likelihood there will be healthy receptivity. Respect must be earned, and healthy respect is not likely to be earned in a fantasized relationship; it is based instead on knowledge of both a person's assets and liabilities. When there is healthy respect, the balance tips in favor of those qualities that engender respect in others. In such situations people recognize another's liabilities but consider them small in comparison to assets. It is only by judicious revelation of deficiencies that such genuine respect is likely to evolve.

Identification with and Emulation of the Therapist

There should be a reasonable desire to emulate qualities in the therapist that would serve the person well in life. (This may be conscious or unconscious.) As a result of such emulation, there will be some identification with the therapist's traits and values. I do not believe that there is any psychotherapeutic interchange that does not involve some attempt on the therapist's part to transmit his or her own values to the patient. It is hoped that the values and qualities so taken on will be in the patient's best interests.

There are many who take issue with what I have just said about identification with the therapist's traits and values. Many have been taught in their training that one should strictly avoid doing or saying anything, either implicitly or explicitly, that involves the communication of, let alone imposition of, the therapist's values on the patient. I believe that this is well-meaning but injudicious advice. I cannot imagine a psychotherapeutic interchange that does not involve, at some level, the process of transmission of the therapist's values to the patient. Even in silence such imposition is taking place. Implicit in the therapist's silence is the message: "What you're saying is all right with me. I don't think it warrants any comment on my part. I don't have any books that say it is unhealthy, inappropriate, unreasonable, or otherwise maladaptive."

When we use the word *values* we refer to that which we consider to be good and bad, right and wrong. The therapist is continually making such judgments. At times, however, the terms sick and healthy may be utilized. But even here, values are intrinsically present in that what we refer to as psychopathological is basically an opinion regarding whether or not the behavior is good or bad, right or wrong. And this is very much determined by the "eye of the beholder." Parents bring a 14-year-old youngster to the psychotherapist with the complaint that, although of superior intelligence, he shows little academic motivation or curiosity. The therapist, after detailed inquiry into the family life, decides that the child has psychological problems that stem from family difficulties. The therapist recommends a therapeutic approach in which the child is treated individually along with active work with the family. The goal here is to reduce those family tensions and pressures that are contributing to the child's difficulties. The goal, as well, is to help the child himself deal with these family stresses in such a way that academic performance returns to the expected level.

By the therapist's agreeing to treat this patient, he or she is implicitly subscribing to the value judgment that education is a "good" thing and that those who do not avail themselves of their educational opportunities are doing a "bad" thing. One could argue that this is only the therapist's personal opinion. One could say (as many in our society do) that all one needs to do in life is to learn how to sign an X on one's welfare check. Under these circumstances, one will receive (in cash, goods, and services) almost as much as the average working man or woman (especially woman) or perhaps 10% to 15% less. By agreeing to treat this child and help this child reach his academic potential, the therapist is implicitly subscribing to the parents' value judgment that education is a "good" thing. I personally happen to share this value, but I am very clear that it is a value nevertheless.

Another example: A 35-year-old man enters treatment with complaints of depression and excessive drinking. He fears that he may become an alcoholic. In the course of the history taking, the therapist learns that the man's father died when he was in grade school and that he is an only child. Although 35, he still lives with his mother. He does not consider this to be a problem; rather he states that he and his mother have agreed that both would be unreceptive to a therapeutic approach that might ultimately result in his leaving home. It may be the therapist's opinion (supported by many books in his library) that this man has an "unresolved Oedipus complex" and that he is far too old to be living with his mother. Consistent with this opinion, one of the aims of therapy should be to help this man "resolve his Oedipus complex," move out of the house, meet a woman, get married, and have children—like other normal, healthy human beings. Although I am in agreement with this goal (even though I might not agree that the man's problems relate to the so-called "Oedipus complex"), I recognize that my position on this subject is still a value judgment. An anthropologist might say that there is an island in the South Pacific where people do this routinely. (There is always an island in the South Pacific where one can justify practically any conclusion regarding human behavior!)

Another therapist might think: "He's right. Stay there living with your mother. You'll never meet anyone who'll treat you as well—no matter how long you live." Still another might take the position: "You're doing a smart thing. Never get married. Women will just take advantage of you. Go out with them; have a good time; enjoy sex with as many as you can; but don't tie yourself down." Yet another says: "Homosexuality is where it's all at. My goal will be to get this guy out of that house into a good relationship with a man who will give him the kind of real love that a woman just can't provide." Yet another thinks that communes are the only sane arrangements and plans to lead the patient in that direction. Last, and certainly not the least common, is the one who says: "I will make no value judgments whatsoever about this arrangement. If he and his mother are happy with this arrangement, who am I to judge it as bad, wrong, sick, or sinful. Unless he expresses some kind of dissatisfaction, I will say nothing at all about it throughout the course of his treatment. I'll just stick to the things that bother him, namely, the depression and drinking." All of these people would be imposing their values on the patient. Even the one who claims to be strictly neutral and nonjudgmental is still going to have an effect on the patient. Under the therapist's influence the patient will maintain the status quo, which is still an option that presents a value. Neutrality is no less a position than advocating either side. It is still a statement; it still has its effects on those who are looking for input from the allegedly neutral person.

One last example. A number of years ago I saw in therapy a man who requested treatment for insomnia, tension, and depressive episodes. He commanded an extremely high salary working for a large and famous advertising agency. He spent most of his day making up songs, jingles, and clever sales pitches. He was viewed by his superiors and clients as one of the most creative men in the business. After working with the patient a few weeks, I informed him that he had to make an important decision. I told him that I considered him to have a formidable problem into which he had practically no insight. Specifically, I considered him to have a deficiency in guilt-evoking mechanisms which, if they were to be present, would produce guilt over the way he was spending his life, namely, trying to engender in people cravings to buy things that they would have little or no use for. I told him that if he were to continue in treatment with me I would try to instill in him guilt and embarrassment over the fraudulent life he was leading. And, if I were successful, he might quit his job and thereby become unemployed. In short, if he were to continue with me he might have to think very seriously about finding another career, one that was more honest and less exploitive—either within or outside of the field of advertising. I was not surprised that the man quit. He told me that he considered me out of touch with the real world and that he would find a therapist who could help him with his problems and not tamper with what he considered to be a healthy life style and ethical (because it was not illegal) career. I fully appreciate that my own personal values were operative here when I confronted the patient; however, I also believe that the next therapist who promised not to tamper with his career (and I am sure he found one) was also operating under a different value system and transmitting *his* value to the patient (in this case by silence on the career issue).

Again, my point here is that the therapist cannot take a position on a therapeutic issue without an implicit attempt to impose his or her own values on the patient. In short we must be honest about the fact that we are "brainwashing" our patients. We must also accept the fact that in the context of such brainwashing, many patients have been done terrible disservices and much grief has been caused by such impositions. In contrast, many have been exposed to healthier values—for some it may have been for the first time in their lives—which have enriched them and made them better human beings, to themselves and those who have the good fortune to encounter them.

Accordingly, therapy is a very "risky business." This problem of value imposition is further compounded by the fact that whether or not one sees something as good or bad is highly individualized and strongly determined by what the therapist brings to the situation, that is, his or her own anticipations, hopes, and even neurotic distortions. The point is well made by the anecdote of the rabbi who dies and finds himself in the hereafter, but he doesn't know whether he's in heaven or hell. He's not experiencing very much pain, so he decides he's probably not in hell. But he's not enjoying very much pleasure either, so he concludes that he's probably not in heaven. As he's groping about, trying to determine where he is, he suddenly sees coming out of the distant cloud none other than Rabbi Isaac Cohen (his mentor from the Talmudic Academy, dead now these 30 years). Rabbi Cohen, he well recalls, was one of the most religious and pious men he ever knew. In his 87 years in life he never broke one rule, so pious was he. Happily, he runs toward his mentor. He then notices that standing next to the old, stooped man's side is a beautiful, young, voluptuous woman—obviously the old rabbi's companion. The two rabbis embrace, tears running down their cheeks, happy to see one another after all these years.

At this point, the younger rabbi states: "Rabbi Cohen, it's so good to see you here. I've been roaming about, lost. I didn't know whether I was in heaven or hell. But it's obvious that if you are here, this must be heaven! A more religious and pious man never lived. It's obvious, also, that this beautiful, young voluptuous woman is God's reward to you for all the good works you've done on earth."

To which the old rabbi replies: "I'm sorry to have to tell you, rabbi, two things. First, this is not heaven, this is *hell.* And second, this beautiful, gorgeous, voluptuous woman is *not* God's reward to me. I am her punishment!"

The anecdote demonstrates my point that the aspirations and hopes that one brings to a situation are going to be an important determinant of how one interprets it. Shakespeare's Hamlet put it well: "There's nothing either good or bad, but thinking makes it so." The point is demonstrated again in a wonderful scene from the Woody Allen movie, *Annie Hall.* In a split-screen vignette, Woody Allen is on one side complaining to his psychoanalyst; and Diane Keaton is on the other side, complaining to her analyst. Woody is complaining bitterly about Diane's lack of sexual receptivity to him. He complains about how "up tight" she is and how painful is his ongoing state of sexual frustration. The deprivation is driving him crazy and he's practically tearing his hair out so distraught is he over his sexual privation. When the analyst asks him how often he is having sexual relations, he replies, "Imagine, only two or three times a week."

At the same time, Diane Keaton is complaining that Woody is continually bothering her with his sexual advances, from the moment he gets up in the morning, throughout the course of the day, until the moment he goes to sleep at night. He rarely gives her any peace. In the course of her complaining she refers to him as an animal. After further complaints about Woody's insatiable lust, her analyst asks Diane how frequently she is having sexual relations. To which she replies, "Imagine, two to three times a week, the beast." It is indeed "the eye of the beholder" that determines whether something is good or bad, right or wrong. Therapists are no exception. Our value judgments are colored by our own experiences, anticipations, and aspirations. And these inevitably will be transmitted to our patients. Let us hope that we don't do too much damage.

Most have heard at some time or other anecdotes about people who are looking for "the secret of life"—the one great wisdom under which is encompassed all the meaning of life's experiences. The jokes and/or stories often involve seeking the secret from some guru, often seated in some mountain cave in India or high in the Himalayas. Finally after a long circuitous route, during which time the individual may be exposed to many dangers, the wise man is finally confronted with the question: "What is the secret (or meaning) of life?" Well, I have the answer here for the reader. (Remember, it was I who told it to you.) The secret of life is this: *Life is a Rorschach test!* Yes, that's it. Life is a Rorschach test. Under this dictum one can subsume all psychological experiences of life. In every experience there is the reality and there is the interpretation that we make of it, depending upon our own psychic structure. There is the Rorschach inkblot, and there is the patient's projection which gives meaning to the inkblot. There is the external reality, and there is the interpretation we give to it. And there is yet another level here, namely, the *interpretation* the psychologist gives to the patient's projection. This reflects his or her values (whether the projection is "sick" or "healthy") and must also be considered part of the reality. There is the glass of water, and there is our interpretation as to whether it is half empty or half full, or whatever other meaning we want to give to it. The reality then is not simply an external entity. Rather, it is a *combination* of an external entity and the meaning and interpretation that our internal psychic structure gives to it. The two together then determine our thoughts, feelings, and actions. Let us hope that our projections and our interpretations of what is good and bad for our patients will serve them well.

Trying to Help Patients vs. Helping Patients

The therapist should have a genuine desire to help the patient. There should be a reasonable degree of empathy (an intellectual process) and sympathy (an emotional resonance) with the patient.

Therapists should have a reasonable capacity to identify with their patients, that is, put themselves in their patients' positions to view situations from their vantage point. The therapist's goal should be that of *trying* to help the patient, but he or she should not feel that the failure to do so represents a failure in him- or herself. I have emphasized the word *trying* because many therapists consider it their goal to "cure" patients or to bring about significant improvements. Many such therapists suffer with what I call *The Statue of Liberty syndrome.* This name is derived from a poem, written by Emma Lazarus, and placed at the base of the statue when it arrived in this country in 1886. It says:

> Give me your tired, your poor,
> Your huddled masses yearning to breathe free,
> The wretched refuse of your teeming shore,
> Send these, the homeless,
> the tempest-tossed to me.
> I lift my lamp beside the golden door.

These lines are certainly inspiring. With the exception of those who are North American Indians and those who otherwise trace their heritage to pre-Columbian days, all of us are either immigrants ourselves, or are the descendants of immigrants, either recent or remote. And these forebears of ours did not generally sail away from foreign shores in their yachts. Rather they often fled a variety of persecutions and other indignities because of their religion, political beliefs, skin color, or poverty. This principle, however noble, is extended by many mental health professionals to:

> Give me your chronic hebephrenic schizophrenics,
> Your alcoholics, your drug addicts, your criminals,
> Your psychopaths, your prostitutes, your criminally insane,
> And all your other rejects from society.
> I will give them sympathy, empathy, and understanding.
> With analytically oriented psychotherapy,
> I will help them gain insight into the underlying psychological processes that cause their disorders.
> And with such treatment I will raise them to new heights of mental health.

Those therapists who exhibit manifestations of *The Statue of Liberty syndrome,* whether they realize it or not, are placing formidable demands upon themselves. They are doomed to suffer frustration because their claims are impossible to achieve. The pathology that we deal with (even the less severe types) is generally generations in the making, and it is therefore grandiose on the part of anyone to believe that he or she can help more than a small fraction of those who come our way.

We generally interview parents of our child patients, and often get information about grandparents. But we rarely get information about earlier generations. Yet, it is naive to assume that the influences of these ancestors have not played a role in our patients' pathology. Furthermore, we are often impotent to change the formidable social and cultural factors that are likely to have played a role in the development of our patients' psychopathology. Accordingly, therapists do well to have very modest goals in regard to the treatment of their patients. We should be comfortable with small changes. To believe that we can do more is to impose upon ourselves goals that may be extremely frustrating for us. The therapist's goal should be that of *trying.* The therapist should be able to say, after a failure, that he or she has worked to the best of his or her ability. That is all that we can ask of ourselves and that is all that our patients should be asking of us.

Those who are afflicted with *The Statue of Liberty syndrome* are welcomed by various individuals in our society. Jails are overcrowded and judges are happy to learn about people who claim that they will bring about the prevention of criminal recidivism. School principals are happy to "get off the hook" by telling complaining parents that a troublemaking child is "in therapy." Even worse is the principal who tells parents that if their child does not go into therapy he or she will be discharged from the school. (This is an extremely misguided statement and compromises significantly the likelihood of the child's being helped by treatment.) Last, therapists who try too hard are likely to defeat their own purposes because the pressures placed on the patient are apt to lessen the likelihood that treatment will be effective.

It is important for the therapist to appreciate how deep-seated the psychopathological patterns can be and that they are often generations in the making. In fact, they may be so formidable that their alleviation or cure might result in the individual's becoming a pariah from the family, so different will the person become. I do not believe that therapists give proper appreciation to this factor in explaining therapeutic failure. If, as a result of the treatment, the individual becomes entirely different from his or her extended family, it is not likely that the therapy will be successful. The so-called "cure" is too heavy a price to pay—entailing, as it will, total removal and isolation from one's family.

This phenomenon was well demonstrated by a 22-year-old young woman I saw a number of years ago. Her presenting complaint was that she found herself gravitating toward young men who would maltreat her; when treated more benevolently, she became tense, anxious, and even found herself provoking her dates into treating her hostilely. She suspected that something might be wrong with her, but wasn't sure. The girl grew up in a blue-collar home in northern New Jersey (pertinent to this discussion). When she was 14 years old, she told her parents that she wanted to go to college. Her father responded by beating her, while accusing her of trying to be superior to the rest of her family. He claimed that no one in their extended family had ever gone to college and there was no reason why she should do so.

Over the next few years she continually prevailed upon her parents to let her go to college and, finally, with some minimal assistance from her mother, her father agreed to let her go with very stringent provisions. The most important of these was that she would have to pay her entire school expenses by working in his gasoline station, which was on the West Side of Manhattan (across the river from New Jersey) in an extremely rough and dangerous neighborhood. Accordingly, she began work at 5:00 in the morning, when he opened the gas station, and worked there until about 8:00 A.M., when she then went off to school. He always paid her the minimum wage and this was the source of the financing of her education. There was hardly a day when she was not propositioned, physically mauled in a sexual way, and even exposed to a few attempted rapes. When she would complain to her father about these indignities, he invariably scoffed and told her that it was her imagination, even though the advances were often made in situations when her father could easily have overheard or even seen what was happening. At the time that I saw her, the girl had graduated college and was working as a secretary in a typical white-collar position.

It is my usual practice to invite the nearest of kin of all of my patients for a family interview, regardless of the age of my patient. In this case, as she was their only child, I invited her parents to join us in one of our early sessions. Her mother accepted the invitation but her father rejected it, claiming that he did not "believe in" psychiatry. Besides, he is reported to have said that he did not think his daughter had any psychiatric problems anyway. Accordingly, I saw the girl and her mother. Early in the interview I asked the mother what problems she considered her daughter to have. She replied, "Doctor, my daughter is perfectly fine. She doesn't have any problems, I don't know why she's coming here." When I asked her what her daughter had told her about the reasons for her visits, she replied, "I know that she thinks she has a problem with boys. She says that she often finds herself trying to get them to treat her badly, and even to hit her. I don't know why she's talking about that as if it was a problem. All men hit their wives. That's normal."

I then asked the mother if she was quite sure that "all" men hit their wives and that there were no exceptions. She replied, "Doctor, my husband's always hit me, all my sisters are beaten by their husbands, and all my brothers beat their wives. My father beat my mother, all my uncles beat my aunts, and all my aunts were beaten by their husbands. My grandfather beat my grandmother, etc., etc." I then asked her if she could conceive of the possibility that there might be marriages in which husbands did not beat their wives. She responded that she would not believe any man who claimed that he didn't beat his wife, nor would she believe any woman who claimed that she wasn't hit by her husband.

With this family background it is not difficult to see what was happening with this girl. When she went to college, she found herself in what was for her an entirely unique environment—different from any she had ever experienced. She found herself with young men who treated her benevolently. With them she was like a "fish out of water." And, when she went into the business world, she found herself in a similar situation. In order to make her relationships with boys more familiar, she would provoke them in the hope that they would treat her badly and even hit her. This is what she knew, this is what she was used to, and this was familiar. What is strange is often very anxiety provoking.

This girl's situation reminded me of the comment of Tevye, the father in the movie and play *Fiddler on the Roof.* In one of his moving soliloquies, dealing with his shock on learning that his daughter is going to marry a Gentile young man, he looks up to the heavens and says, "I could understand, God, how a bird might fall in love with a fish. But where would they live?" This girl was basically a masochist. All known females in her extended family, back as many generations as one could go, were masochists. And all of them found sadists for husbands. One could almost predict at the time of her birth that she too would become a masochist. Certainly, other factors were probably operative in bringing about her masochism. However, what I have described above was, I believe, the most formidable and significant component.

I describe this patient's situation here because it demonstrates so well my point that a patient's symptomatology, although presented as an individual problem, may be deeply rooted in family processes—processes that may go back many generations. With such a heritage, with such powerful contributing factors, the therapist must have very modest goals in the treatment of such symptoms. And even when close work with the family is possible, the chances of alleviation may be minimal.

It is important for the reader to appreciate that pathological modes of interaction between and among family members are not 100 percent detrimental. They are derived in an attempt to establish some kind of an equilibrium and generally provide benefits in spite of the pains and discomforts attendant to their perpetuation. They may contain constructive and cohesive elements—the patient's complaints about them notwithstanding. Such appreciation should lessen therapeutic fervor and reduce also the therapist's tendency to develop manifestations of *The Statue of Liberty syndrome.*

An example from my military experience demonstrates this point quite well. An elderly couple once came to me for consultation, at the initiation of the wife. He was 86 and she 83, and they had been married 63 years. They lived near a central military hospital in Frankfurt am Main, Germany, where I was stationed. (Retired military people often choose to live near military hospitals where they can receive free medical care and live close to other military retirees.) The wife described things as having gone well during the first 61 years or so of the marriage, stating that her husband was a good man, and did not gamble, drink, run around with other women, or engage in other behavior traditionally disruptive to a marriage. Furthermore, he was a devoted husband, father, grandfather, and greatgrandfather. Accordingly, they had never sought counseling before. (I always like a "fresh case," so that I don't have to deal with statements like, "Well, Doctor so and so said . . ." and "You know, Doctor, the other person we saw has a very different opinion.")

The wife then went on to tell me that during the previous two years her husband had become progressively more preoccupied with accusations of infidelity. It was not simply that he was perpetually accusing her of being unfaithful, but he was accusing her of having a special attraction for young recruits, ages 18 to 20. His suspicions reached the point where he would hardly leave her alone and when with her his allegations were continual. When she would go shopping at the PX, for example, on her return he would confront her: "Well, as I figure it, it should have taken you an hour and a half. It should have taken you a half hour to get there, a half hour to shop, and a half hour to get back. It's taken you an hour and three-quarters. I know you had a 'quickie' in the alley with one of those young soldiers." No amount of reasoning on the wife's part was successful in dispelling her husband's delusion. Her argument that she had no such inclinations proved futile. Her attempts to prove that her absences did not take longer than necessary were again responded to with incredulity and accusations that she was lying.

By the end of the interview it became apparent to me that if I had a pill that could magically dispel this old man's delusions, I would have done both him and his wife a disservice. Both of them were deriving important psychological gratifications from the symptom, their ostensible complaints notwithstanding. From the husband's point of view, it was not that he had a wife who was old and less attractive than she was 63 years previously. Rather, his wife was still so attractive that young men in their late teens would prefer her over far younger women who were clearly available. The symptom, therefore, enabled him to deny the unpleasant reality of his wife's aging. It also provided him with the enhanced self-worth associated with his belief that at his age he had such an attractive wife. And there were similar gratifications for the wife. Her protestations notwithstanding, she was flattered by her husband's belief that she was still so pretty that young men would prefer her over their peers. And both of them utilized the discussions over the delusions as a way of filling up the vacuum of their empty lives. Accordingly, as mentioned, if I indeed had a pill to dispel this delusion I would have deprived them both of valuable psychological benefits. It was from this recognition that I advised them to try to fill their lives more meaningfully by taking advantage of the many services that the military had available for such individuals. Furthermore, I advised them to involve themselves in various programs for the elderly back in the United States where they were soon planning to move.

Therapy—An Educational Experience

In the context of a good therapist-patient relationship, the therapist helps the patient learn better how to deal with the fundamental problems and conflicts of life with which we all are confronted and must deal in the course of our existence. After a detailed study of the factors operative in bringing about change in psychoanalysis (one form of psychotherapy), H. Strupp (1975) concluded that the most important elements in bringing about therapeutic change were the "lessons in constructive living" that the patient learned. I am in full agreement with Strupp on this point. The more judiciously and intelligently a person deals with the problems of life, the less likely it is that the individual will resort to pathological modes of adaptation. Therapy, more than anything else, should enhance one's capacity to deal with life's challenges. Therapy, more than anything else, involves helping people learn how to deal with these inevitable problems. The younger the patient, the more guidance, advice and instruction the therapist should be willing to provide, and the older the patient, the more the therapist should facilitate the patient's finding his or her own solutions to these problems. However, even with the most mature adults, some guidance and instruction is warranted *after* the patient has made every reasonable attempt to resolve the problem him- or herself. Accordingly, the therapeutic process is very similar to the educational.

The Therapist as Teacher

This similarity between the educational and therapeutic processes goes further. An important determinant of whether a student will learn from a teacher relates to whether the student will identify with the teacher. Teachers who are bored with teaching or unmotivated and watch the clock throughout the day are not likely to teach their students very much. In contrast, teachers who are enthusiastic, who genuinely enjoy learning and teaching what they themselves have learned, are much more likely to impart knowledge to their students. The former teach little, the latter are likely to create an atmosphere in which their students are swept up in the learning process. An important factor in this process is that of identification with the teacher. Children in the classrooms of the enthusiastic teacher want to "join in on the fun," and they thereby imitate the teacher in order to derive similar enjoyments. We learn best from those we admire and respect, and we are going to learn little from those who produce little desire for identification and emulation. Worse yet is the teacher who is feared. She not only teaches her students little, if anything, but may contribute to a generalized revulsion for the educational process and the development of psychopathology as well.

The Levels of Therapeutic Learning

Intellectual and Emotional Learning The therapeutic learning process occurs at many levels. I believe that the *least* efficacious is the intellectual. An intellectual insight acquired by the patient is, however, more useful than one provided by the therapist. Classical analytic treatment focuses heavily on the intellectual. It is based on the theory that the primary way of bringing about clinical change is to help the patient gain conscious insight into the unconscious processes that are bringing about the psychopathology: "Where there is unconscious, there shall conscious be." As will be discussed in detail throughout this book, I believe that this focus on intellectualization robs both the therapist and the patient of more predictably therapeutic experiences. When emotions are associated with intellectual learning, there is a greater likelihood of change. Classical analysts appreciate this and recognize that an emotional loading adds clout to an intellectual insight and increases the likelihood that it will be remembered. However, classical psychoanalysts focus excessively on the role of emotions in enhancing the insight-gathering process (an intellectual endeavor) and do not give proper attention to their value as therapeutic facilitators in other areas—many of which do not rely on the development of conscious insight. I describe these below and throughout the course of this book.

The Metaphor Metaphorical communications are especially potent. Aristotle recognized this long ago and considered the metaphor to be the richest and most valuable form of verbal communication (*Poetics,* 1459a):

> The greatest thing by far is to be a master of the metaphor; it is the one thing that cannot be learned from others; and it is also a sign of genius, since a good metaphor implies an intuitive perception of the similarity in the dissimilar.

A metaphor is basically a figure of speech in which two entities, which have no intrinsic relationship with one another, are equated. An example of a metaphor would be: "He is a rock!" There is no intrinsic relationship between a rock and a particular man. However, when one equates them, one provides a statement that is richer than the two separate entities that are being equated. The whole here is indeed greater than the sum of its parts. "She is a flower" is another example of a metaphor. Probably the greatest creator of metaphors in the English language was William Shakespeare. One of my favorites is from *Macbeth.* One could say that life is transient and that before you know it, it's over. However, one could also say, as does Macbeth (v, 5):

> Out, out brief candle!
> Life's but a walking shadow, a poor player
> That struts and frets his hour upon the stage
> And then is heard no more: it is a tale
> Told by an idiot, full of sound and fury,
> Signifying nothing.

The same message, but obviously Shakespeare's way of putting it makes the initial statement weak and sterile. I do not believe that the creation of metaphors can be taught. The ability to see linkages where others do not and to make the proper selections so that rich metaphors are formed is a talent that I believe to be inborn. It is a testimony to Shakespeare's genius that he was able to discover a relationship between the course of life and the mundane: a candle, a shadow, an actor, and the tale. Of course, we therapists do not have the creative capacity of William Shakespeare, and our ability to form metaphors is far more limited. However, to the degree that we can utilize them in our work, to that degree we will enhance the efficacy of our therapeutic communications.

Metaphors become even more enriched when incorporated into the context of allegories, anecdotes, and other narrative forms. This is not only true of children who traditionally enjoy stories, but of adults as well in that they will often learn better from a well-selected anecdote or the relating of an experience by the therapist. M. Erikson (J. Haley, 1973) was especially appreciative of the value of the metaphor in therapy. My main criticism of his work, however, is that the metaphors he would present to his patients appeared to be "pulled out of the sky" and were not, I suspect, as carefully tailored to the needs of the patients as he professed. I say this because the information upon which he would select his metaphor was often minuscule and, accordingly, his metaphorical presentations often had a high degree of speculation.

Conceptualizations and Abstractions vs. Concrete Examples Conceptualizations and abstractions are far less potent vehicles for clarifying issues than specific concrete examples, especially examples that relate to the patient's immediate experiences. Many therapeutic interchanges are quite sterile and therapeutically unproductive because the therapist and the patient are speaking at abstract levels. It is much harder to pay attention to an abstraction, which cannot be visualized, than a concrete example, which can. One of the reasons why philosophy textbooks are so boring to students is that they dwell to a significant degree on abstractions. In contrast, the traditional detective story is very specific and concrete regarding the details it provides and is therefore much more likely to maintain the reader's interest. If a patient, for example, talks about being depressed, the patient is speaking at a conceptual level. The therapist does well, in response, to ask the patient what he or she is specifically depressed about, what in concrete terms are the exact thoughts and feelings that the patient is experiencing and, even more important, to focus on the specific situations that have brought about the depressed feelings. The best way to alleviate the psychogenic components in the depression is to focus in detail on the specific concrete events that have contributed to it. In this chapter, as well as throughout this book, I follow this principle. I present general theoretical principles (abstractions) and then provide concrete clinical examples (readily visualized) that enhance, I believe, the likelihood that the reader will recall what I have written.

The Experience The most potent mechanism for modifying behavior is the experience. The old proverb, "A picture is worth a thousand words," is well known. I would add to this, however, that "An experience is worth a million pictures." To the degree that the therapist can provide experiences, to that degree will he or she be able to bring about clinical change. This hierarchy of the efficacy of the various forms of learning is well epitomized by the following comparisons. Let us take, for example, the experience of reading a play. Reading the play is purely a visual experience, both at the level of reading the written page and the visual imagery that is engendered by such reading. It is primarily an intellectual experience, although some emotions may certainly be engendered. Let us compare this with attending a theatre and observing the play being acted. It is likely that the individual will be more affected by the play because an auditory modality of input has now been added to the visual experience associated with reading the play. If one becomes an actor in the play, then one is even more likely to remember its messages. The reason for this is that one is now adding physical action to the visual and auditory modalities of input. With each additional modality, there is a greater likelihood that the story will have an impact. However, the emotions being exhibited in the play are feigned. No matter how convincing the actor is, the emotions are still turned on and off in accordance with the dictates of the script. The actor is still playacting. Compare this with emotions that are caused by an actual experience. Here, the reactions are engendered by reality and even more likely to be recalled in the future.

Therapy, more than anything else, should be an experience. It is an experience that is one slice of life. It is a living experience in which one has an ongoing encounter with a person who is more honest than any other individual with whom one may be involved in one's lifetime. Our best friends may hesitate to criticize us, lest they hurt our feelings. Therapists criticize benevolently with the purpose of helping remove those behavioral manifestations that alienate others and that interfere with our dealing most effectively with the problems in life with which we are all confronted.

Although the therapist's specific knowledge and experience may increase the likelihood that an involvement with him or her will be therapeutic, such encounters were taking place long before Sigmund Freud was born. Let us take, for example, a young woman, in her late twenties, who comes to therapy because she is not yet married and is concerned that she may never meet a man with whom she will have a satisfactory marital relationship. Let us assume that the therapist is a man in his late fifties, approximately the age of her father. Let us assume further that she reports early in treatment that her father was particularly cruel and rejecting and that she learns in therapy that her anticipation of similar rejection from young men is playing a role in her avoidance and rejection of them. In the course of her treatment she discusses with the therapist her male relationships, and this insight helps her avoid a repetition of her childhood experiences. The therapist is sympathetic, understanding, sensitive, and kind. At no point does he treat her in a way similar to her father. Let us assume that her treatment was successful and she ultimately marries a man with whom she has a stable and rewarding relationship.

I believe that the *insights* this woman gained in her therapy were far less important in bringing about the therapeutic change than the *experience* she had with the benevolent and sympathetic therapist. Without necessarily having any conscious insight into the process, the experience with the therapist enabled her to reduce and possibly even remove her generalization that all men would treat her badly. Similarly, the therapist's discouraging her from involving herself in the same pathological pattern with other young men increased the likelihood that she would have *experiences* with men who were more kindly disposed to her. In short, then, I believe that the major elements in bringing about change in this woman had less to do with intellectual insights and more to do with the quality of the therapist and the men that she subsequently encountered. Had the therapist been aloof, cool, and unsympathetic, she probably would not have changed—all her insights notwithstanding. I would speculate further that this experience was had by a multiplicity of women long before Sigmund Freud's birth. With similar upbringing they too had difficulties in their relationships with young men. However, if they had the good fortune to form a relationship with an older man (an uncle, teacher, or mentor, etc.), then this might have modified their views of men and lessened the likelihood that they would carry the generalization over into their courting patterns. All this may have occurred without conscious awareness and was certainly much more likely to have taken place outside of conscious awareness in the days prior to psychoanalysis. In short, it was the experience that was the best teacher, not the insight.

WALT DISNEY'S PINOCCHIO AS A METAPHOR FOR THE PSYCHOTHERAPEUTIC PROCESS

I consider the story of *Pinocchio* to be an excellent metaphor of the therapeutic process. I suspect, however, that it is not generally recognized as such. A powerful statement of what goes on in psychotherapeutic treatment may be found especially in the Walt Disney version of the original Carlo Lorenzini (pen name, Collodi) story written in 1883. It begins with Geppetto, a woodcarver, who makes a wooden boy puppet he calls Pinocchio. As he looks at his creation he begins to wish that his Pinocchio could be turned into a real boy. He goes to his window, gazes up at the heavens and prays:

> Star light, star bright,
> First star I've seen tonight.
> I wish I may, I wish I might,
> Have the wish I wish tonight.
> I wish my Pinocchio were a real boy!

Geppetto's prayer is overheard by Jiminy Cricket who feels sorry for the old man because he knows that Geppetto's wish could never come true. However, much to the surprise of Jiminy Cricket, a shimmering light suddenly fills the room, a beautiful lady dressed in shining blue appears, raises her wand and says:

> Wake Pinocchio, and live.
> To you the gift of life I give.
> Be good and give Geppetto joy.
> And grow to be a real live boy.

Suddenly, Pinocchio blinks his eyes, raises his wooden arms, and joyfully exclaims, "I can move! I'm a real boy!"

"No," says the Blue Fairy sadly, "You have life, but to become a real boy you must prove yourself, brave, truthful, and unselfish."

"But how can I do that?" asks Pinocchio, discouraged.

"You'll have a Conscience to help you!"

Looking around, the Blue Fairy beckons Jiminy out of his hiding place. "Sir Jiminy Cricket," she says, "I dub you Lord High Keeper of Pinocchio's Conscience!"

Basically, what is happening to Pinocchio is that his transformation from a wooden boy into a real boy is a two-step process. The first step, enabling him to move, has already been accomplished by the Blue Fairy. However, he is still essentially made of wood; he is not yet a real, live boy. In order to accomplish this final goal he must "be good and bring Geppetto joy" and he must prove himself "brave, truthful, and unselfish." In short, he must develop human virtues. To help him accomplish these goals Jiminy Cricket will assist him in forming a conscience. Jiminy's purpose will be to help him develop internalized guilt-evoking mechanisms that will help him deal in a civilized way with his primitive impulses. This, of course, is what therapy is all about for the vast majority of people. Some, for example those with antisocial problems, have weak consciences and so they do not properly suppress their primitive impulses. Others have consciences that are so rigid that they inhibit themselves inordinately when suppressing and repressing their primitive impulses. The goal of the therapist (here symbolized by Jiminy Cricket) is to provide the patient with help in developing a reasonable conscience—neither too repressive nor too lax.

The next day Geppetto tells Pinocchio, "But now, Pinocchio, you must go to school . . . Study hard! Then you'll soon become a real boy!" Basically, Geppetto is telling Pinocchio that another thing that must be accomplished if he is to develop into a real boy is that he become an educated individual. And so Pinocchio goes off to school, trailed by Jiminy Cricket. En route Pinocchio encounters a fox named J. Worthington Foulfellow and his cat friend Gideon, who have the reputations for being "the worst pair of scoundrels in the whole countryside." They tell Pinocchio that he is much too talented to waste his time in school and that he should join a theatrical troupe. They recognize what a find they have in a spontaneously moving puppet. Pinocchio is easily taken in. Jiminy implores him not to become involved and asks, "What will your father say?"

Pinocchio rationalizes his going off with the scoundrels, "Oh, father will be proud of me."

Foulfellow and Gideon then sell Pinocchio to Stromboli, the owner of a marionette theater. At the end of his first day of extremely successful performances Pinocchio is ready to take leave of Stromboli. Before he realizes what is happening, however, Stromboli locks him in a bird cage. As Pinocchio is sitting in the cage, while being lectured to by Jiminy Cricket on the errors of his ways, the Blue Fairy suddenly appears. She asks, "Pinocchio, why didn't you go to school?"

Pinocchio responds, "I *was* going to school until I met someone . . . two big monsters!" At this point Jiminy claps both hands to his head and frowns. At the same time Pinocchio's nose begins to grow longer. Pinocchio then continues and tells the good fairy that the monsters tied him up in a big sack. His nose grows even longer. Pinocchio notices what is happening to his nose and becomes upset.

The Blue Fairy then says, "Perhaps you haven't been telling the truth, Pinocchio. You see, a lie keeps growing and growing until it's as plain as the nose on your face."

Pinocchio is *ashamed.* "I'll never lie again—honest, I won't."

"Very well," says the Blue Fairy. "I'll help you this time, because you are truly sorry. Be good now, Pinocchio."

This interchange is worthy of analytic scrutiny. It is probably the most famous part of the story. Many Freudian psychoanalysts consider the interchange between Pinocchio and the Blue Fairy to be basically an oedipal one. The nose, as a projection from the anterior surface of the body, lends itself well, they claim, to symbolizing the penis. The Blue Fairy, as an "older woman," lends herself well to symbolizing Pinocchio's mother. Geppetto, we presume, is a bachelor, in that no wife ever appears in the story. The idea that Pinocchio is being sexually turned on by the Blue Fairy is certainly possible. However, I consider another explanation to be more likely. We are told that Pinocchio is "ashamed" and that his lying is apparent to everyone about him. I believe that reference is being made here to the experience children have that when they lie adults generally can see through their duplicity. Many children are startled by the apparent wisdom of adults in this area. Pinocchio's change here, I believe, relates to the shame stage in the development of conscience that I described in Vol. I (1999a). In this phase, the child is deterred from engaging in antisocial behavior by the fear of invoking the alienation and rejection of significant figures who observe or learn of the transgression. Pinocchio has not yet internalized the mechanisms that will deter him from engaging in unacceptable behavior. The Blue Fairy is serving as another therapist (in addition to Jiminy Cricket) and provides Pinocchio with information which will serve him in his maturation into a real boy. Because he is "truly sorry" (as opposed to using the sorry excuse as a manipulative device to exonerate himself from punishment), she excuses his transgression, waves her wand, and removes him from the cage. Jiminy and Pinocchio proceed again along the open road.

Soon afterwards, Pinocchio and Jiminy once again encounter those low-life characters, Foulfellow and Gideon, who symbolize primitive drives which press for gratification and ignore potential future consequences of wanton self-indulgence. The sly fox and sleazy cat feign sympathy when Pinocchio tells them about his tribulations at the hands of Stromboli, and they persuade him to take a "rest cure" on *Pleasure Island.* Again, Pinocchio rejects Jiminy Cricket's warnings not to get involved with these unworthies. He replies to Jiminy, "Foulfellow says I need a rest after my terrible experience. Just think of Pleasure Island. Bands, circuses, ice cream mountains!" Pinocchio appears to have forgotten his promise to the Blue Fairy and happily anticipates the opportunity to indulge himself in primitive pleasures.

Pinocchio then boards a coach bound for Pleasure Island. The coach is pulled by small donkeys and is filled with impudent, noisy boys. The Coachman surreptitiously gives Foulfellow a bag of money in return for his passenger. Again, unbeknownst to Pinocchio, the fox has sold him to an individual who ultimately exploits the naive boy. After a long journey they finally arrived at Pleasure Island. "Here were bands playing, streets paved with cookies and lines of donut trees, and fountains spouting lemonade. And always the Coachman kept urging the boys 'Have a good time—while you can!'" All the bad boys are encouraged by the Coachman to indulge themselves. However, there is the ominous warning of future consequences implied in the "while you can" comment. The seed is being planted here that unbridled self-indulgence is not without its penalties. The boys continue their wanton and hedonistic lifestyle: "They climbed the Ice-cream Mountains and sailed down the Lemonade River. They smashed windows, burned school books, and teased the poor little donkeys. Pinocchio made friends with the very worst of the boys, a young bully called Lampwick, and he was always in the middle of the mischief." Lampwick epitomizes the juvenile psychopath who serves as a model for those who wish to engage in a life of guiltless self-indulgence. He is the antithesis of Jiminy Cricket and the Blue Fairy. As the fun at Pleasure Island escalates the boys become increasingly rowdy and antisocial. One day Jiminy Cricket finds Pinocchio shooting pool in Tobacco Lane. Lampwick is smoking a cigar and Pinocchio a corncob pipe. Jiminy exclaims, "Throw away that pipe! Come home this minute!" At Lampwick's prodding Pinocchio mocks Jiminy and blows a puff of smoke in his face.

Soon afterwards the bad boys are suddenly afflicted with "donkey fever," an illness characterized by rapid transformation into donkeys—starting with the sprouting of donkey ears. The Coachman starts rounding up the boys who have been newly transformed into donkeys to do slave work in the coal mines and other kinds of donkey labor. With Jiminy Cricket's help Pinocchio narrowly escapes—with only his ears turned into those of a donkey. Fortunately, the rest of his body is still intact.

After an arduous journey they finally reach home. Unfortunately, the house is empty and inside they find a letter from Geppetto informing them that he had learned that Pinocchio had gone off to Pleasure Island and he had left home to find Pinocchio. It also informs Pinocchio that while he was on a small boat headed to Pleasure Island the giant whale Monstro gobbled him up, boat and all, and that he is now living in the belly of the whale. Pinocchio then decides that he is going to save his father, even though Jiminy warns him about the dangers. This time Pinocchio's failure to heed Jiminy's warning is a healthy sign in that he manifests a willingness to take risks and suffer pain on behalf of another person. After a series of adventures, Pinocchio and Jiminy finally encounter the whale Monstro. Soon thereafter Monstro swallows Pinocchio, Jiminy Cricket, and their boat in one massive gulp. Inside the whale's huge stomach they find Geppetto, and Pinocchio devises a plan for their escape. He builds a fire, which forces the whale to sneeze. This results in the ejection of them all. But escape from Monstro is not so simple. The angry whale relentlessly pursues his former captives, obsessed with destroying them. At one point it is Pinocchio who saves his father from drowning—helped by the enhanced flotation power of his wooden body. Although finally safe from the jaws of Monstro, the ordeal so incapacitates Pinocchio that he is washed ashore, rendered still, cold, and motionless. Geppetto is heartbroken, weeps bitterly, and is sure that his son is dead. He carries the boy's limp body back to his cottage and prays for him. Suddenly a ray of starlight appears and the voice of the Blue Fairy is heard. She repeats her earlier prophecy: ". . . and some day, when you have proven yourself brave, truthful, and unselfish, you will be a real boy. . . ." Pinocchio suddenly recognizes that he has been changed. Joyfully he realizes that the Blue Fairy's promise had come true. Pinocchio was no longer a puppet. Pinocchio was a real, live, flesh-and-blood boy! The Blue Fairy then presents Jiminy Cricket with a reward for his labors. It is a badge of gold on which is stated:

> Awarded to a Good Conscience
> Who helped make
> A Real Boy out of a Wooden Head

And this is the role of the therapist, to make real boys out of wooden heads. They do this primarily by contributing to the development of the internalized guilt-evoking mechanisms, commonly referred to as the conscience. But such development does not occur quickly. It takes place only after a long series of adventures in life—both painful and pleasurable—in which lessons are learned and there is a gradual process of internalization of those dicta, values, and principles that society considers crucial for the perpetuation of a civilized world.

As mentioned, the story outlined here is taken from the Walt Disney adaptation. Disney took many liberties with the original, the most important of which—for the purposes of my analysis—relates to what happened to Jiminy Cricket. In the Disney version, Jiminy's work is successfully completed and he enjoys the ego-enhancement of having contributed significantly to the transformation of a wooden head into a real boy. In the Collodi version, Pinocchio kills Jiminy by crushing him to death with a mallet! I leave it to the reader to decide which rendition he or she prefers.

CONCLUDING COMMENTS

The material presented in this chapter represents a statement of my views regarding the basic factors that contribute to the development of psychogenic symptoms and the fundamental elements operative in the psychotherapeutic process. This "blind man" sees the elephant this way in the late 1980s. It was not the way I saw things in the 1950s, 1960s, and 1970s. I have learned things over the years, and I suspect some modifications of my present position by the 1990s. My purpose here has been to present a relatively short statement of my views on these issues. Throughout the course of this book, however, I will be elaborating on all of these points with many clinical examples. Throughout this book, as well, I will be making reference to these principles because they are the basic foundation of just about everything that is described herein.

There is an old Hasidic saying: "A good man is one who knows what he feels, says what he means, and means what he says." The statement could very well serve as a central therapeutic goal in that it epitomizes the kinds of qualities that therapy attempts to engender in patients. We want our patients to know what their feelings are and to be able to use them judiciously. We want them to be forthright and express themselves honestly. And we want them to be viewed as credible human beings who have the courage to follow through with their convictions. Therapists who possess these qualities themselves are more likely to engender them in their patients.

Passive therapists, those who hide behind "blank screens," those who are fearful of appropriately revealing themselves, and those who are vague and/or indecisive, are not likely to be of much assistance in helping their patients reach these goals.

TWO

THE THERAPIST-PATIENT RELATIONSHIP AND THE PSYCHOTHERAPEUTIC PROCESS

In this chapter I discuss in specific detail the ways in which the therapist-patient relationship contributes to the changes that may be brought about in adolescent psychotherapy. The material here is an elaboration of the therapist-patient relationship discussion in Chapter One – with particular focus on elements relevant to adolescent therapy. As emphasized previously, I consider the good therapist-patient relationship to be at the foundation of treatment; without it there can be no meaningful psychotherapy. There will be no identification with the therapist, emulation of him or her, or receptivity to what the therapist has to say. The orientation here is psychodynamic and the kinds of problems focused on will be those that I consider to be psychogenic. Thus the term *psychotherapeutic* in the title of this chapter. This is a comprehensive chapter and will cover, in depth, the important basic principles of treatment for a wide variety of adolescent psychogenic disturbances. It is presented as a foundation upon which the treatment of specific disorders, and specific patients, may rest.

Some readers may consider my failure to discuss in detail the treatment of a wide variety of disorders to be a deficiency in this book. My response is that I am not presenting a comprehensive statement of treatment details of *all* the forms of adolescent psychopathology. I do not believe that one individual can possibly claim to be competent enough to write such a volume. Because I have had significant experience working with antisocial patients, I have devoted a chapter to their treatment. However, as the reader can readily see, both in this chapter and elsewhere, I do discuss in some detail the treatment of many other common disorders seen in adolescents. Readers interested in works that cover the wide variety of treatments for the various disorders of adolescence do well to refer to such collections as *American Handbook of Psychiatry* (1974), *Basic Handbook of Child Psychiatry* (1979), and the more recent *Psychiatry* (1986).

THE ADOLESCENT PATIENT'S PERSONALITY

Insight and Motivation

Psychotherapists generally hold that the patient must exhibit insight and motivation before meaningful psychotherapy can be engaged in. The patient must have insight into the fact that the problems are indeed psychogenic and that their psychological pain is not merely the result of external factors or physical illness. Furthermore, the patient must have the motivation to deal with these problems via psychotherapy. But this is not all. The therapist as well must have the conviction that the problems are indeed psychogenic, that the patient is properly motivated for psychotherapeutic inquiry, and is willing to suffer the pains, embarrassments, and discomforts attendant to the process of self-inquiry. The more analytically oriented the therapist is the more likely he or she is going to subscribe to these *desiderata* of effective psychotherapeutic treatment. Some therapists even recommend an initial preparatory phase in which the patient is groomed for therapy. In this early phase an attempt is made to help the patient gain the insight that he or she has psychiatric problems. Next the patient is helped to become motivated for the treatment.

My experience has been that very few adolescents (especially early adolescents) have such insight and motivation. Those who ultimately do get to us represent a small fraction of all those who have difficulties. And even those who are willing to come to our office are not generally committed to the aforementioned principles of insight and motivation. Rather, most who come to us must often find a rationalization to justify their being in treatment. The most common such rationalization is that the youngster is being coerced into therapy and is submitting to irrational and punitive parents who are forcing him or her to see the therapist. D. Holmes (1964) is well aware of this phenomenon and speaks of it frequently in his superb book *The Adolescent in Psychotherapy:* "The adolescent...is so desperately aware of his need for help that he dare not call it by that name. He must represent it to himself and to others as an abominable infringement upon his personal rights by a meddling adult (p. 209)." The adolescent often needs what Holmes refers to as "a face-saving show of resistance (p. 186)." In fact, Holmes goes further and states that when the adolescent professes motivation for psychotherapy it is generally wise to be somewhat incredulous: "A youngster's direct request for psychiatric treatment, his sincerely expressed wish to cooperate in psychotherapy even before he has the least idea what it is, or his sober appraising of the therapist's abilities, are all representative of the kind of resistance which sends shivers of apprehension through the therapist who is experienced in treating adolescents (p.117)."

With regard to the adolescents' claim that their parents are forcing them into therapy, the realities are that no parent can actually force an adolescent to come to treatment. In fact, a parent cannot even force a younger child to attend treatment on an ongoing basis. Younger children may be physically carried into the consultation room but even then, if the child is adamant enough in his or her refusal, the likelihood is that the therapist will ultimately give up. And the adolescent cannot even be physically brought into the consultation against his or her will. Even if the parent is sick enough to physically overwhelm the adolescent and bodily coerce the patient into the therapist's office, the therapist is not likely to go along with this method of bringing the youngster to treatment. The therapist does well to accept the patient's excuse and not attempt to help the youngster gain insight into the fact that it is a rationalization. To do so may result in losing the patient.

Dealing with the Adolescent Who Refuses to Attend the Initial Visit

On a number of occasions I have received telephone calls from parents stating that they want their youngster to go into treatment, but that he or she refuses to come. Often I have told the parents that they should inform the adolescent that an appointment has been made and that if he or she does not come at least two or three times there will be repercussions such as disciplinary measures and various kinds of privations. Sometimes this is just what the adolescent needs and then, after a few sessions, the youngster finds that the anticipated repercussions of coming to a therapist were not realized and then he or she can more comfortably continue the treatment voluntarily. On other occasions this approach has failed and either the youngster hasn't even come to the first session (the punishments notwithstanding) or has gone through the motions of attending the required number of sessions and then promptly refused further involvement with me. Under such circumstances I have generally seen the parents a few more times, provided some counseling, and then discontinued the treatment with the understanding that they would return on a request basis in the future. I cannot recall having conducted ongoing treatment in a situation in which the youngster was threatened with punishments for nonattendance throughout the whole course of the therapy. Although I recognize the possibility that there may be rare situations in which this is warranted, I believe that it can easily result in the youngster's using the therapy as a way of expressing hostility toward the parent. By coming, and not cooperating and not using the sessions meaningfully, the youngster knowingly wastes the parents' money. Therapists who are party to this hostile maneuver are not only contributing to the perpetuation of the patient's psychopathology but "ripping off" the parents as well.

Using Anger as a Vehicle for Self-Revelation

Sometimes the adolescent needs the vehicle of anger to reveal him or herself. D. Holmes states: "If given the opportunity to rear up on his hind legs a little, he is able to confide much information about himself without experiencing the serious loss in self-esteem which would come from submitting helplessly to an omnipotent adult and poring out his heart like a baby (p. 109)." Holmes continues: "When arguing, he (the adolescent) is able to reveal things about himself which he could not possibly speak of in a quiet, expository tone." However, Holmes also recommends that the therapist, in response, argue with the patient: "Getting into arguments with the adolescent, patient or not, is both inevitable and useful. It does not signify either a loss of dignity for the therapist or a disruptive lapse in treatment (p. 109)." Although I am in agreement that adolescents may need anger to reveal themselves, I am not in agreement that therapists do well to argue with their angry adolescent patients. Although such arguments may prolong the adolescent's self-revelatory anger, I believe that arguing back with the adolescent does produce a "loss of dignity for the therapist." A therapist's arguing implies that the therapist has some strong need to convince the adolescent that the therapist is right and the youngster is wrong. Such responsive arguing suggests that the therapist's self-esteem will be lowered if the adolescent is not convinced of the wisdom of the therapist's position. However, a therapist's arguing would be justifiable in a situation where the therapist does indeed have something to lose if the argument is not won, such as the situation in which there is a threat to the therapist's life, property, etc. But under those circumstances meaningful therapy may no longer be possible.

Final Comments on the Adolescent's Personality

Throughout the course of this book I will be making many comments about the adolescent's personality traits and how they affect the therapist-patient relationship. Furthermore, in the next two sections I will also be commenting on adolescent personality patterns that are likely to improve or work against the development of a good therapist-patient relationship. Before closing this section I would like to focus on the personality pattern of the psychopathic youngster. As I have described in detail in Vol. I (1999a), patients with a fully developed psychopathic personality pattern are not likely to be candidates for meaningful therapy. They have not developed the capacity to relate meaningfully to significant figures in their environment, and so it is not likely that they are going to relate to the therapist. Accordingly, the therapist does well to recognize the unsuitability of such prospective patients at the outset. We cannot relate therapeutically to all human beings; we cannot help patients with every psychiatric disorder; and it behooves us to differentiate between those we can help and those we cannot. Not to do so is to cause both patients and ourselves a significant waste of time, effort, and in many cases money.

THE THERAPIST'S PERSONALITY

Here I discuss those elements in the therapist's personality structure that I believe are desirable for him or her to possess if a good therapist-patient relationship is to develop. It is important for the reader to appreciate that these personality qualities all exist on a continuum from therapists who have little capacity in any of these areas to those who are significantly strong. To the degree that the therapist exhibits these to a significant degree, to that degree is it likely that the therapist-patient relationship will be a strong one. In the next section I will describe exactly what the factors are in the therapist-patient relationship that bring about therapeutic change.

The traditional view of psychotherapy is that it is a process in which the patient comes into the therapist's office and speaks voluntarily about his or her problems. Hollywood movies, especially, have promulgated this notion of the psychotherapeutic method. Typically, the patient is highly motivated to speak to the therapist who is continually kind, sympathetic, understanding, and rational. Like many other things depicted on movie screens, this is a myth.

Many therapists (including this author), when seeing such movies, are often envious of the motivation and cooperation of such patients and may even suffer with feelings of inadequacy when they compare themselves with the therapist on the screen. These screen therapists often exhibit a degree of sympathy, empathy, and toleration that we therapists in the audience are not likely to possess. And their patients often eagerly involve themselves in treatment and pour forth their innermost secrets from the outset. The realities are that the vast majority of adolescents who come our way do not profess any particular interest in unburdening themselves. In response we generally become impatient, discouraged, and even wonder whether we are defrauding the parents by continuing a therapeutic process that is so far below what we may consider to be the ideal.

Liking Children and Adolescents

The first, and possibly most important quality, is that of genuinely liking children. I cannot imagine someone's involving him- or herself meaningfully and effectively in the field of child and adolescent therapy without basically liking young people. I am not suggesting that the therapist should like children *all* the time; in fact, I would be distrustful of those who claimed that they did. Children and adolescents inevitably cause us periods of resentment and exasperation. Rather, I am only suggesting that a significant percentage of the therapeutic experiences with them should be benevolent and moderately enjoyable.

Projection of Oneself Into the Patient's Position

Therapists must have the capacity to project themselves into the patient's situation, to see the world through the patient's eyes—and probably to feel the way the youngster feels. We know little of this phenomenon. Why is it easy for some and for others impossible? Piaget's panoramas (in which the child is asked to determine which card shows the view that the little model man in the center of the panorama sees as his position is changed) could give us information about this quality. Some would easily be able to see the view of the model, and others would have trouble. But this is only part of the phenomenon. It describes only a *visual-mechanical* aspect of the projective process; the *human elements* are far more complex. We use such terms as *sympathy* and *empathy* in our feeble attempt to describe this quality, but we still have much to learn about it—its mechanics, its psychodynamics, and the factors that play a role in its development. Does an accurate memory of one's own childhood play a role in this capacity? I think so, but as far as I know this has not been tested. And, indeed, it might be hard to evaluate accurately. Egocentricism inhibits this quality. Therapists who lack this capacity to a significant degree are ill-equipped to help their patients. If they cannot view the world through their patients' eyes (not necessarily agree with their patients, however), then they are handicapped in helping them. (Gardner, 1973c).

Frustration Tolerance

Adolescent therapists must be willing to tolerate certain frustrations that their adult counterparts need not contend with. One potential source of frustration is the youngster's parents. They often feel threatened by the therapeutic process. Having a child in therapy may be considered proof of the parents' failure, and many defenses may be utilized to avoid coming to terms with this notion. Many parents come not because they have seen the problems themselves (they have often denied them for months to years), but because some outside agency (most often the school) has suggested psychiatric consultation. Such parents often hope to hear that the youngster is completely normal and the referrer was in error. Once the youngster is in therapy, their ambivalence may manifest itself through forgotten appointments, lateness, cancellations with meager excuses, withholding payment of bills, failure to follow through with recommendations, hostility toward the therapist, and other gambits that are consciously or unconsciously designed to undermine the treatment. Sudden withdrawal of the patient is therefore common.

At any particular time the therapist who works with adolescents has to keep three people involved: a youngster who would prefer being with friends; a mother whose life is hectic enough caring for the house and other children without having to bring the patient to the therapist; and a father who could find much better ways to spend his money. If, at any point, any one of these three develops significant psychological resistances, the others are dragged down and the project fails. I often feel as if I'm juggling three greased balls and that when one of them drops, the whole act is over. Some therapists get fed up and gradually confine themselves to adult work. In residency, one of the definitions we had of a child psychiatrist was: "someone who used to do child psychiatry." The humor stemmed from the recognition that many of our supervisors were no longer doing child and adolescent therapy, merely supervising it. The consensus was that people got tired of doing such therapy after the age of 40 or so. I passed that landmark uneventfully (with regard to my enthusiasm for child and adolescent therapy) and also passed the age 50 landmark. As I write this, I am 56 and starting to get tired. Perhaps it's my age, perhaps the frustrations of the field are finally getting to me. At the same time, my interest still appears to be quite high. Then once every week or two, I have a really good and valuable session and it all becomes worthwhile again.

The frustrations of doing child and adolescent psychotherapy may be more than counterbalanced by certain gratifications that the adult therapist may not so frequently enjoy. The satisfactions of therapeutic success are more easy to come by in child and adolescent work than in adult therapy. These patients' problems are generally of shorter duration than the adult's and may be less deeply imbedded in the psychic structure. In addition, more change can be effected in the patient's environment. The deleterious influences to which the youngster is being exposed can be altered more readily: parental attitudes modified; misconceptions rectified; management advice provided; and schools, clubs, and camps recommended. Adults who come for treatment are usually deeply entrenched in their life situations. They may be locked into a bad marraige from which it is difficult to remove themselves because of children and the financial privations attendant to a divorce. And their work situation may be similarly rigid in that quitting a job or changing one's field may not be viable for them.

The Therapist as Parent

The question is sometimes raised as to whether it is necessary for child and adolescent therapists to have had children of their own. It is certainly possible to be an effective and accomplished child psychotherapist without having had such experiences, but I believe that the lack may compromise one's therapeutic abilities. The child, when seen in an office setting, is in an artificial situation. The childless therapist has not had the experience of living and growing with children in their natural setting; fathering and mothering; worrying and scolding; changing diapers; seeing them through physical illness; handling their fights with siblings and peers; and involving themselves in the thousands of other activities that enrich one's knowledge and appreciation of children. Childless therapists, no doubt, gain many of these experiences vicariously through their patients. They may, indeed, be able to involve themselves with their patients to a greater degree than therapists who have children of their own. These considerations notwithstanding, I still hold that having one's own children enhances a child therapist's efficacy.

Memory of One's Own Childhood

The ability to remember one's own childhood experiences deserves emphasis. There are people who will say with all honesty that they cannot remember a thing about their lives before the age of eight, or ten, or even twelve. People who are so repressed regarding memories of their childhood experiences are not likely to be effective child therapists. If they are to appreciate optimally the youngster's situation, therapists have to be able to recall how it was when they were the same age as their child or adolescent patient is at the time of treatment. Child and adolescent therapists have to be able to put themselves in the positions of their patients if they are to be successful. They need to be able to project themselves back in time. In addition, child and adolescent therapists must be able to involve themselves in both processes, i.e. present and past projections. Their task, therefore, is much more difficult than that of the adult therapist.

Comfort with Patients' Anger

One of the complaints I have about the people who taught and supervised me during my training period is that they didn't warn me about one of the most important stresses attendant to practicing psychotherapy. I am referring to the stresses of continual bombardment with patients' anger. Therapists must indeed have a thick skin. And those who work with children and adolescents must have even thicker skins. Children generally don't want to be in the therapist's office and express their irritation directly at their therapists for their central role in requiring them to be brought (often dragged, coerced, and bribed would be better terms) to the therapist's office. And the parents who bring their youngsters would much prefer spending time doing other things as well as spending money elsewhere. And then there is the anger that the parents have toward the therapist for not living up to their expectations for quick and magic solutions to their problems. Most parents have such expectations and most parents blame the therapist for not bringing about rapid change. And the parents most likely to do this are those who are most uncooperative in the therapeutic process.

Then there is the obvious fact that we are dealing with sick people. Under such circumstances there should be no surprise that people are going to be angry at us, often irrationally so. Therapists must appreciate that when they go into practice (whether it be in a clinic or private practice setting) they are basically putting a sign outside their door which says: *Welcome crazy people! If you are insane, disgruntled, bitter with life, frustrated over your lot, feeling rejected, isolated, lonely, or have any other dissatisfactions with life, come in here and tell me about it. If all others reject you, don't worry, I will accept you. All others may find your behavior noxious and alienating, I will not.* When one puts out such a sign, one shouldn't be surprised if one becomes the scapegoat of irrational people who are going to do irrational things. The therapist who takes most of this personally is in the wrong field. But even people such as myself, who believe that we have not made an incorrect professional choice, find it wearying. I often find myself drained at the end of the day and am envious of those who have the opportunity to work with more congenial individuals.

Comfort with Therapeutic Failure

It is important that therapists be comfortable with therapeutic failure. Therapists who think that it behooves them to alleviate the difficulties of all (or most) of those who come to them, will suffer significant frustration and a deep sense of failure. Children and adolescents often present with a total life of exposure to the detrimental influences that have contributed to their difficulties. Their parents generally have been living with their own problems for many years as well. But things do not stop there. Not only may the pathological processes have been transmitted down numerous generations, but social and cultural processes have usually contributed as well. It is therefore grandiose of therapists to consider themselves capable of rectifying all these pathological influences, and they are assuming unrealistic obligations if they consider it their responsibility to do so. The best attitude therapists can take is to commit themselves to the therapeutic process and try their best to do what they can. If they can say to themselves, with regard to the unsuccessful case, that they have tried their best and possibly learned a few things that will serve them in good stead in the future, they should be able to accept therapeutic failure without undue guilt and self-recrimination. I have spoken previously (Chapter One) about *The Statue of Liberty syndrome.* Therapists should ask themselves whether they are exhibiting manifestations of this disorder. If they are, they do well to cure themselves as soon as possible; otherwise, they are doomed to lead very frustrating lives.

The Therapist's Sex

The sex of the therapist is sometimes given significant attention. I believe that in most cases this is a minor factor, less important than the personality qualities of the therapist and whether or not they dovetail with those of the patient. Also more important is the skill of the therapist and his or her insight into the patient's difficulties. This is not to preclude the possibility of the therapist's sex having some importance in certain situations. For example, a youngster whose father has been out of the home might do better with a male therapist. Girls in early adolescence are sometimes quite uncomfortable with a male therapist, and they probably do better with a female during this period. Most (but not all) adolescent boys who are dealing with homosexual problems probably do better with a male therapist because, as discussed in Vol. I (1999a), I believe that most of these youngsters have had significant impairments in their relationships with their fathers and a male therapist may be useful to help rectify this difficulty. But these examples (and there are others) represent a small fraction of patient needs. More important than the therapists's sex are the therapist's talent, skills, and personality.

Therapists Who Are Still Adolescents Themselves

In the 1960s and early 1970s many therapists who treated adolescents considered it useful if they took on the attire that would be appealing to adolescents. These gurus often sported beards, hung beads around their necks, wore fancy shirts, and sat yoga style on the ground when conducting therapy. They generally espoused the same philosophies as the hippie adolescents of the times and even went so far as to smoke pot and use other drugs with their patients. These were often people who had difficulty with the aging process and were fixated at or had regressed to the adolescent level of development. I consider the youngsters who went to these "therapists" to have been shortchanged. I believe they did them more harm than good. Although they were attractive to the youngsters and thereby may have drawn them out more quickly than more conservative therapists (such as this examiner), I believe that they also fostered antisocial acting out and deprived their patients of what I consider to have been a healthier adult model. I am not claiming that every philosophical position held by these people was unhealthy, only that many of them were so. The adolescent needs a traditional (I am not saying slavishly traditional) parent figure against whom he or she can rebel but who, at the same time, can serve as a healthy model. These therapists provided neither opportunity. Fortunately, at the time of this writing, they are not very much in vogue, but they still can be found. They may not wear the same "uniforms" as their contemporaries in the sixties and seventies, but their reflex idealization of and identification with adolescent values in vogue at the time have the same detrimental effects on their patients.

Concluding Comments

I do not claim to have covered all the factors in the therapist's personality that are important for the establishment of a good therapeutic relationship. There are many subtle factors that we know little about. When we say that the therapist and the patient have "established rapport" we are being quite vague. However, this vagueness relates to our ignorance of the process. We say that they are "on the same wavelength." Again, we cannot define exactly what we are talking about when this term is used, but it does have significance. When this rapport is referred to in a male-female romantic relationship we say that the "chemistry" between the two individuals is very good. We cannot define what these particular chemicals are, but obviously they have something to do with the sex hormones. And this factor may be operative in some therapist-patient relationships when the parties are of the opposite sex. Pretty girls are likely to get more attention from their male therapists than those whose male therapists consider them less attractive. And pretty mothers are likely to get more attention from male therapists of their children and adolescents. And there are many other factors—conscious and unconscious, healthy and pathological—which may have a profound influence on the relationship.

FACTORS IN THE THERAPIST-PATIENT RELATIONSHIP CONDUCIVE TO BRINGING ABOUT THERAPEUTIC CHANGE

Possessing certain qualities requisite to doing effective work with children is of little value if these qualities are not utilized in building a good relationship with the child. A good therapist-patient relationship is crucial to successful therapy. It is the focal point around which the various therapeutic experiences occur, and it is difficult to imagine successful psychotherapy if the relationship between the patient and therapist is not a good one.

A meaningful relationship with other human beings is vital to survival. Provide a newborn infant with food, clothing, and shelter, but deprive it of the tender loving care of a mother (or her substitute) and the child will lose its appetite, become unresponsive to the environment, and may actually waste away and die. Others similarly deprived may survive infancy but may develop such severe withdrawal from others that they become effectively nonfunctioning individuals, living in their own mental worlds, and gaining whatever little gratification they can from their fantasies. The parental deprivation need not be overt (such as physical abandonment) but can result from psychological rejection in the form of parental withdrawal, hostility, lack of interest, or other kinds of detrimental interaction with the child. In short, it is only through meaningful and gratifying involvement with others that we develop into human beings; without such exposure we may survive, but we cannot then be called truly human.

Meaningful relationships with others are the stuff of life. More than anything else they enrich us; without them we become shells—mere imitations of living individuals. From the moment we are born until the time of our death we need others—necessary times for solitude notwithstanding. The child in treatment has generally suffered some difficulties in the ability to form and gain gratifications from involvement with others. It is hoped that therapy will help the child accomplish this. But I cannot imagine its being successful if a meaningful relationship hasn't been accomplished between the therapist and the patient.

The Therapist's Affection for the Patient

The therapist's affection for the child can serve to compensate for some of the privations the patient may have experienced in relationships with others. However, there are significant limitations in the degree to which the therapist can do this. Although the parents may exhibit formidable deficiencies, they most often are providing the child with food, clothing, shelter, protection, and guidance. Even though they may have serious psychological problems, they are in all likelihood more bonded with the child than is the therapist and they probably will always be. The youngster who has been severely deprived—so much so that there are and there never will be any bonds established with any human being—is not likely to benefit from the therapist's affection. The youngster who has suffered some (but not formidable) deprivation in this area is more likely to profit from the therapist's affection. Such affection can be ego-enhancing to the child and therefore therapeutic. In a way, it is easier for the therapist to provide the patient with the unadulterated affection that the parents and others may not be able to give. The therapeutic situation is so structured that therapists need not have to do much of the "dirty work" entailed in raising children. Therapists don't have to change diapers, get dawdling children dressed in the morning, bring them to emergency rooms in the middle of the night, worry about them when they are not home on time, etc. They, like the grandparents, can enjoy children in the most relaxed situations—when few demands and restrictions are placed on any of the parties—and so there is less chance that there will be conflicts, power struggles, and other difficulties.

I am not suggesting that the therapist should like the child all the time. It is unrealistic to expect anyone to like anyone else more than a significant percentage of the time. Children will do things at times that will irritate their therapists, bore them, and alienate them in a variety of ways. It is hoped that the therapist will use these negative reactions in constructive and therapeutic ways. I do not agree with those who hold that therapists should have "unconditional positive regard" for their patients. Those who claim that they do are either lying or just not in touch with the inevitable frustrations and irritations we experience in our relationships with all human beings—patients included. Patients who are told that the therapist "accepts" them (a condescending remark if there ever was one) regardless of what they do or say, will distrust the therapist (and justifiably so). They will recognize the duplicity inherent in such an attitude and this must be antitherapeutic. I will elaborate on the concept of "unconditional positive regard" in the next section. Accordingly, the optimum experience youngsters can have with regard to their therapist's affection is that they view the therapist as someone who likes them most of the time and that when they do things that alienate the therapist, the latter will use his or her negative reactions benevolently in the service of helping them.

Intimately associated with the affection the therapist has for the child is the feeling of pleasure that the therapist may experience with the child. The child's appreciation, at some level, that he or she is capable of providing another individual with pleasure on a continual (but not necessarily uninterrupted) basis is gratifying and ego-enhancing. And this is yet another element in the therapist-patient relationship that can be therapeutic.

There are some therapists who actually believe that they can provide children with significant compensatory affection for that which they have not received from parents and other caretaking individuals. I believe that this is unrealistic. The amount of time the therapist spends with the youngster is an extremely small fraction of that which even the more deficient parents spend with the patient. Most therapists generally see their patients once or twice a week. But even classical psychoanalysts, who see their child patients four or five times a week, are still involving themselves with the youngster a smaller fraction of the time than the parents are. Only if the therapist is willing to go to court and litigate for transfer of the child to him or herself, adopt the child both legally and psychologically, provide the child with food, clothing, and shelter, and then over years provide significant love and affection, perhaps then will the bond between the patient and the therapist be stronger than that which the child had with the parents—even the more deficient ones. Also, the therapist has not generally seen the child during the earliest years of life when the deepest bonds have been formed. And, as discussed at the outset in Vol. I (1999a), if there has been significant deprivation of parental affection, the therapist, no matter how loving and giving, is not likely to be able to compensate the child anyway. The child has gone beyond what I consider to be the critical period for the development of the capacity to gain from the affection of others.

It is also important for the therapist to appreciate that children do not generally develop the kinds of deep bonds with their therapists that many adult patients form. Let us take the example of children's relationships with their teachers. Although children may spend five to seven hours a day, five days a week for approximately 180 days (the duration of the school year) with their teachers, and although they may miss their teachers somewhat at the end of the school year, they generally are not devastated by the disruption of the relationship. It is a rare child who goes into mourning or depression over the fact that he or she will no longer have a particular teacher. If this is the nature of the bond a child can form with a teacher—a person with whom the youngster spends much more time than with the therapist and a person with whom the child may have much more benevolent experiences than enjoyed with the therapist–then it is unlikely that the youngster is going to mourn or grieve after the disruption of the therapist-patient relationship. Most of the children and adolescents I see do not have any strong, painful reactions after the termination of the treatment–whether the termination be appropriate or premature. This is another statement of the weakness of the depth of the bond between therapist and patient and another reason why I believe that the therapist's capacity to provide significant compensation for parental deprivations is limited. This does not mean, however, that no therapeutic work can be done. It only means that the relationship I am discussing here, the relationship that is the foundation for the youngster's treatment, at best is weaker than that which the patient has with the parents. But this does not preclude effective therapy taking place within its context.

"Unconditional Positive Regard"

Related to the issue of the therapist's affection for the patient is the concept of "unconditional positive regard." The term was introduced by Carl Rogers who considered this attitude by the therapist toward the patient to be central to his therapeutic approach, which he referred to as *nondirective therapy* or *client-centered therapy.* I have always considered the term *client centered therapy* to be somewhat condescending in that it implies that other therapists are less concerned with their patients than Carl Rogers. It reminds me of those individuals who have bumper stickers which state "I brake for animals." Again, the implication here is that the driver of a car bearing this sign is somewhat superior to others who couldn't care less if they ran over an animal. Probably the most well known therapist to apply Rogerian techniques to children was V. Axline (1947, 1964). The basic assumption of Rogerian theory is that there resides within all of us fundamental knowledge about what is best for us, but that social inhibitions suppress and repress the expression of these healthy forces. The primary goal of treatment is to help people bring about a state of "self-actualization" via which the blocked impulses are given free expression. The optimum atmosphere in which to realize this goal is one in which the therapist is basically nondirective and provides the patient with "unconditional positive regard." Technnically, this is best accomplished by the therapist's serving a catalytic role in which the last fragments of the patient's statement are repeated back to him or her. If one looks at psychology textbooks of the 1950s and 1960s, and turns to the chapter on psychotherapy, Rogerian treatment is often presented as psychotherapy per se–often with few alternative psychotherapeutic methods described. At the time, psychoanalysis was viewed as the supreme form of treatment by psychiatrists and Rogerian therapy as the optimum form of treatment by psychologists. One element in this development probably related to the fact that the classical psychoanalytic institutes were not permitting psychologists admission–a situation that still exists, to some extent, to this day. However, this too is changing as fewer physicians are demonstrating interest in psychoanalytic training. This new receptivity to psychologists' entering psychiatric psychoanalytic training programs has not been brought about by true insight into the contributions psychology can provide; rather, it stems from the desire for self-preservation. Without such input from the realm of psychology, most analytic institutes would be defunct from lack of new recruits and acolytes.

Although Rogerian therapists claimed that the treatment was quite complex and not a simple one in which the therapist, in parrot-like fashion, repeated the last fragments of the patient's statement, in practice that is what generally went on. I recall an anecdote that was making the rounds during my residency about the man who goes to a Rogerian analyst. The following interchange takes place:

> *Patient*: Boy, I'm feeling depressed today.
>
> *Therapist*: So, you're feeling depressed today.
>
> *Patient*: I'm feeling so depressed, I feel like killing myself.
>
> *Therapist*: So you're feeling so depressed, you feel like killing yourself.
>
> *Patient*: I'm feeling so depressed, I could jump right out of that window, even though we're on the 23rd floor.
>
> *Therapist*: You're feeling so depressed, you could jump right out of that window, even though we're on the 23rd floor.

Patient: Yes, that's how I feel. (At this point, the patient gets up, walks to the window, opens it up, and stands on the window sill.)

Therapist (Now looking at the patient, who is standing on the ledge of the open window): So that's how you feel.

Patient (Now leaps off the ledge and a few seconds later the sound of his body—splat—is heard as it splatters on the sidewalk.)

Therapist (Now walks to the window and peers out, looking down at the sidewalk): Splat!

The reader may view this anecdote to be a mockery of Rogerian treatment, consider it a *reductio ad absurdum*, and argue that only the most simple-minded therapists would respond in this manner. I am in agreement that most Rogerian therapists would not go so far as to let the patient jump out of the window. However, I do believe that the overwhelming majority of Rogerian therapists were not doing much more than "splat therapy."

Not only am I in disagreement with the technical maneuver of catalyzing the patient's comments by repeating the last fragment, but I have other disagreements with the Rogerian approach as well. First I do not have the conviction for the existence of an inborn pool of knowledge and feelings which is basically healthy, and that it is the suppression of these thoughts and feelings that brings about psychopathology. And I do not believe that simple release of these pent-up feelings—whether by nondirective therapy or any other approach—is the primary therapeutic ingredient (although it can help a little). In fact, when people who have completed such treatment are "self-actualized" they appear to be quite similar to others who had self-actualized themselves at the same time. In the 1960s this often took the form of going to Vermont, joining a commune, and engaging oneself in eating natural foods and weaving baskets.

Furthermore, I am not in agreement with the notion that a therapist should provide a patient with "unconditional positive regard." I consider this to be a disservice in that it ill equips the patient to function in a world where this is rarely if ever provided. In fact, one's mother does not even give one unconditional positive regard. For the therapist to do so must involve some fabrication and/or suppression of the therapist's thoughts and feelings in that there must be times when the patient's behavior is irritating and alienating. Allowing the patient to believe that his or her farts smell like perfume is not providing the patient with a healthy life experience. The rest of the people in the world generally remove themselves from us when we alienate them and do not give us the reasons why. I believe that the therapist—rather than being nondirective and providing unconditional positive regard—should be more directive and should provide "negative regard," when such is warranted. One must differentiate between criticism given benevolently and criticism given malevolently. Patients need benevolent criticism and direction to help them in life. If they cannot obtain these from their therapists, then who else is going to provide them in as objective and benevolent a way.

Treatment of the Projected Self

This phenomenon has broad implications for many aspects of treatment, for both the patient and the therapist, and has not been given the attention it deserves. For example, adults in individual therapy who tend to view most of the people they encounter as harboring or exhibiting certain alienating qualities are usually denying these same characteristics in themselves by projecting them on to others. Similarly, those who do group therapy frequently observe patient A suggest an interpretation of patient B's behavior that is totally irrelevant to B, but a clear statement of A's difficulties. This defense is well known to therapists and we most often have little difficulty detecting it. When we ourselves utilize the mechanism, we are less likely to be aware of it. I believe that all of us use it to varying degrees. When properly utilized, it can enhance the efficacy of our work; improperly used, it can seriously interfere with it.

Practically every therapist has been asked, at some time or other, "How can you listen to that shit all day long?" If the question is benevolently asked (and it often isn't) and if the therapist is inclined to respond seriously (and he or she is not often so inclined), one of the completely honest answers is: "In treating my patients, I treat vicariously my projected self, and this is an important determinant of my interest." Although many factors certainly contribute to one's choice of psychotherapy as a profession, one that is central for most, if not all, is the desire to cure one's own psychopathology. Rarely is personal analysis, or other forms of therapy which the therapist may have engaged in, enough to accomplish this goal. We are still at too primitive a level in our knowledge to use the word *cure;* at best, we usually strive toward significant *alleviation* of our own and our patient's difficulties. And whether previously treated or not, the therapist, I believe, continually attempts to alleviate his or her own psychological problems through psychotherapeutic endeavors in which the vicarious treatment of the projected self is operative. The pathological processes within us are disowned and projected onto the patient. It is as if each time we ameliorate the patient's problems, we are vicariously alleviating our own. Without this factor operative, I do not think the therapist would maintain for long interest in the psychological minutiae that patients in treatment can often endlessly discuss. In fact, if one could indeed *cure* a prospective therapist of all psychopathological problems (whatever that really means), then I question whether he or she would continue on as a therapist—so vital do I believe this mechanism to be as a motivating factor for those who do psychotherapy. There are certainly other motivating factors operative—and many of these are far less self serving—but it is a vital one that is not given the attention it deserves. The child therapist is, in all likelihood, treating vicariously his or her own childhood problems that have yet to be resolved.

If therapists are using patients to treat themselves vicariously, may this not be detrimental to the patient? Doesn't this interfere with the patient's therapy? Couldn't this be considered exploitive? Doesn't this tendency result in the therapist's seeing things in the patient that do not exist? The questions are rhetorical. They describe real dangers in the therapeutic situation—dangers that we have not studied enough to enable us to avoid them effectively. Yet, if what I have said is true—that a certain amount of this factor is necessary if the therapist is to be meaningfully interested in the patient—what is the solution to this problem? It lies, I believe, in determining that level at which the salutary use of the therapist's treatment of the projected self ends and the pathological begins. How can we learn then to make this important distinction between the helpful and detrimental use of this mechanism? It is not within the scope of this book to discuss in detail possible methods that we might utilize to make this important distinction. Elsewhere (1973c) I have proposed some techniques by which we might be able to differentiate between healthy and pathological treatment of the projected self.

Taking the Patient's Side in His Or Her Conflict with the Parents

Some therapists believe that taking the patient's side against parents or other authority figures is a good way of engaging the youngster in treatment and entrenching the therapeutic relationship. One of the earliest and most well-known proponents of this approach was August Aichhorn, a Viennese schoolmaster who tried to apply Freudian psychoanalytic techniques to the treatment of delinquent boys. In his classic *Wayward Youth* (1925) he described the difficulties that arose in such boys' treatment because they were very defiant of authority and tended to see him as another authority against whom to rebel. He found, however, that if he looked at the world from their vantage point and identified with them in their antisocial attitudes, he could gain their admiration and thereby form a relationship with them. In words, but not in acts, he expressed sympathy for their antisocial behavior. He would become a psychological ally in order to win their confidence. Once such a relationship was established, he would gradually shift his position and attempt to bring about a stronger superego in the youngsters. An intrapsychic conflict would thereby develop, in short, a psychoneurotic process. His hope was that their desire to maintain their relationship with him would then motivate the youngsters to follow along with him as he encouraged them to remain in the treatment and tolerate its pains and frustrations. His hope also was that he would then become a model for prosocial behavior.

There is an obvious duplicity involved in such an approach, and I myself would not be comfortable utilizing it. I think that most youngsters would sense the therapist's artificiality when supporting antisocial behavior and would thereby lose respect for him or her—and this could not but be antitherapeutic. Most therapists today would not utilize this approach.

There are therapists, however, who consider themselves to be the protectors of their child and adolescent patients against the indignities they suffer at the hands of their parents. Such a position has a divisive effect on the family. It puts the patient between the therapist and the parents in a tug-of-war and is thereby antitherapeutic.

I believe that the ideal therapeutic situation is one in which children come to view their therapists as impartial, as criticizing them benevolently when such criticism is warranted and equally ready to criticize the parents when the therapist considers them to be in error. In the context of such impartiality, the therapist can still serve to protect youngsters from irrational and inapropriate attitudes and reactions they may be exposed to. In such situations youngsters may feel quite helpless; having someone whom the parents respect and who can bring about a reduction and even elimination of parental detrimental exposures can be most salutary for the patient. It reduces tension and anxiety, takes a heavy burden off the child, and removes environmental influences that may be significantly contributory to the patient's symptoms. Similarly, such an impartiality makes it more likely that the therapist will be in a position to protect the parents from the youngster's irrationality and indignities they suffer as a result of it.

Ideally, the therapist's position should be one of providing information and advice to both parents and children. It is hoped that the parents will be receptive to the therapist's recommendations. If not, therapists should listen with receptivity to the parents' disagreements. If modification is justified, the therapist should be comfortable doing so. If the therapist remains unconvinced that his or her suggestions should be altered, the following statement should be made: "Well, this is what I think would be in the best interests of your child. Perhaps one of us may change his or her opinion in the future."

Children should not view the therapist as someone who controls the parents, but rather as one who provides advice and information and leaves it up to the parents to decide whether or not they wish to accept the therapist's opinions and implement his or her recommendations. If the therapist is seen as the manipulator of the parents and if the patient sees the parents as being unduly dependent on the therapist, as people who hang on the therapist's every word and put them into action, the parent-child relationship is likely to be compromised. In addition, such a situation may produce in the child some discomfort with the therapist because he or she is jeopardizing the respect that the patient has for the parents.

Ideally, both parents and patient should come to view the therapist as truly impartial, as attempting to be as objective as possible, and as not favoring anyone. They should come to view the therapist as someone who sides with healthy behavior—regardless of who exhibits it—and benevolently criticizes unhealthy behavior—regardless of who manifests it. Generally, the criticisms tend to balance out and no one tends to feel that the therapist is prejudiced against him or her. In such an atmosphere, both the patient and parents will generally come to respect the therapist. In contrast, when therapists routinely attempt to favor the youngster, they will alienate the parents and lose the respect of the child, who senses the duplicity—a situation that is definitely antitherapeutic.

The Resolution of the Transference Neurosis

Of the innumerable patterns of human interaction each person tends to select a few favorites. From earliest childhood (primarily as the result of our interaction with our parents) we develop a constellation of patterns of relating to others that are unique. As we grow older these patterns become strengthened and we tend to utilize them in preference to others that may be either absent from our repertoire or have lower priority for utilization. Some of these patterns of interaction are healthy and enhance our effectiveness in life. Others are maladaptive and often cause us significant difficulty, both personally and in our interaction with others. These patterns are strongly repetitive—almost reflexly so. Accordingly, in new situations we tend to use the old patterns, even though we may suffer significantly because of our injudicious reactions.

Using psychoanalytic terminology, we tend to *transfer* onto others reactions that we had toward our parents in infancy and childhood. We tend to interact with others in a manner similar to the way we interacted with our parents. When these modes of interaction are neurotic—and they exhibit themselves in the therapeutic relationship—they are termed *transference neuroses*. Specifically, patients try to involve the therapist in the same pathological patterns with which they were involved with their parents and with which they try to involve others as well. Those who comply with these requests (because of their own pathological needs) maintain their relationships with the patient (they may call such individuals their "friends"); those who do not comply with the psychopathological overtures for involvement, avoid or sever ties (and may be regarded as "unfriendly"). When the therapist refuses to involve him or herself in the pathological pattern, the patient will generally react with resentment, anxiety, or other divisive thoughts and emotions. At such a point the patient may leave therapy and consider the therapist uncaring, unloving, uninterested, hostile, etc. Or, the patient may choose to try to gain insight into what is going on and attempt to change the maladaptive pattern. Such working through is referred to as the *resolution of the transference neurosis* and is an important step in the alleviation of the patient's difficulties. It is to be hoped that once the pathological pattern of interaction is alleviated in the context of the patient's relationship with the therapist, he or she will more readily develop healthier modes of interaction in relationships with others as well.

Although child analysts differ regarding whether a child can exhibit what can justifiably be termed a transference neurosis (M. Klein, 1932; A. Freud, 1965), I believe that most children will do so if they get involved with the therapist. In other words, the deeper the child's relationship with the therapist the greater the likelihood the child will exhibit the pathological patterns of interaction and the greater the chance the child will try to involve the therapist in them. For example, a 13-year-old girl, who uses coyness and seductivity to get her way with adults, may try to involve the therapist similarly. In response to the therapist's failure to react with the expected "affection," she may become angry, consider him or her to be mean and unfriendly, and refuse to return. However, if such a youngster can be engaged (and it is the purpose of this book to help the therapist accomplish this), she may be helped to appreciate and experience that there are more effective and predictably gratifying ways of relating to others. If a good relationship is not established, the patient will be less willing to tolerate the frustrations attendant to the therapist's refusal to comply with pathological requests. And the youngster will thereby be less likely to gain this important therapeutic benefit that can be derived from the relationship.

Last, I wish to emphasize the point that the aforementioned changes relating to the resolution of the transference neurosis are less accomplished from insights and more from experiences within the therapeutic relationship. The insights the patient gains into the fact that the transferential patterns are often replays of early childhood involvements is less important than the *experience* the patient has with the therapist. *Learning* that the neurotic overtures will not be successful with the therapist is less important than having the *experience* that the neurotic goal will not be accomplished. When these therapeutic involvements are expanded into the world outside of the consultation room, a similar process occurs.

The Transference Cure

When patients, very early in treatment, exhibit a sudden and dramatic alleviation (and even cure) of presenting symptoms, they are described by psychoanalysts as having exhibited a *transference cure*. Specifically, because the patient hasn't delved into the unconscious roots of the pathology and worked out the basic problems that underlie it (something that generally takes a long time to do), the therapeutic change is usually considered specious. When this occurs extremely early in therapy (such as after the first or second session), it is understood to reflect the patient's resistance to entering into treatment:

> *Patient* (at the beginning of the second session): You are, without doubt, the most brilliant doctor I've ever met. Since I saw you last time, I'm one hundred percent better. I'm feeling so good that I'm wondering whether I need any more treatment.
>
> *Therapist*: But all I did last time was ask you some questions about your problems and get some background history.
>
> *Patient*: Oh, it was much more than that, doctor. There was something about the way you asked me those questions—I don't know what it was—that made me feel so much better. In fact, I don't know what I'm going to talk about today. I don't even know why I came. I'm feeling so good.

When the "cure" occurs a little later in treatment, it often relates to an attempt by patients to get the therapist to like or even love them. After all, if the primary goal of the therapist is to cure the patient, then it is reasonable to assume that the therapist will love someone who helps him or her achieve quickly this goal. Of course, both of the aforementioned factors may be operating simultaneously, and others as well. Rarely is there a simple explanation for anything that occurs in psychoanalytic treatment—or any other kind of psychotherapy as well.

These specious kinds of cures are well known to most psychotherapists. Because they are generally manifestations of a pathological pattern, the term *transference cure* is generally spoken of with a certain amount of derision. This, I believe, is unfortunate because there is a useful, and often unappreciated, element in the transference cure. All patients, I believe, change partly in the attempt to ingratiate themselves to the therapist. From the very first encounter the patient has with the therapist he or she wants to be liked. (This doesn't differ in any way from all other first encounters with nontherapists.) The anxiety the patient experiences in the first session is, in part, a manifestation of the fear that he or she will be considered loathsome and unworthy by the therapist because of the things that will be revealed. As the relationship intensifies, there is usually an even greater need to be liked by the therapist. The patient has invested much time and (often) money in the project and the reliance on the therapist to help the patient alleviate his or her difficulties is great.

I believe that *one* element that plays a role in patients' exhibiting therapeutic change is the desire to get the therapist to like them. Others are certainly operative. But this factor is, I believe, an important one in the early phases of alleviation of a symptom. Patients know that when they tell their therapists that improvement has occurred, the therapists cannot but feel good about themselves for their contribution to the success. (Some therapists, in accordance with their theoretical position, deny having any such gratification. I don't believe them.) If the patient has it within his or her power to make the therapist feel good, then it follows that the therapist will like the patient who provides such gratification. After all, we generally like most those who have the good sense to provide us with the pleasures we seek. It is to be hoped that the new mode of adaptation will subsequently become more deeply entrenched as the patient gains greater insight into the causes of the symptoms and has the experience that the newer way is the more judicious and gratifying. Then, the patient is likely to maintain the healthier adaptation because, through knowledge and/or experience, he or she will have developed the inner conviction that it is the preferable alternative. Ideally, the patient will then no longer need to maintain the improvement for the purpose of pleasing the therapist (whom he or she will probably never see again anyway after the treatment is over—psychological ties, fond memories, gratitude, and other positive feelings notwithstanding).

The younger the patient the greater the likelihood he or she will change behavior in order to please the therapist. Children are constantly concerning themselves with the approbations of parents, teachers, and other authorities. They are constantly being told about whether what they do and say is "good" or "bad," "right" or "wrong." And the therapist is just another authority from whom they usually wish to gain acceptance. It behooves the child therapist to make use of this phenomenon. It can enhance significantly the efficacy of the treatment. Accordingly, the therapist does well to praise the patient for newly gained healthier modes of behavior. Such praises, however, must be genuine; if they are artificial and/or contrived, the patient will sense this and they are not likely to "work." It is hoped that the earlier experience with the somewhat artificial venture into healthy behavior will help the youngster reach the point where he or she engages in the healthier adaptations—both from the inner conviction and the *experience* that life is much more gratifying when he or she does so. Although adolescents are less desirous of pleasing the therapist than younger children, they are still not immune to the process. Accordingly, the therapist can still rely on the benefits ultimately to be derived from the transference cure phenomenon.

The Corrective Emotional Experience

In the process of working through or resolving the transference neurosis a particularly effective therapeutic phenomenon that may occur is the *corrective emotional experience* (F. Alexander and T. French, 1946; F. Alexander, 1950). Essentially, the patient has a living experience (often associated with a significant upheaval of emotional reaction) that alters significantly a previous pattern. For example, a 14-year-old girl whose father has been very punitive may generalize and expect similar treatment from all men, including her male therapist. The therapist's telling such a youngster that he will treat her differently will not generally be very effective because intellectual processes only are involved in the communication. However, if the girl has the living experience– over an extended period–that the therapist indeed does not react punitively, then her view of men may indeed change. Her fearful reactions lessen and relaxation and trust gradually replace them. It is this combination of insight, feeling, and experience that brings about some of the most meaningful changes that can occur in psychotherapy.

When a boy cheats during a game I may say: "You know, it's no fun for me to play this game when you cheat. If you do that again I'm going to stop playing and we'll do something else." To simply discuss why the patient cheats may have some value. However, if this discussion takes place in a setting in which the patient experiences some frustration over the alienation his symptom causes, the conversation is more likely to be therapeutically meaningful. In such a discussion we might talk about whether this may be one of the reasons why others don't like to play with him, or about the futility of this way of trying to compensate for feelings of inadequacy, or about other aspects of the problem which may be of psychological significance. But, without the emotional reactions attendant to the threat of alienating the therapist and/or interrupting an enjoyable experience, such discussions are not likely to be very effective.

The Patient's Identification With the Therapist

Just as children imitate their parents and acquire many of their traits (both adaptive and maladaptive), they will tend to identify with the therapist if the relationship is a good one. It is to be hoped that the personality qualities that the patients acquire in this way will serve them in good stead. There are, as stated earlier, those who believe that what I am saying is risky business–that such a process is dangerous and antitherapeutic. They hold that therapists must do everything possible to present themselves as a blank screen upon which the patient's fantasies can be projected. Some believe that the therapist should encourage the patient's realizing his or her "true self." Central to such a theory is that there exists such an entity – that each individual has within him- or herself a personality pattern that is blocked from free expression by environmentally induced inhibitions and that such blockage is central to psychopathological behavior. They hold that an important aspect of treatment involves helping the individual express freely these hidden personality characteristics.

Although I certainly agree that many people in treatment are repressed and need to be helped to express themselves (although there are many who need some repression more than anything else), I believe most people usually need to express some *specific* pent-up thoughts or feelings. I am somewhat dubious about the concept of a whole personality being hidden inside, knocking for release. Rather, I believe that some aspects of our personality may be genetically determined (such as activity level, assertiveness, passivity, and curiosity); most, however, are environmentally induced (and even the genetic ones are subject to significant environmental modification). I see core *potentials,* not core personalities. Most of our character traits, I believe, are derived from the environment – more specifically from what we learn from those in the world around us and what we acquire by imitation of significant individuals in our lives. The therapist becomes another in the series of individuals whom the child may imitate, emulate, and identify with. Even the kind of therapist described above, who tries to provide the patient with a neutral atmosphere to facilitate "self-actualization," sends many subtle cues that encourage the patient to proceed in specific directions. In addition, the therapist still has a personality, and no matter how much he or she may try to suppress and hide it, much is still revealed – much that the patient may identify with.

As mentioned, it is obviously preferable that the qualities of the therapist that patients identify with will serve them well. For example, a 15-year-old boy's father may have operated in accordance with the principle that admitting any deficiencies to his children will lessen their respect for him. The boy, then, may take on this similar maladaptive pattern and find himself having trouble with his classwork because he cannot tolerate admitting errors. If his therapist, however, is the kind of person who can, without discomfort, admit errors when they naturally arise, the patient may come to appreciate that this is a desirable and effective pattern and may take on the quality him or herself. However, the therapist's admission of errors must be genuine. To do so in a contrived situation is not only therapeutically worthless but may be antitherapeutic because it is basically dishonest. Another example. A 14-year-old girl may have acquired the pattern of lying (in both subtle and overt ways) as a significant part of her interactional repertoire. In the course of treatment, she observes the therapist to be a person who is consistently honest. As a result, she recognizes that the therapist's life becomes less complicated and that such honesty enhances the esteem the therapist enjoys from others. As a result of the process of identification and emulation, she may acquire this valuable asset herself.

Therapists traditionally encourage their patients to express their pent-up thoughts and feelings from the appreciation that such expression, properly directed and utilized (not often the case), can be therapeutic. However, many therapists attempt to do this in a setting where they exhibit little if any such expression themselves (Gardner, 1968, 1973a). They thereby serve as poor models for their patients and so impede the process they are attempting to achieve. Therapists who express themselves in situations where such expression is appropriate, and in the best interests of the patient (as mentioned, without artificiality), have a much better chance of getting their patients to do so as the latter identify with them. Therapists who assert themselves and do not allow themselves to be taken advantage of serve as good models for patients who are inhibited in these areas. And it is only in the context of a good patient-therapist relationship that such salutary identifications can occur. As mentioned in Chapter One, such identification with the therapist's values can be risky. It is to be hoped that such values will be healthy; otherwise the therapy will do the patient more harm than good (a not uncommon occurrence, unfortunately).

The Therapist as Educator

We learn best from those whom we respect and admire. Disliked, hated, or disrespected teachers will teach their students little of educational value (although they may teach them something about having to tolerate a despised person in certain situations). Therapists who are basically respected can teach patients much that can be of therapeutic value. One does well to compare the relationship between a therapist and a patient with that which exists between a teacher and a pupil. Teachers who are enthusiastic about their work and genuinely enjoy teaching will communicate to their students the message that learning can be fun. The student will thereby emulate the teacher and attempt to gain the same gratifications. In such a setting, the youngster will be willing to endure the frustrations and drudgery that are necessary if one is to truly learn. The identification with the teaching person is a central element in the healthy educational process. A teacher who basically dislikes the work is not likely to serve as such a model and is not likely to teach her students very much. Even worse, a teacher who instills anger and fear in children not only is going to teach them little, but may very well contribute to the development of psychopathology.

I believe that therapy is, more than anything else, an educational process. Although we certainly try to help our patients learn as much as they can on their own, we are also providing a significant amount of information in the course of the therapeutic process. Good teachers try to get their students to derive as much information as they can on their own. It is only after their students have reached the limits of their capacity to acquire information and expand from the foundations they have built that the teacher supplements that which has been self-acquired. We don't want to spoon feed our patients and entrench their dependency; we want to help them become self-sufficient human beings, who learn how to learn, but who still can supplement the knowledge they have acquired with input from others with more knowledge and experience in a particular area.

A. Freud (1965) strictly warned therapists against submitting to the temptation to provide child patients with information and educational communications. Such advice is like warning an internist not to submit to the temptation to provide patients with penicillin. I am in full agreement with H. Strupp (1975), who considers the central element in adult psychoanalytic therapy (and other forms of psychotherapy as well) to be what he calls "lessons in constructive living." The more competent one is in dealing with the problems in life, the less likely one will be to form symptoms in an attempt to resolve the inevitable conflicts and problems with which we are all confronted. Whether therapists provide such communications directly, symbolically, or through insights into the unconscious they help their patients gain, the educational element regarding more effective living is ever there. When therapists are admired and respected, their patients will be receptive to what they have to say and treatment is more likely to succeed. When the therapist is bored, just putting in time to get payment, or otherwise going through the motions, little is likely to happen.

The Correction of Distortions As part of the educational process the therapist helps the patient correct distortions. For example, all of us carry into adult life distorted concepts of the world that we blindly accept. Adherence to these dicta may cause us many difficulties, yet they may never be questioned. It is one of the purposes of treatment to help patients examine (sometimes for the first time in their lives) these premises that guide their behavior. Some of the more common ones that adult (and often adolescent) therapists must deal with are: "No one is to be trusted," "Sex is bad," "Fun is sinful," "I must do everything to avoid criticism because all negative comments about me must be correct," "I must do everything possible to avoid anyone's getting angry at me," and "If there's a choice between another person's being inconvenienced and my being so, rather it be me." Some common dicta of childhood (which may continue into adolescence and even throughout life) are: "Mother and father are always right," "Nice boys and girls never have hateful thoughts toward their parents," "Thoughts can harm, i.e., wishing that something bad will happen to someone can make it happen," "If my mother and/or father doesn't love me very much, I can't be very good and no one can ever love me," "One fault makes you totally worthless," "There are perfect people who never make mistakes and never do anything wrong or bad," and "An unacceptable thought is as bad as an unacceptable act."

I believe that emotions related to fight and flight follow cognition and that many feelings of guilt, fear, anger, etc. can be alleviated if notions such as the aforementioned are corrected. A. Ellis (1963) holds that the correction of such cognitive distortions are the basic issues to be focused upon in psychotherapy and has coined the term *Rational-Emotive Psychotherapy* for this type of therapeutic approach. I am in agreement with Ellis that emphasis on this element is important in practically everyone's treatment, regardless of age. However, I believe that things are more complex and that many other factors contribute to symptom formation. (Although Ellis admits to other factors, he considers them far less important than cognitive distortions.)

Decreasing or Increasing Guilt From the earliest days of psychoanalysis S. Freud and J. Breuer (1895) considered reducing the patient's guilt to be one of the analyst's most important tasks. With less guilt, there is less repression and hence symptoms are less likely to develop and persist. Although Freud's subsequent experience convinced him that things were far more complex (some have yet to read his later work), the concept is certainly still valid if one considers it to be *one* of the possible contributing factors in *some* patients' difficulties. Partly by virtue of the therapist's position of authority and his or her experience in matters of things such as guilt, patients become convinced that their unacceptable urges are very common, if not universal, and that the difference between themselves and others is not so much that they have the particular thoughts and feelings, but that they feel more guilty over them. In essence the analyst communicates to the patient: "You're still acceptable to me, even though you have those ideas." (Condescending elements in the communication notwithstanding, the message is often helpful.)

In my work with youngsters who need some loosening up of their superegos, I will make such comments as: "Most people I know would get very angry when something like that happens. I guess you must have been pretty mad also," "I can't believe that somewhere, someplace, you weren't a little bit angry when that happened," or "So what's so terrible about *wanting* to do that? You know wanting is not the same as doing."

Many adolescents I see, however, do not need any loosening up of their consciences. They have what A.M. Johnson (1949, 1959) calls "super-ego lacunae," i.e., like Swiss cheese they seem to have holes in the part of the brain where the superego is (I speak figuratively, of course). If their treatment is to be useful, attempts should be made to increase such youngsters' guilt. Some comments that I may make in the service of this goal: "That's terrible. She really must have felt bad after you ripped up her new kite," and "I really don't think you could have felt very good about yourself getting 100 percent on that test after copying most of the answers from the kids around you."

To the 14-year-old bully I might say: "I know you think you're quite a big shot when you beat up those little kids. But deep down inside, you know that there's nothing so great about it and that must make you feel kind of bad about yourself. You think the kids think you're hot stuff when you go around beating up lots of kids. Some of them may; but others, I am sure, don't like you at all. They feel sorry for the children you're hitting and I'm sure you've noticed how they stay away from you." Although these comments can be very bitter medicine to swallow, they are accepted if the patient has a good relationship with the therapist. In addition, as mentioned, the therapist's attitude is more important than the content in determining whether his or her comments will alienate a patient. When benevolently communicated in the context of a firm relationship the most painful confrontations are likely to be accepted.

Acquiring a More Accurate View of One's Parents All patients, regardless of age, have to be helped in treatment to gain a clearer view of their parents. As children, we tend to operate on the principle: "If it's good enough for them, it's good enough for me." We tend to incorporate most if not all of their traits—healthy and unhealthy. We swallow the whole bag, without separating the good from the bad. Therapy, in part, involves making (often very belatedly) these vital discriminations. The child and adolescent therapist has the opportunity to provide these corrections at a time when it can do the most good, at a time before the deleterious results of such indiscriminating incorporation and acceptance have had a chance to become deeply entrenched. Children and adolescents have to be helped to appreciate that their parents, like all other human beings (including the therapist), are not perfect. We all have our deficits. Helping youngsters become clear regarding which personality traits of their parents are assets and which are liabilities can be very useful. And the therapist is in a unique position to provide such information. This, of course, may require some advance work with the parents; but if the relationship with them is a good one their cooperation can often be relied upon.

The phobic child of a phobic mother can be told: "You know that your mother has many fears that she herself realizes are not real. She knows that there's nothing to be afraid of in elevators or crowded places, but she just can't help herself. She'd prefer not to have these fears and that's why she's seeing a psychiatrist." Ideally, it can be helpful to get the mother herself to verbalize to the child comments such as these. (The reader interested in a detailed account of such parental divulgences in the therapy of a phobic child may wish to refer to Chapter Sixteen of my *Therapeutic Communication with Children,* 1971). The child of divorce can be told: "Your father can be counted upon to give your mother the money she needs to take care of herself and the children. However, as you know, he's not very reliable when it comes to showing up for appointments on visiting days. This doesn't mean that he doesn't love you at all. It does mean that he has less love for you than a father who does show up all the time. This doesn't mean that you are unlovable or that no one else can love you more. You still have many people who like being with you and you can spend time with them when your father doesn't show up." Elsewhere (1976, 1977, 1979), I have discussed in detail the wide variety of cognitive distortions that the therapist can help correct for children of divorce.

Acquiring a More Accurate View of Oneself I introduce my next point anecdotally. A number of years ago *Listerine* mouthwash was advertised with the slogan "Your best friend won't tell you." In the typical pitch a young girl cannot understand why dates persistently reject her even though she is bright, pretty, etc. Finally, she realizes that *bad breath* is driving them away! Happily, she chances on *Listerine* , washes her mouth with it, and the boys come flocking. I believe that therapists should be better than one's best friend. They should be able to tell their patients things that even their best friends will hesitate to reveal. And if the therapist's motivation is benevolent and his or her timing judicious, he or she should be able to do so with only occasional dificulty or hesitation.

To put it another way. Robert Burns (1786) once wrote:

'O wad some Pow'r the giftie (small gift) gie (give) us
To see oursels as others see us!
It would from many a blunder free us
And foolish notion.

It is the therapist's job to help patients see themselves as others see them. And this is one of the significant benefits that all patients, regardless of age, can derive from treatment. Such increases in self-awareness can indeed free individuals from unnecessary burdens and protect them from the detrimental effects of harboring foolish notions about themselves. Patients should be able to gain, as well, what H.S. Sullivan (1953) called "consensual validation" of their views of the world. For example, a youngster can be told: "You think that the kids really like you when they play with you after you give them money. If you think about it, I think you'll agree that they don't spend time with you *unless* you give them money. I suspect you're doing things that turn them off." And if the patient agrees, the therapist might say, "I wonder what those things might be?"

The boy who feels unpopular may attempt to gain respect and admiration by boasting about various exploits, travels, etc. However, the fear of exposure and possible guilt he may feel ultimately result in his feeling even worse about himself than before. And if (as is often the case) others learn of his duplicity, his social position is further worsened. As part of the therapy of such symptoms the therapist does well to inform the youngster of the injudiciousness of his mode of compensation. For the lonely 13 year-old boy who "clowns" in the classroom, I might say: "I know you think that clowning around in class gets the kids to like you. And I know you think that their laughing at you proves this. However, I believe that although you're good for laughs, they really don't like you in other ways. They still don't seem to invite you to parties nor do they seem to want to see you after school."

Another youngster can be told: "You always seem to want your way when you're here in the office. You always seem to want to do only those things you want. You never seem to care about what your mother or father or I would like to do or talk about. If you act this way with friends, maybe that's why they don't want to be with you." Another example: "You say you're sorry in the hope that a person will no longer be bothered or angry about what you've done. Although people may *say* that they accept your apology and that they're not angry, *deep down inside they really still are*. Even though you've told your father that you're sorry that you broke the television set, I think he's still angry that it's cost him all that money to fix it." I often suggest that youngsters who utilize this common manipulative device (invariably taught by parents) read my story "Say You're Sorry" in my book of psychologically oriented children's stories, *Dr. Gardner's Stories About the Real World* (1972b).

Part of the confrontational process involves helping children gain a more accurate picture of their assets and liabilities (both inborn and acquired). The child with a neurologically based coordination deficit should be discouraged from intensive involvement in competitive sports (although special training and exercises preparing for minmal to moderate involvement may be indicated). In the earliest years children's views of themselves are acquired from what H.S. Sullivan called "reflected appraisals" (P. Mullahy, 1970). In essence, children come to view themselves in accordance with information about them provided by significant figures in their lives, especially their parents. A four-year-old boy runs into the house crying, "Mommy, the kids all call me stupid." Mother replies, "You're not stupid. You're very smart. Although you're four you can write your name, count to 25, and you know nickels, dimes, and quarters. *He's* the one who's stupid, if he calls you stupid." Tears are kissed away and the child leaves the house reassured. The criteria for self-assessment here, however, are externally derived. He *is* what his mother (the final authority on him) says he is. As the boy grows older, he generally gathers information from others (teachers, neighbors, peers, etc) that may modify and expand the information derived from his parents. These facts become his own internal criteria for judging self-worth. It is to be hoped that the accumulated data (derived from parents and others) will be accurate and it is one of the therapist's jobs to help correct any distortions that may have arisen. And this is more easily done in adolescence than in adulthood.

Introducing Alternative Modes of Adaptation Last, it is part of the therapeutic educational process to introduce to patients alternative modes of adaptation to those pathological and self-defeating ones that they may be utilizing. These options may never have occurred to the patient, nor may he or she ever have been introduced to them. For example, in a boy's family, denial of or flight from awareness of one's deficiencies may have been the only reactions. Such a boy must be helped to appreciate the value of dealing directly with one's deficits and he must be encouraged to try this alternative to see for himself its advantages. Throughout the course of this book I provide many examples of the therapist's introduction of alternative modes of adaptation.

Intimacy and Self-Revelation

When we use the term *intimacy*, we are generally referring to a close personal relationship. I consider a central element in the intimate relationship to be the revelation of personal thoughts and feelings which one would generally not reveal indiscriminately to others. The revelation, however, is made in a situation where one anticipates a benevolent and/or understanding response by the listener. Without the freedom for such self-revelation the term intimacy does not apply. Intimate divulgences tend to bring people closer. The one to whom the information is revealed generally feels flattered by the revelation, especially because he or she has been selected from many possible listeners. Also, intimacy cannot be a one-way arrangement. Both individuals must feel comfortable with such revelations. Unilateral divulgence is not properly called intimate. Accordingly, many, if not most, therapist-patient relationships are not, by the above definition, intimate. They are generally one-way arrangements in which the patient reveals all (the ideal to be achieved) and some therapists believe that it behooves them to reveal nothing (or as close to nothing as is humanly possible). Whatever benefits may be derived from such an arrangement (and I do not deny that there are some), it cannot reasonably be referred to as an intimate relationship.

This situation presents dilemmas for therapists. If they reveal more of themselves, in order to enhance the intimacy of the relationship, they are going to contaminate blank-screen associations. In addition, there is the risk that the patient's time will be used more for the benefit of the therapist than the patient—especially if the revelations focus on problems of the therapist's. This easily becomes exploitive of the patient. In contrast, therapists who strictly hide behind the couch in order to provide their patients with a blank screen, who strictly avoid any self-revelation, may achieve many benefits derived from their patients unadulterated free associations. However, these patients are robbed of the psychotherapeutic benefits to be derived from a close and intimate relationship. I believe there is some point between these two extremes where there is a proper balance of self-revelation by the therapist and self-revelation by the patient. The vast majority of the revelations should be made by the patient, but not every divulgence provided by the therapist need be viewed as unnecessary utilization of the patient's time or exploitation of the patient by the therapist. Such revelations by the therapist–judiciously provided–can be therapeutically beneficial. They bring the two individuals closer, entrench the relationship, and strengthen thereby the foundation upon which therapy rests.

It is difficult to state specifically when the revelations are judicious and when they are not. There are some guidelines however. As mentioned, a revelation made by the therapist–whose primary purpose is to use the patient for assistance in dealing with the therapist's own problems–is clearly contraindicated. Also, if a significant amount of the patient's time is used for such therapist revelations, then this too is exploitive of the patient. One of the best guidelines is that the revelation should have immediate and obvious benefit to the patient's treatment. A personal experience of the therapist's that may help the patient gain insight into his or her problems at that point would be in this category. As mentioned in Chapter Five, metaphorical, anecdotal, and experiential communications often provide a useful vehicle for communicating important therapeutic messages. And the experiences and anecdotal material provided by the therapist can be very much in this category.

Another guideline is that the divulgence of such material should not be contrived or artificial. Rather, it should flow from the natural course of the material provided in the session. Obviously, this guideline is not being followed if the therapist initiates such divulgences at the beginning of the session. My *The Talking, Feeling, and Doing Game* (1973b), to be discussed subsequently, provides therapists with many opportunities to divulge information about themselves in a noncontrived manner. Game cards provide the therapist with the opportunity to make such revelations and, in accordance with the rules of the game, if the therapist doesn't answer the question, he or she does not get a reward chip!

There is another aspect to the therapeutic benefits of the therapist's self-revelations that is particularly applicable to child and adolescent therapy. Children generally enjoy thoroughly hearing details about events that occurred in their parent's lives during their childhood. A child will commonly ask a parent, "Mommy, tell me about how things were with you when you were my age and living with grandma and grandpa." Such information is generally of great interest to children and the divulgence of it strengthens the parent-child bond. Similarly, therapists who judiciously provide such information about their own childhood and adolescence can also strengthen the therapist-patient relationship. What is lost by the resultant contamination of the blank screen is more than counter-balanced by the advantages related to the strengthening of the therapist-patient bond that such divulgences create. Furthermore, when providing such revelations the therapist is serving as a model for the youngster to reveal his or her own feelings and will thereby increase the likelihood that the patient will be freer to provide such revelations. Last, when such revelations involve the therapist's describing shortcomings and deficiencies of his or her own (in a noncontrived way), this too can be therapeutic. It helps reduce the idealization and idolization of the therapist that can be antitherapeutic. It makes the therapist more of a real human being who has both assets and liabilities—just like the rest of the world. Viewing the therapist as perfect will contribute to patients' lowering of feelings of self-worth as they invariably compare themselves unfavorably with their perfect, or nearly perfect, therapist. This too is antitherapeutic. Children and adolescents, especially, already feeling so impotent in their relationships with adults, are therefore likely to benefit significantly from such divulgences.

THREE

CONFIDENTIALITY

Adolescent psychopathology, like all forms of psychopathology, is best understood as a manifestation of intrapsychic and interpersonal factors. Although social, cultural, and genetic factors must certainly be considered, most of the therapeutic work focuses on the interpersonal and intrapsychic elements because there is little if anything that can be directly done by the therapist in the consultation room about the other contributory factors. Outside the office, the therapist may be devoting himself significantly to changing these external factors, but this is not of immediate value to the patient's treatment. In order to address oneself to the interpersonal elements, it is important that the therapist work closely with other individuals who may have contributed to the development of the youngster's difficulties and who may still be playing a role in the perpetuation of the problems. Most often this involves members of the immediate family and, on occasion, other individuals such as grandparents, aunts, and uncles. I cannot discuss the specific ways in which I involve myself with these other individuals without first discussing the issue of confidentiality. Obviously, the guidelines I utilize in deciding whether or not I will reveal what the youngster tells me must be understood before one can discuss meaningfully when and when not to discuss and divulge information. In this section, I will consider the general issue of confidentiality and the principles presented here will be followed in my subsequent discussions of individual treatment, group therapy, and work with parents.

Many therapists believe that the active involvement of a parent in a child's treatment will compromise significantly the youngster's confidentiality, the preservation of which is crucial to meaningful therapy. I believe that such therapists are placing too much weight on confidentiality. The patient is coming primarily for treatment—whether the patient is a child, adolescent, or an adult. The patient is not coming primarily for the preservation of confidentiality. To the degree that the preservation of the confidential relationship serves the ends of treatment, to that degree should it be respected. To the degree that strict adherence to confidentiality will undermine, subvert, or work against the goals of therapy, to that degree should confidentiality be ignored or compromised. One must not lose sight of the primary aim of therapy: to do what is in the best interests of the patient. In order to describe my position more specifically, I will consider the confidentiality issue as it pertains to the treatment of the adult, the adolescent, and the child. Although there are differences with regard to confientiality in these three areas, there are basic similarities that hold for all three categories.

CONFIDENTIALITY IN ADULT THERAPY

If the adult is to have a successful therapeutic experience, he or she must have the feeling that the therapist will not disclose to others what is revealed during the course of treatment. Otherwise, the freedom to reveal will be significantly compromised—to the point where therapy may become meaningless. Most therapists would agree, however, that there are certain situations in which strict adherence to confidentiality may be antitherapeutic. Such is the case when there is a strong suicidal or homicidal risk. Basically, when a human life is at stake, concerns about confidentiality are reduced to the point of being trivial. If the patient is suicidal, it behooves the therapist to enlist the aid of family members and close friends to do everything possible to protect the patient. This usually involves their active participation in hospitalizing the suicidal patient. It would be unconscionable to "respect" such a patient's request that the suicidal danger not be divulged to the nearest of kin. Similarly, when there is a homicidal risk, the therapist should do everything possible to warn the potential victim and to take every reasonable precaution to prevent the murder.

When an adult patient in treatment raises the issue of confidentiality, I will openly state that he or she can feel secure that I will not reveal what is divulged—with the exception of situations in which there is a homicidal or suicidal danger. In most cases, the patient is thereby reassured that confidences will not be divulged because neither of these eventualities seems likely. On occasion, however, a depressed patient will be told that I might divulge the suicidal danger. In such cases I will assure the patient that everything will be done to avoid such disclosure. However, I inform the patient that there might be an occasion in which I might divulge the suicidal risk, if such revelation might prove lifesaving. Interestingly, most patients are not upset by this. Some healthy part of them appreciates that they could conceivably "go crazy," and that at such a time they might impulsively commit a self-destructive act that could cause irreparable damage and even death. My position provides reassurance that should such a situation occur some healthy and stabilizing intervention will take place.

A good example of this phenomenon occurred many years ago when I saw in treatment a 35-year-old man who came to therapy with chief complaints of depression and excessive drinking. Early in the treatment he told me that he suspected that his wife was having an affair. She was coming home at 2:00 to 3:00 am with various excuses regarding why she was so late. None of these were convincing. Finally, he told me that he had hired a private detective to help him determine whether his suspicions were justified. About two weeks later, he telephoned me in a state of agitated rage. The detective had confirmed his suspicions. He had many details about his wife's visit to various hotels and motels with her lover—who turned out to be a "friend" of his. He told me that he planned to go home immediately and kill his wife with a gun that he had in the house. He stated that this was the only way he could "save face." He agreed, however, to come to my office en route home to discuss the matter further.

In our discussion the patient told me that he was terribly humiliated and that the knowledge that his wife was having an affair caused terrible damage to his self-esteen. He reiterated that the only way he could possibly regain a sense of self-worth was to kill his wife. I sympathized with the blow to his ego that the knowledge of his wife's affair caused him; however, I tried to impress upon him my belief that his reactions were definitely exaggerated. I told him that too much of his self-worth was dependent on external events, events that he had no control over. Specifically, if his self-worth were significantly determined by his wife's sex life outside the home, then he was putting himself in a very precarious position because his self-worth was thereby dependent on events over which he had absolutely no control. Furthermore, I told him that I did not agree with him that killing his wife would thereby enhance his feelings of self-worth. Again, it was another example of an external event that was being used in the service of changing an intrapsychic process.

After about two hours of discussion, the patient remained unconvinced and insisted that he was going home to kill his wife. I then confronted him with the various options that were open to me: two of which were to call the police and/or call his wife. He angrily informed me that I had no right to inform his wife because we had a confidential relationship. He went further and threatened that he would sue me for malpractice as well as report me to my psychiatric and medical societies for unethical conduct. The following interchange then ensued:

> *Therapist*: Let me ask you this. Why did you first come here to see me?
>
> *Patient*: Because I was depressed and had a drinking problem.
>
> *Therapist*: Yes, that's my recollection also. And what did you ask me to do?
>
> *Patient*: I asked you to help me with these problems.
>
> *Therapist*: Yes, that's my recollection. Now, did I ever say to you that I would never, under any circumstances, reveal to others what you told me.

Patient: No, but I didn't think it was necessary. I assumed that I wouldn't even have to raise that question. I assumed that you, as my psychiatrist, would never reveal anything that I said to you. I assumed that we had a confidential relationship.

Therapist: Yes, I agree with you. I never did promise you that I would not reveal what you said to me. I am in agreement with you that if you were to have the feeling that I were to frivolously reveal what you told me, that you would not have the kind of comfort and confidence necessary for good therapy. However, if you had asked me about confidentiality, I would have told you that under certain circumstances I would not respect it—especially in situations where there is a risk of homicide or suicide. And this is one of those situations.

Furthermore, I believe that divulgence in this situation will really serve the ends of your treatment, especially the goals that we set out for ourselves. I believe that if you kill your wife it will not only *not* enhance your self-worth but will result in your going to jail for many years. I believe, as well, that while incarcerated you probably will become even more depressed and your craving for alcohol will probably increase enormously. Accordingly, I believe that I am serving the goals of your treatment by doing everything possible to prevent you from killing your wife.

After further discussion, I told the patient that I thought the best option was to call his wife, invite her to the office, and the three of us would then discuss what we would do. Reluctantly, the patient said nothing while I called his home. Fortunately, his wife was at home and I told her the reasons for my call. She agreed to come to the office. I told her that I thought it would be a good idea for her to drop the gun off at the police station en route to our meeting. The patient suddenly chimed in and asked me to tell his wife that she should drop the gun off at his brother's house. I responded, "No way. The police station." The wife agreed and joined us. After a few hours of further discussion, I felt I could safely let the patient return home with his wife. (By that time I think he was too exhausted from psychotherapy to even lift a gun, if he had one.) Before leaving, arrangements were made for intensive counseling for the two of them.

I believe that this man was basically ambivalent about murdering his wife. Had he been fully resolved to kill her, he would not have called me. In his scheme of things, the only way to preserve his masculinity was to take revenge. However, healthier and more rational forces were operating; otherwise, he would not have called me and, in addition, agreed to discuss the matter with me. It was to these healthy forces that I appealed to when I decided not to respect his confidentiality. What I did, however, was to demonstrate what I considered to have been a greater respect for my patient, namely, I did everything to interrupt an act for which he would probably have suffered regret for the rest of his life.

In recent years there have been a number of cases in which the litigation has centered on this issue. Psychiatrists were sued for malpractice because they preserved patients' confidences, and there was a resultant suicide or homicide that could conceivably have been prevented. The usual defense was that the therapist was respecting the patient's confidentiality and the doctor was acting in the highest ethical traditions of the medical profession. Even in former years, I did not subscribe to this view. It is not in the highest ethical tradition of the medical profession to sit by and do nothing when there might be a suicide or homicide taking place. It is in the highest interests of the medical profession to protect human life. Fortunately, the courts and ethical committees in medical societies are shifting in the direction of supporting divulgences in such cases. This is a good trend.

CONFIDENTIALITY IN ADOLESCENT THERAPY

It is not uncommon for me to have the following conversation with an adolescent:

> *Patient*: Everything I say to you is just between me and you, right? You'll never tell my parents anything I tell you, right?
>
> *Therapist*: Not right.
>
> *Patient*: You mean you're going to tell my parents everything I tell you?

Therapist: No, I didn't say that either.

Patient: But my friend goes to a shrink, and his shrink told him that everything they speak about is strictly confidential, and his shrink says that she'll never tell my friend's parents anything about what goes on in a session.

Therapist: Yes, many therapists work that way. But I don't. Let me tell you how I work. As long as you don't do anything dangerous, to either yourself or others, you can be quite sure that what we speak about here will be held strictly confidential. I'm in full appreciation of the fact that it's important that you have the feeling that what we talk about is confidential. However, there are certain exceptions. And these exceptions hold for anyone, regardless of age. My policy is the same for all. It's not just for teenagers. It's the same whether you're 5 years old or 85 years old. The basic policy is this: As long as you're not doing anything dangerous, either to yourself or others, you can be sure that I won't reveal what you tell me. However, if you're doing something that's dangerous, I reserve the right, at my discretion, to reveal to your family whatever I consider important to reveal to help stop you from doing the dangerous thing. I may need their help. What do you think about what I've said?

At that point the patient may ask me to tell him or her what things I would reveal. I will not then provide "food for thought." I do not wish to give the youngster suggestions for various forms of antisocial and/or self-destructive behavior that may not have entered his or her head. Rather, I ask the adolescent to tell me what things he or she might do that might warrant such divulgence. I may then use this as a point of departure for a therapeutic inquiry. However, I do have a "list." It includes: heavy use of drugs (not occasional use of marijuana), heavy use of alcohol, dangerous driving (especially when under the influence of drugs or alcohol), criminal behavior, and for girls, a desire to have an out-of-wedlock child (occasional sexual intercourse is not a reportable item). I also impress upon the adolescent the fact that should one of these dangerous situations be arising, I will not automatically discuss the problem with the parent. Rather, I will exhaust all possibilities of discussion with the patient and the adolescent group before divulging the risk. Usually, such discussions are enough. However, when they are not, the youngster usually knows beforehand that I am going to divulge the information.

There is another aspect of the confidentiality issue in adolescence that warrants comment. The parents have a reasonable right to know whether there is a significant risk of dangerous behavior. When this issue is broached, generally in the initial evaluation, I will tell them that they should know that "no news is good news," i.e., that I *will* divulge dangers to them, and if there are no such divulgences, they can feel assured that no great risks are imminent.

I am fully appreciative of the fact that the adolescent needs a special, separate relationship with the therapist. This is part of his or her developmental need to establish a separate identity from that of the parents. This autonomy is necessary if the adolescent is to grow into an independent, self-sufficient adult. Active participation of the parents in the adolescent's therapy can compromise this goal. However, the goal can still be achieved by some participation on the part of the parents. Occasional joint sessions in which the youngster is seen along with the parents need not interfere with this goal. There can still be a significant percentage of sessions devoted to the adolescent alone, and the confidential relationship can also serve the purpose of enhancing separation and autonomy. The potential divulgence of a dangerous situation need not interfere with this sense of autonomy so important to the adolescent's development.

CONFIDENTIALITY IN CHILD PSYCHOTHERAPY

Although my focus in this book is on adolescent issues, I present here my views on confidentiality in child therapy because many of the principles are applicable to the treatment of adolescents. By child psychotherapy I am referring to the treatment of children between the ages of about four and ten. In my opinion, the confidentiality issue has little if any place in the treatment of most of these children. There are many therapists who will say to such children something along these lines: "Whatever you tell me here in this room is just between you and me. I promise I'll never tell your mother or father what you tell me. You can trust me on that." Many children might wonder exactly what the therapist is referring to. They know of no great secrets that they have from their parents. And this is especially the case for younger children. The parents know quite well that the child is soiling, stealing, lying, truant, etc. They more than the child are aware of these problems, and it is they who initiated the treatment. So the statement must be confusing and even irrelevant to many children.

In addition, the statement sets up a structure in which there are "we" (the therapist and the patient) and "they" (the parents). "We" *and* "they" can easily become "we" *versus* "they." With such an approach the therapist introduces the notion that something undesirable or bad will occur if "they" find out about certain therapist-patient confidences. This cannot but produce or add to the child's hostility toward and/or distrust of the parents. And this concept can introduce new schisms in the family. The family has enough trouble already; it does not need an additional problem brought about by a therapeutic program that adds a new pathological subsystem to the family. The "secret club" that the therapist creates with the patient also impedes open communication. Generally, communication impairments contribute to the development of and perpetuation of psychopathology. The confidential relationship with the child is likely to increase the communication problems of the family. The thrust of the therapy should be to encourage open expression of the issues that are causing people difficulty. A conspiracy of silence usually serves only to reduce communication and defeats thereby an important therapeutic goal.

The therapist should attempt to create an atmosphere in which all things pertinent to the child's treatment are discussed openly with the parents. I do not make any statements about this; I do it as a matter of course. In work with children I generally make no mention of confidentiality. If the child says to me that he or she does not wish me to tell his parents something, I will get very specific about what it is he or she wishes me not to divulge. Almost invariably it is an issue worthy of being discussed with the parents. Usually the child fears repercussions that are unreal or exaggerated. Encouraging the child to express to the parent(s) the forbidden material, either in my presence or at home, is usually therapeutic. It can teach all concerned that the repression (unconscious), and suppression (conscious) of thoughts and feelings is likely to perpetuate problems, whereas civilized discussion is the best way to resolve family problems.

A boy, for example, will say to me that he doesn't want me to tell his parents something. On further inquiry the issue almost invariably is one that should be discussed with the parents, and the child's fears of what will happen if such information is disclosed are unrealistic. Encouraging the child to express the forbidden material to the parents can provide him with the living experience that the hidden thoughts and feelings are not as terrible as he considered them to be and the anticipated consequences are not forthcoming. The therapist can serve as a catalyst for such expression, and his or her presence can make the atmosphere a safer one for the child to first make such revelations.

There is an aspect of S. Freud's famous Little Hans case (1909) that is pertinent to my discussion here. During the one joint session that Freud held with Little Hans and his father, Hans expressed some hostility toward his father that he had not previously revealed. I believe that it is unfortunate that Freud did not direct his attention to this in his report of the case. I would speculate that the reason why Hans had not expressed the hostility previously was that he was afraid to do so because of fears of his father's retaliation. However, in the presence of "Professor Sigmund Freud," a man of whom both the patient and his father were in awe, Hans could safely reveal his anger because of his awareness that his father was not likely to react with severe punitive measures in Freud's presence. I suspect that Hans' having had the living experience that his father would react to his hostility in a civilized manner made it easier for him to express his resentments elsewhere. And this, I believe, was a contributing factor to the alleviation of his symptoms.

Classical psychoanalysts, in particular, are strict adherents to the confidentiality principle. It is they, more than other therapists, who make it a point at the outset to emphasize to the child that they will respect confidences. It is of interest that Freud did not consider confidentiality to be an important issue in his treatment of Little Hans. Hans' father was the therapist and Freud was the supervisor. When reading the transcript of the treatment, one learns that Hans was easily led to discuss bowel movements, urination, masturbation, interest in observing his mother's toilet functioning, sexual fantasies toward his mother, and so forth. If he were indeed hiding material that a child might be ashamed to reveal, I would find it hard to imagine what such material might be. Little Hans knew that his father was revealing their discussions to Freud. In the one joint session that Freud had with Hans and his father, there was open discussion of these intimacies. Classical analysts often point to the case of Little Hans as proof that Freud's theories of infantile sexuality, the Oedipus complex, and castration anxiety are valid. Libraries have been written on these theories—which are supposedly proven by the Little Hans case. However, the structure of Freud's therapeutic program is often ignored by the same psychoanalysts. They do not utilize the parents as assistant therapists (as did Freud), and they enter into a strictly confidential relationship with the child (which Freud did not). In both cases, I believe, they do the child and the family a disservice. Elsewhere (1972a), I have discussed in detail this and other aspects of my understanding of the Little Hans case.

FURTHER COMMENTS ON CONFIDENTIALITY IN ADOLESCENT PSYCHOTHERAPY

Although there are differences in my approaches to the confidentiality issue among adults, adolescents, and children, there are some basic principles applicable to all three age levels. And the most important of these principles is that the patient is coming primarily for therapy. To the degree that respecting the patient's confidences serves the higher goal of the treatment, it should be respected. To the degree that "respect" for the patient's confidentiality is a compromise of the therapeutic goals, it must be ignored. In my discussion of confidentiality in adults and children, there is much that is pertinent to this issue in the treatment of adolescents. For example, an adolescent may say to me: "Don't ever tell my parents what I'm going to tell you now." Here, too, I will not promise in advance that I will respect the confidence. At most, the adolescent will not tell me what it is. Most often, however, with some reassurance that I will lean in the direction of nondisclosure, the youngster will provide me with the divulgence. In most cases I conclude that it will not serve the purposes of treatment for me to reveal the information to the parents and we may go on with our discussion. In extreme cases, in which there is a homicidal or suicidal risk, then there is no problem regarding my providing the revelation. In some situations I will discuss the issue of divulgence, but not belabor the point. Rather, I want to quickly provide the youngster with the *living experience* that such divulgence will not bring about the anticipated repercussions. It is for this reason that I generally advise the parents of my adolescent patients to be available to join in the session by remaining in the waiting room throughout the course of my patient's session. In this way, they are "on call" for quick involvement in our discussions.

There are some older adolescents who come to the session alone. Some of these live close enough to ride to my office on their bicycles. Others are old enough to drive to my office. In such cases, I still advise the parents to frequently (every third or fourth session) come to the sessions because there are usually issues that I wish to discuss with one or both parents. On occasion, youngsters who come alone may miss a session and not tell their parents about it. And they may even try to discourage me from informing their parents that the session has been missed. They recognize that the parents will be billed for the missed session, but hope that my bill will not make a differentiation between missed and attended sessions. I have not yet been in a situation where there is a healthy reason for the request that I not divulge to the parents that a session has been missed and they have therefore wasted their money. Generally, the youngster has a pathological reason for making this request. Usually the session is missed out of hostility and/or self-indulgence. The youngster's request derives from the desire to avoid repercussions from the parents for their having wasted their money. To "respect" confidentiality under these circumstances is to perpetuate psychopathology. It goes against the basic reason for the patient's being in treatment and is a disservice to both the patient and family.

On occasion I will receive a telephone call from a parent who wishes to make an appointment for an adolescent. However, the parent informs me that the youngster has agreed to go for treatment with the proviso that the therapist promise that there will be absolutely no contact at all with the parents, either by direct interview or even by telephone. The parents have reluctantly agreed to such an arrangement because it is the only way that the youngster will go for treatment. I have never agreed to see a patient with such a restriction. I cannot conceive of their being a healthy reason for such a proviso. It generally serves to promulgate some form of psychopathology. The therapist here, in advance, is being used as an ally in the creation of some form of pathological family subsystem. Unfortunately, there are therapists who are willing to see a patient with this restriction. I believe that such therapists are doing both the patient and family a disservice. I generally inform such a parent that I will not agree to such a constraint. I might agree to see the youngster first alone and hear the reasons why family involvement is not desired, but I let the youngster know beforehand (through the parent) that I consider it unlikely that I will be convinced by the arguments and that there is an extremely high probability that I will want to have at least some contact with the parents.

I have never in my experience had a therapeutic situation with an adolescent that justified *total removal* of the parents from the youngster's treatment. I am sure that there are such situations, but I have not yet seen them in my private practice. This is probably related to the fact that if parents are willing to pay for treatment, they are likely to have a degree of involvement that warrants their seeing the therapist—at least sometimes. Generally, I suggest to the mother that she communicate my refusal to the youngster and to tell him or her the reasons why. Sometimes the youngster will then agree to come under the conditions I proposed to the parent and other times he or she will not. I suspect that in the latter case the parents have found a therapist willing to work with this restriction. This is a good example of the principle that patients will always be able to find a therapist who will do their bidding, regardless of how sick the request is and how much the therapist perpetuates psychopathology by complying with it.

FOUR

INDIVIDUAL TREATMENT

Three therapeutic modalities can be useful to the adolescent who warrants psychotherapy. These are individual sessions, adolescent group therapy, and work with parents. An adolescent who is a candidate for individual therapy will receive one or more of these in varying combinations, as warranted. It is rare for a youngster to receive only one of the three; rather, some combination is generally utilized. I am not referring here to family therapy. That may also be useful to the adolescent. In this and the next two chapters, I will focus on the individual therapy aspect of this treatment program. In Chapters Seven and Eight I will focus on the other two modalities. Although I divide these into three separate sections, it is important for the reader to appreciate that I am actually referring to three facets of the patient's therapy. The division is somewhat artificial because even in an individual session I may ask a parent to join us. Conversely, a situation in which I am seeing the adolescent with both parents may be transformed into an individual session, when warranted. In short, any possible combination of the three therapeutic modalities is utilized throughout the course of the treatment—or even in the course of a session.

ADOLESCENCE AS A PERIOD OF THERAPEUTIC RECEPTIVITY

As a group, children of four to six may very well be the ones who are most receptive to the therapist's comments. This is a period of rapid superego development when youngsters are very receptive to the comments of authorities (such as a therapist). Teachers will agree that kindergarteners and first graders are typically in awe of their authority, and episodes of nonreceptivity notwithstanding, are generally far more compliant than, for example, fourth graders, eighth graders (they may be the worst), and twelfth graders. Many classical psychoanalysts believe that the rapid superego development that takes place from ages three to five results from the need to repress oedipal fantasies and designs. I am in agreement with Freud that this is indeed a period of rapid superego development, but I do not believe that such growth has anything to do with the Oedipus complex in the vast majority of children. Rather, it relates to the fact that children, during this phase, are expanding their horizons outside the home at a very rapid rate. They are sleeping over at the homes of other children for the first time; they are entering nursery school and kindergarten; and they are doing many more independent things. Accordingly, they are being exposed to a new army of authorities, each of whom has his or her own rules. If they are to adjust in this new, more complex world they have to learn quickly the rules that each of these giants has. And the therapist, coming into the child's life at that time, may also be able to enjoy the benefits of the child's receptivity to rules and regulations. If I say to a five-year-old boy that I'm very sorry but I'm going to have to write down in his chart that he is once again engaged in certain transgressions, he is usually crestfallen and will be quite unhappy that his unacceptable behavior is being so recorded. If I say the same thing to a nine-year-old boy, who exhibits similar behavior, his general reaction would be something along these lines: "I don't give two shits what you write down in my chart." Although he may not use these exact words, every cell in his body is transmitting that message to me.

My statement that adolescence, too, can be a period of therapeutic receptivity may come as a surprise to the reader. Even though it is characteristically one of rebellion, and even though some of the rebellion may be against the therapist, it can be, at the same time, a period of very high receptivity to the therapist's comments. One explanation relates to the quest for identity. As discussed in Vol. I (1999a), most adolescents suffer from significant identity confusion and are ever collecting data to provide them with information about what their identity really is. Accordingly, even though quite antagonistic to a therapist, they are likely to be receptive to long discussions on their appearance, hairstyle, attractiveness to others, whether or not a certain defect can be seen from a distance, cosmetics, clothing styles, etc. Fifteen or twenty minutes can easily be consumed on a discussion of whether or not the youngster's ears stick out too much or whether or a girl's eyes are set too far apart. The conversation may include the opinions of peers on these particular subjects and it is not uncommon for a certain amount of controversy to be raging on whether or not a youngster's almost invisible skin blemish is "turning off" the boys. Once the therapist has shown receptivity to discussing these important issues, he or she is more likely to be heard on subjects that may appear initially to be of less importance to the youngster. These discussions, therefore, serve as a good bridge to issues that are uppermost on the therapist's agenda (even though lowermost on the patient's).

With regard to their receptivity to individual sessions, one can divide adolescents into two groups. As a rule, younger adolescents (13–15) are unreceptive to face-to-face confrontations in individual sessions. They are generally made uncomfortable by therapists who ask them to sit alone with them in a room for 45 to 50 minutes, asking them to talk about their problems. Such youngsters, in this regard, are more like pre-adolescent patients. The older adolescents (16 and up) are likely to be more receptive to direct discussion. Actually, this division is somewhat artificial in that there is a continuum between the less talkative and the more talkative youngsters. I will begin this section with a discussion of the more talkative ones and then describe techniques I utilize to engage those less receptive to discussions on a one-to-one basis. For the latter category I will be giving particular emphasis (Chapter Five) to *The Talking, Feeling, and Doing Game* (1973b) because it has proved to be a valuable instrument for drawing out less talkative adolescents. But even the more loquacious may occasionally find the instrument useful.

Furthermore, the therapist does well to appreciate that many adolescents need to defend themselves against the realization that they have psychological difficulties and may need to have some kind of an excuse to justify their being in the therapist's office. The most common excuse is that the youngster is only there because the parents have forced him or her to attend the sessions. As mentioned previously, the therapist does well to support such a rationalization and provide some sympathy for the youngster's plight. The youngster is voluntarily attending—professions of coercion notwithstanding—and once the "body is in the room" the therapist must do what he or she can to keep the patient there.

BASIC TECHNICAL CONSIDERATIONS

Here I focus on some of the technical and structural aspects of the individual session that may serve as guidelines for these interviews. I generally begin with the youngster alone. This is in contrast to the procedure I use with pre-adolescent children, with whom I generally start the session with the child and parent together. The adolescent needs a sense of autonomy and routinely bringing the parent in with the patient may be therapeutically contraindicated. However, this does not preclude my requesting that the parent stay in the waiting room throughout the course of the session and be "on call."

Beginning the Therapeutic Session

Once seated, I generally begin with the traditional psychoanalytic question "So, what's on your mind?" or "What would you like to talk about today?" Although I have many criticisms of psychoanalytic theory and technique, I still believe that this open-ended question is quite useful (but I don't go too far with it). For example, as mentioned in Vol. I (1999a), I don't use this opening with a new patient at the beginning of the first interview. It is much too anxiety provoking at that time. Nor would I use it in a situation where something is obviously going on that demands my attention. For example, if a boy comes in on crutches and his leg is in a cast, I am not going to begin with that question. In such cases I might start with: "I'm sure that I'm not the first person to ask you this question. What happened to your leg?" The reader could argue that I am contaminating the blank screen with such a question. I don't deny it. In my defense, however, I believe that not to ask it has its obvious drawbacks. First, to inquire about the leg is the *human* thing to do. The boy just broke his leg and it is not only reasonable and sensitive of me to inquire about it, but would be somewhat insensitive and even cruel not to ask about the situation that resulted in the trauma. In addition, it is a good principle of therapy not to talk about something while being distracted by something else. Often the distraction may be more important to discuss than the issue under consideration. The leg in a cast would be just such a distraction. In addition, inquiry into the causes might be therapeutically useful in that the injury may have related to psychopathological processes operative in the youngster, e.g., driving when inebriated, show-off antics, or some manifestation of the youngster's delusions of invulnerability. Another example of such a distraction would be the adolescent girl who is being seductive to me. The therapist cannot concentrate on the issues at hand if the patient is being seductive. One does well to discuss the seductivity, get whatever therapeutic mileage one can out of it, and then switch back to the original issue under consideration. But these are exceptions. Most often the situation warrants my beginning with the open-ended question in order not to contaminate the "blank screen."

The Therapist Bringing Up a Subject

In the course of the session, as well, I may again depart from traditional psychoanalytic practice by bringing up a subject. If after a significant portion of the session has been used and the youngster hasn't raised up what I consider to be significant material left over from the previous session, I may refer the youngster back to it. If we are moving along in a meaningful way on another subject, I certainly will not rob us of the benefits to be derived from discussing something "hot," i.e., something that is highly emotionally charged. In such cases I will not bring up extraneous material because of my belief that the present material is now taking higher priority. However, if the present material appears to be low priority, and/or even resistance material, I will make some inquiries regarding why the more important issues from the previous session have not been brought up. Generally, I do not specify at the outset what the particular issues are. Rather, I will introduce the subject with a comment such as this: "I don't have the feeling that what you're talking about now is particularly important to you. In addition, we discussed something last time that I think is much more important and you haven't mentioned it yet. Do you know what I'm referring to?" In the formulation of the question, I try to get the patient to recall the issue, rather than my mentioning it myself. To bring up the issue would be "spoon-feeding" and would entrench the patient's dependency on me to do his remembering for him. Also, I want to get some idea as to how deeply repressed and "forgotten" the original issue is. Furthermore, the aspect of the issue that may seem important to me, may be less important to the patient. My making specific reference to it might shift the youngster away from the more psychologically meaningful material. If, after these general introductory questions, the patient still has absolutely no recollection of what I am referring to, I may provide the patient with clues and reminders, but generally will not present the whole issue. Usually one clue will serve to catalyze recollection of the issue. I am generally least prone to bring up past issues in adult therapy, more prone in adolescent therapy, and most prone in the treatment of young children. Young children are not famous for their memories and not to bring up the material (such as is the practice of many child psychoanalysts) is a disservice to the patient.

Dealing with Silences

If the youngster has nothing to talk about and if, in addition, there were no "burning" issues from the previous session, I will allow for a minute or two of silence, but not much more. Many analysts consider this to be a technical error. They would claim that it would be more beneficial for the patient to sit silently, even for many sessions. Many articles have been written in the psychoanalytic literature about the benefits of silences and how much both the patient and the therapist can learn from them. I am dubious. I am not claiming that silence provides no information whatsoever; nor am I claiming that silence is of absolutely no therapeutic benefit. I say only that it soon reaches the point of diminishing returns—after which it becomes a waste of money. Besides which, even if it were highly beneficial therapeutically, and even if it cost the patient nothing, it is quite boring and I like myself too much to subject myself to such masochistic treatment over time—especially 45–60 minutes. Life is short, and I am not the kind of person who comfortably will sit for many hours doing nothing, staring into space, even if some therapeutic benefit might be derived by the patient.

Accordingly, after a few minutes of silence I will generally say something along these lines to the patient: "Well, if you have nothing to talk about why don't we bring in your mother (father) and see if she (he) will have something to tell us." Generally, the parent does have something to contribute and the issue that the parent brings up serves as a point of departure for discussion among the three of us. If, however, the parent has nothing to bring up (rarely the case) then I will generally ask a question about the original complaints and whether or not they still exist. I may even go back to the list of complaints presented by the parents in my questionnaire and described during the first meeting. It may be that things have gotten so much better that therapy is no longer warranted. In such cases we then discuss the question of winding down and even stopping. There are parents (and even youngsters) who continue coming without having any particular clinical problems. They believe that the therapeutic program is designed to go beyond the point where symptoms are no longer present. There are some therapists who also subscribe to this principle. Although it is the more lucrative one, I do not believe that it is the most judicious one from the therapeutic point of view. The clinical symptoms are the "handle" for our treatment. They are the points of departure for our therapeutic interchanges and maneuvers. Without them the therapy becomes sterile, intellectualized, and theoretical. To talk at length, over many sessions, about *why* the patient *had* the symptoms and *why they no longer exist* is a relatively fruitless endeavor. Few if any emotions may be tied to the discussion and it therefore becomes even less therapeutic. This does not preclude spending some time on the subject, especially in the period just after the patient reports significant reduction and even removal of symptoms.

Another reason for avoiding long silences is that one may lose the adolescent patient. Adults, interestingly, are often more naive in this regard and will continue to pay for sessions in which most if not all of the time has been spent in silence. They gullibly believe the analyst that such sessions can be therapeutically useful. Adolescents are not so gullible and will generally not attend more than a few such sessions. They are likely to say that the whole thing is boring and a waste of time and the parents, with justification, are likely to agree with them. Accordingly, engaging in long periods of silence is a good way of losing the patient and depriving him or her of the opportunity to gain some therapeutic benefit.

For patients who do not seem to have much of an agenda, I will often suggest that they make lists between sessions. Again, classical analysts would take issue with this approach, claiming that it is likely to contaminate the blank screen. They claim that they want to know what it is at the forefront of the patient's mind–at that particular point. I cannot deny that the making of lists may result in such contamination. However, if the choice lies between nothing being said and speaking from a list, I would far prefer the list because it is much more likely to be therapeutic. If, however, the therapist suspects that the list is being made as a resistance maneuver, and that the issues being written down are selected because they are likely to provide discussion on issues that are less touchy and anxiety provoking, then the therapist does well to discourage such utilization. This, however, has not been my experience. Most often the youngster who makes lists is one who has a serious commitment to the treatment and genuinely wants to make the best use of the therapeutic time. In addition, I will generally instruct the adolescent to write down his or her dreams. In Chapter Six I will discuss dream analysis for those youngsters who are candidates for such therapeutic inquiry. Usually, these are the older adolescents.

Dealing with Preoccupations Of Parental Blame

A common topic for adolescents in treatment is blame of their parents. Many youngsters will come in, and when asked what is on his or her mind, will quickly start talking about the various indignities they suffer at the hands of their parents. Even those who profess that they have problems and want to change themselves, are likely to talk at length about the reasons why their difficulties are caused by their parents. This is another time when it is good to have the parents available. Accordingly, I might say to such a youngster: "Well, I've been listening to you for 15 minutes now and all you've been doing is telling me about how terrible your home situation is and how your parents are causing you all these difficulties. It may be that some of your points are valid, but it may be that some aren't. I always find it useful to get the other person's opinion on subjects like this. So let's have your mother come in and get her opinions about what's happened." I do not ask the youngster's permission to have the mother brought in; rather, I rise as I am talking, go to the door, and bring the parent in–before the youngster has a chance to object. This is not to say that I will never listen to, discuss, and try to get therapeutic mileage from such objections; rather I want the pattern established that the parent's participation is crucial if we are to find out exactly what went on at home.

In the course of such a discussion, I may point out what the parent's deficiencies have been, try to get therapeutic mileage out of a discussion of such deficiencies, and make recommendations to the parent about effecting the appropriate changes. In addition, I will point out to the youngster what his or her role has been, try to get the youngster to focus on such defiencies as a point of departure for therapeutic inquiry, and similarly will make suggestions regarding the youngster's changing those contributing factors that have originated within him or her.

In the course of my discussions with patients and their parents–especially discussions in which the patient is particularly insensitive to the parents' affection, willingness to sacrifice, and dedication – I will present what I refer to as the *kidney transplant principle*. This is a typical way in which I present this important concept: "I know you have many criticisms of your parents. I suspect that you believe that you had bad luck when God gave out parents, but I can tell you this: If you were in the hospital and needed a kidney transplant—so much so that your life depended on it—I am positive that of the five billion people on earth your parents would be the first ones on line. Where do you think all the others would be at that time, all those whom you call your friends, all those whom you claim treat you far better than your parents?" Although many youngsters' delusions of invulnerability lessen considerably their appreciation that they will *ever* be in such a position, the message does sometimes have the effect of enhancing some patients' appreciation of their parents. In contrast, parents will generally find it a useful reminder for the youngster who is being particularly callous to them—a common situation when raising an adolescent. Some would be critical of the obvious attempt at guilt evocation when utilizing the *kidney transplant principle*. I have no problem with this. I do not subscribe to the theory that the therapist should never try to enhance guilt. Most adolescents (like most people in this world) need more guilt, not less. And therapy is an ideal situation in which guilt should be engendered when it is sorely lacking.

Asking the Patient to Repeat What I Have Said

Another useful technical maneuver in the individual therapy of adolescents is to ask the patient to repeat what I have just said, especially if my comments have been somewhat complex. My purpose here, of course, is to ensure that what I have said has been "registered." Patients (regardless of age) are not famous for remembering the details of anxiety-provoking confrontations, no matter how carefully, benevolently, and sympathetically presented. It is only via their reiteration by the patient that we can be sure that we have been "heard." I recognize that the patient may consider such a request demeaning, but I ask the question anyway. I believe that the benefits to be derived from ensuring that my message has been heard far outweigh the possible antitherapeutic elements associated with the patient's feeling of embarrassment associated with the question. And even here, most adolescents do not claim that I am embarrassing or otherwise putting them down by asking them to relate to me their understanding of what I have just said. The question is posed benevolently and the patient appreciates that my request for reiteration is in the service of the goals of the treatment.

Typically, I will use questions such as this: "What I have said may be quite complicated. In order to be sure that you've understood, I'd like you to tell me what I just said." and "Many people find that when I talk about things that relate to their problems it is hard to understand what I'm saying. If you're like most people, there's probably some confusion about what I just said. Any questions?" The patient's questions may enable me to determine whether or not I was understood. If they indicate I was not understood, I might say: "From your questions it's clear to me that some of the points I made might have been a little difficult for you to understand. I'm going to say it again and then I'm going to ask you to tell me what you understood me to have been saying. I'm doing this because we're talking about something that's *very* important." Adolescents who may feel demeaned by this approach may be reassured by the knowledge that I work similarly with adults. Although adults are more likely than adolescents to respond with some indignation to my request for reiteration, most ultimately come to appreciate the judiciousness of the request.

Asking to See My Notes and/or Chart

On occasion a patient will ask what I have just written down or, even further, ask to see my notes in the chart. Only in my residency days would I have considered such a question inappropriate and would have taken great pains not to show the patient his or her chart. My fear then was that the information contained therein might be misinterpreted by the patient and might prove too anxiety provoking for him or her to handle. However, it was during my residency days that I had an experience that taught me something important on this point. Specifically, a borderline patient of a colleague of mine left my colleague's office with his chart and ran out of the hospital. A staff conference was held and various speculations were made regarding the possible detrimental effects of his having read his chart. No one, even the senior supervisor, considered the possibility that good could come from such an act. A few days later, the patient returned with the chart, told his therapist that he had read it completely, and then began to discuss certain points that he disagreed with. It was clear that the points raised were useful and that he had gained much from the experience. I am not claiming that such experiences can be useful for *all* patients; I do believe, however, that reading one's chart can be useful for most.

After the completion of my residency I spent two years in the military service in Germany. I was stationed at a large military hospital in Frankfurt am Main, Germany. The hospital serviced many satellite dispensaries. The soldiers routinely came with their charts in hand because it would have been extremely difficult to arrange for the charts to be sent separately. Furthermore, having each soldier carry his own chart lessened the likelihood of charts being lost, displaced, or sent to the wrong place. This was the practice with all medical services, and psychiatry was no exception. Accordingly, the soldiers routinely sat reading their charts as they waited to see me. In my two years in the service I never found one soldier who suffered from such an opportunity. Rather, most found it useful and their discussions about what they had read provided me with useful data about what was going on with them.

It was from these early experiences (which occurred in the late 1950s and early 1960s) that I developed a much more relaxed attitude about patients seeing their charts. Accordingly, if an adolescent says to me that he wants to see what is in his chart, I will generally respond along these lines: "You know, there is absolutely nothing in that chart that you don't know about. It's all information that you and your parents have told me about yourself. If you'd rather spend your time reading the chart, that's okay with me. However, I think you could make better use of your time. That stuff is all past history, even though some of it was what you said to me during our last session. I think you'd do much better to talk about the things that are on your mind now. But I leave the choice to you." It is rare for the youngster to spend the time looking through his or her chart.

Preventing the patient from seeing the chart promulgates the idea that the therapist has some information about the patient which he or she does not know. This has the effect of giving the patient the notion the therapist has some magic powers, the supernatural ability to know things about the patient that the patient doesn't even know about him- or herself. I believe that promulgating such a view of the therapist is antitherapeutic. My experience has been that once the patient is told that the freedom to look at the chart is his or hers, the whole situation becomes decompressed and the curiosity to see what is contained therein often evaporates immediately. The most predictable way to engender such curiosity is to tell the patient that he or she is strictly prohibited from viewing the material between the chart's covers. Such a position just sets up a morbid situation that generally is going to contaminate the treatment. Last, after the first few sessions, I generally do not take any notes on the vast majority of my patients. I work on the principle that I will remember those things that are important and not remember those that are not important. This is the same principle that exists between friends. Accordingly, no notes are being taken and so no morbid curiosity is being engendered.

The Use of Contracts

There are therapists who draw up "contracts" with their patients. Often these contracts are made along with the parents. A list is made of the various things the youngster will not do, especially antisocial behavior. Sometimes a list of rewards is included in the contract. I have never yet seen a contract which provides meaningful disciplinary and punitive measures if the contract is abrogated. The theory is that the youngster—by sheer dint of will—will adhere to its provisions. The youngster is placed on his or her honor to do so. I have never yet seen a youngster live up to such a contract. I believe that drawing it up is naive on the part of the therapist and is derived, in part, from the hope that the various psychopathological forces that have contributed to the aberrant behavior will somehow be suppressed and repressed in compliance with some vow to subscribe to the provisions of this document. And, the addition of the signatures of all the concerned parties is supposed to add a certain sanctity to it that will increase the likelihood that the vows taken will be subscribed to. This is a naive view of treatment and does not give proper respect to the power of the unconcious forces operative in bringing about the psychopathology. Unfortunately, the whole experience then becomes antitherapeutic because there are no repercussions for breaking the contract. The youngster then has the living experience that the failure to live up to one's promises is not going to be followed by meaningful consequences and so frivolous attitudes towards one's vows is promulgated.

Soda, Pretzels, and Candy

Some therapists believe that it is crucial for the adolescent therapist to have a refrigerator of soda pop as well as pretzels, potato chips, and candy readily available for them. One of the arguments given for this is that food is a symbol of love and providing such is likely to entrench the therapist-patient relationship. At best, the therapist can provide the youngster with some affection in compensation for some of the privations he or she may have suffered. This, if it is in any way to be meaningful, must evolve from an ever-deepening relationship. At best, soda, food, and candy can play an insignificant role in bringing about such a relationship. The therapist must appreciate that food is a *symbol;* it is not a replacement for the real thing. There are therapists who are somewhat deficient in providing that degree of affection optimum in the therapeutic situation and who may try to compensate for their deficiencies in this regard by providing food, soda, etc. Such therapists may be entrenching a common parental problem in which the parents use food to compensate for their deficiencies in providing genuine affection. Such therapists, therefore, are promulgating and perpetuating a pathological use of food. Accordingly, I do not routinely supply food, candy, and soda to my adolescent patients. This does not preclude my occasionally having such available, but it is not in any way planned; nor do I feel that I have to stock my refrigerator and pantry with these items for special distribution for my adolescent patients.

The Value of Philosophical Discussions

With an adult patient, I generally discourage significant time spent on such issues as religion, politics, and philosophy. General ly, such discussions are likely to serve as resistances against focusing on more important personal issues. This is not the case with the adolescent. Normally adolescents are preoccupied with these issues as part of their developmental process. They may spend hours thinking about "the nature of things." They may be deeply absorbed in whether or not they still subscribe to their parents' religious beliefs or whether they should embrace doctrines of another religion, especially one that is quite remote from their parental heritage. In the 1960s and 1970s Zen Buddhism was the most popular alternative religion for adolescents of all ages. Adolescents often preoccupy themselves with some of the traditional questions that have plagued philosophers throughout the ages: questions about God, existence, the purpose of the universe, etc. And they often enjoy talking with anyone at length about these issues. Therapists who refuse to engage in such discussions because of their view that they are thereby sidestepping, circumventing, or avoiding discussions about the more basic pathological issues are making an error.

From the adolescent's point of view, what could be more important than a discussion about the meaning of God and the purpose of the universe? Accordingly, therapists do well to spend time with these youngsters discussing such topics and presenting their own views on them, *after* the youngster has expounded on his or her opinions. I am not suggesting that every minute of every session be spent in such discussion, only that these topics should not be viewed as off limits for the therapist. These discussions bring the therapist on the same wavelength as the patient, especially if the therapist has some views that the adolescent finds of interest and value. They thereby entrench the relationship and provide a foundation for receptivity to the therapist's comments on other subjects. It is as if the adolescent reasons: "He seems to know a lot about the philosophy of religion and the meaning of existence. He's probably worthy of being respected on other topics as well." Although the therapist may not be viewed by experts in these areas to be anything but a novice, from the adolescent's point of view the therapist may be viewed as a *maven*. The groundwork, then, is laid for greater receptivity on issues that are more directly relevant to the patient's problems.

In addition, in the context of such discussions, the issues of values and ethics are likely to arise and this may bring the therapist much closer to the patient's actual problems. In discussing what is right and wrong, good and bad, it is difficult not to touch on aspects of the patient's life relative to these considerations. These need not be discussed directly with the patient as the example. Rather one can discuss these issues theoretically, about third parties, or about people in general, and yet the messages are likely to be received in such a way that the adolescent saves face. The discussion of ethical behavior, again on a theoretical basis, is not likely to be unrelated to the patient's own problems in this area. Ethical considerations in politics will relate to ethical considerations among family members, regarding how they treat one another. And religious ethical doctrines, as well, can easily be related to intrafamilial relationships—again, without necessarily discussing the patient's particular family.

Learning from the Patient

A few years ago, when my three children were then in their adolescence, I was having dinner with a group of colleagues. In the course of our conversation one of them said to me: "Gardner, I want to ask you a question. What do you consider the most important thing a parent can do when raising adolescents?" The colleague was by no means a simple-minded person, recognized that there was no simple answer to his question, and knew that many factors are involved in raising an adolescent. It was a question raised in the course of a dinner conversation and it would not have been proper for me to have started giving a lecture on the multiplicity of factors that would be important to consider. He was basically asking me what factor I would put at the top of the list. He was also asking me to state that which sprung first into my mind, without giving too much thought to the question—in the hope that I might thereby come out with the most important one.

My response was: "Try, if you can, to find something that they can teach you. Try to find an area in which they are genuinely superior to you and avail yourself of the opportunity to learn from them." As discussed in Vol. I (1999a), adolescents suffer with significant feelings of inadequacy. Although physically adult and capable of procreation, they are basically still children. They do not have the wherewithal for independent functioning in our complex, industrialized society and are basically quite dependent on their parents for food, clothing, shelter, and even guidance (although they may try to deny their need for the latter). Many of their irritating behaviors are compensatory for these feelings of inadequacy. If the youngster genuinely has an area of expertise, which will enable him or her to serve a useful purpose for the parent, then he or she will not only enjoy an enhanced sense of self-worth but will not have to resort so quickly to injudicious and sometimes pathological forms of compensation for feelings of low self-worth.

A youngster, for example, who is knowledgable about computers, will appreciate that his father is functioning at "the idiot level" in this area. By "educating the poor slob" he not only can lord his superiority over his father but perform a useful service for a "retarded person." Some youngsters may be able to gain these gratifications from having superior knowledge about repairing the family car. Many school subjects allow for the exhibition of such superiority: science, social studies, foreign languages, literature, etc. Parents do well to avail themselves of the "wisdom" of their adolescents and to praise them when it is so imparted. They do well also to express their gratification over having the good fortune for having a youngster who is so knowedgable. The adolescent is likely to consider him- or herself an expert on a particular subject on the basis of the fact that he or she has written a report on it that received an A grade. Although the parent may recognize that the expertise so gained is specious and that the youngster still remains abysmally ignorant about the subject, the parent still does well to learn what he or she can (most often the case) about what the adolescent can teach. I have previously used the word *genuine* when referring to this issue. This is an important point. This is no time for "buttering up" the youngster and professing that one is learning something when one really isn't. The parent does well to find some area in which the adolescent can realistically provide information that the parent is ignorant of. If the adolescent has absolutely nothing that he or she can provide, then that youngster is not going to be able to derive the benefits of this experience.

Therapists are no exception here. They too do well to try to ascertain areas in which the adolescent is indeed superior to them. Here again, school subjects may serve this purpose. If the therapist can make statements such as: "I don't know much about that," "You know much more about that than I do," and "I'd like to hear what you can tell me about that, because I know very little about that subject," he or she may be able to provide a useful therapeutic service for the patient. Again, I am not suggesting that all sessions be devoted to the adolescent's educating the therapist; I am only saying that some time spent on these kinds of conversations can be therapeutically useful. It enhances the patient's self-worth and this cannot but contribute to an alleviation of the wide variety of psychogenic symptoms that derive from feelings of low self-esteem. It entrenches the therapist-patient relationship, the foundation upon which the therapy rests.

Relating One's Own Personal Experiences to the Patient

Many children enjoy immensely hearing about the events in their parent's lives that occurred in their own childhood: "Tell me Mommy, how were things in your house with Grandma and Grandpa when you were nine, when you were my age." When parents provide their children with details about their early lives they entrench their relationships with them. The divulgences also are a manifestation of the intimacy of the relationship enjoyed by both. Although adolescents are less interested in such conversations (they are people of the present and future, not the past), they still have some interest in and can benefit from them. Therapists, too, can provide such revelations and enjoy thereby the therapeutic benefits to be derived from them. As mentioned previously, such revelations about the therapist—judiciously made—can entrench the therapist-patient relationship because they bring the patient and the therapist closer to one another. However, these revelations should not be made indiscriminately. They should always be made with the purpose of helping the patient in his or her treatment. A divulgence should be selected which has direct relevance to the patient's problems. Otherwise, the therapy may degenerate into a situation where the patient is being used for the therapist's treatment—an exploitation if there ever was one. The therapist's experience may serve as a metaphor for the patient's experience and provide a useful therapeutic communication to the patient without his or her realizing that such is the case.

For example, in the context of a conversation relating to the patient's devastation over being jilted by a girlfriend for another boy, the therapist may relate his own experience in this area when he or she was an adolescent. Obviously, all the details need not be divulged. Rather, the therapist does well to select those aspects that might be of use to the patient. Just knowing that the therapist has had similar experiences can lessen the boy's burden. Knowing that the therapist, whom the youngster may have viewed as being perfect and therefore beyond rejection, has also had this experience makes it easier for him to bear the pains of his rejection. Telling the youngster that his has been a common experience may be helpful. Telling the youngster that the therapist has also had the experience is a little more helpful. But providing some specific details about one or two such rejections can be even more therapeutic in that the concrete example generally has more clout than a theoretical statement. Similarly, if the youngster is dissappointed over not having gained admission to a particular college the therapist might tell about his own experiences in this area. If, however, the therapist has not had that experience then he does well to choose another area of disappointment. (If the therapist had no such disappointments, rejections, etc., he or she would probably not have become a therapist.)

Discouraging Pathological Use of the Treatment

One of the dangers of psychoanalysis and psychoanalytically oriented therapy is that patients will come to see themseves as helpless victims of their unconscious processes. The notion of conscious control becomes less important in modifying behavior than control by the unconscious. Therapists do well to avoid such a misinterpretation of the psychotherapeutic process. We never know more than a small fraction of the numerous unconscious factors that may be operative in bringing about a particular symptom. We really are not certain how much the insight process brings about therapeutic change. We do know, however, that most patients (even those who are psychotic) have some degree of conscious control over their behavior. Accordingly, I believe that therapists do well to err on the side of assuming that their patients have control over what they are doing. Because of our ignorance of where the line can be drawn between control and noncontrol, we do better for our patients to assume that they have this control and only accept the fact that they haven't when the evidence is overwhelming that this is the case. In short, therapists do well to take a hard line against patients' comments that they are sick and therefore cannot control their behavior. It is important for the reader to appreciate that such an approach is not warranted when the patient is indeed psychotic and really cannot control his or her behavior. But even some psychotic symptoms are controllable. Often, psychotics will not exhibit their symptoms in situations in which they might be put in jail or committed to a hospital. Of course, there are others who are so sick that deterrents do not operate.

When communicating with the nonpsychotic patient's school, either directly or through the parents, school authorities should be told that the patient should not be given any special considerations because he or she is in treatment. If the school is providing such indulgence, it is likely to entrench the pathology by providing secondary gains for its perpetuation. Many teachers will be hesitant to impose traditional disciplinary measures because they "feel sorry" for the youngster who is in therapy. This is a mistake. Some youngsters are given higher grades than they deserve, again because of the misguided belief on the part of school personnel that the patient is less capable of handling the disappointments associated with a low grade. Failing marks become suddenly transformed into Cs and Ds on the day of the last report card. I call such marks "mercy grades" and strongly discourage teachers from giving them. Also, I generally advise parents to request that the patient's teachers give only those grades he or she deserves—nothing higher and nothing lower. And if, at the end of the school year, a course is not passed then the youngster should be required to repeat it over the summer. And if a few courses are not passed, then the youngster should be required to repeat the grade. Promoting on to the next grade is a terrible disservice. The patient is ill-equipped to handle the more demanding material and may then deal with this embarrassment by dropping out of school entirely. Repeating a grade is certainly embarrassing; but more humiliating is the experience of being over one's head in a higher grade and suffering thereby the daily embarrassments of being significantly behind one's peers. The former mortification is generally acute and short-lived; the latter may very well result in lifelong embarrassment. Similarly, at home, disciplinary measures should be imposed in accordance with traditional household practice and the patient should not be given any special dispensation because he or she is in treatment. Providing such indulgence does not prepare the youngster to function in the real world, which will not provide such special considerations. Accordingly, it is a terrible disservice. Again, my comments here are relevant to the nonpsychotic youngster. Patients who are so sick that special considerations are warranted regarding grading and class placements should be in special classes and even special schools. My comments here are relevant to the healthier youngster, the more common adolescent patient one sees in treatment.

"If You're Going to Take Something Away From Someone, You Should Give Him (Her) Something Back in Return."

This is an old saying which has applicability in many situations, but is especially applicable in therapy. In a sense, many of the things that we do in therapy is a taking-away process. We are being asked to "take away" symptoms and we may make the assumption that this can be done without giving something back in return. As mentioned previously, symptoms are not 100 percent destructive and maladaptive. They also have cohesive value and their constructive factors must be appreciated by the therapist. I believe that therapists with a deep commitment to behavior modification as the primary therapeutic process do not give proper attention to this factor when they consider the symptom and the disease to be the same. I am not claiming, as some did in the early stages of psychoanalysis, that removal of a symptom would automatically result in another one popping up unless the underlying problems were completely resolved. Rather, I am saying that we must appreciate that symptoms arise as an attempt to deal with fundamental life conflicts and removing them without giving proper attention to the underlying problems is not likely to work as well as a therapeutic approach that takes unconscious factors into serious consideration. Throughout this book I have been critical of many aspects of psychoanalytic theory and treatment. However, there are many aspects of the psychoanalytic approach that I have deep conviction for and incorporate into my work. My criticism of psychoanalysis notwithstanding, I believe strongly that unconscious factors play an important role in the development of psychogenic psychopathology and that a therapeutic approach that does not give serious consideration to them is far less likely to be effective than one that does.

Adolescents need to rebel. Therapists must differentiate between healthy and unhealthy forms of rebellion. We should not be trying to squelch rebellion entirely. Rather, we should attempt to make a shift, to change pathological forms of rebellion into neutral and even healthy ones. At the same time that the therapist is trying to discourage a youngster from antisocial acting out that is destructive and dangerous, he or she should take a supportive position regarding the utilization of age-appropriate innocuous forms of rebellion such as wearing hair and clothing styles that are "in" for adolescents and viewed as noxious by adults, espousing rebellious philosophies (without acting out), and professing political views that are directly at variance with those of the parents and extended families. A girl with strong sexual urges who is engaging in promiscuous sex is not likely to be helped by the therapist's merely discouraging sexual behavior. One certainly wants to go into the psychodynamic factors operative in the sexual promiscuity and help her work out these problems. No matter how successful the therapist may be toward attaining this goal, the facts are that the girl is still likely to have sexual urges that require release. Dance, sports, and other forms of sublimation may allow for some gratification. But generally these are not enough. Accordingly, the therapist would still do well to encourage selectivity, exclusivity, and masturbation.

Such substitution, unfortunately, cannot always be easily accomplished. For example, a youngster may be drinking heavily. Of the many factors operative in the formation of this symptom an important one might relate to the fact that all of the youngster's friends drink as well. To advise such a patient to stay away from friends who drink is not likely to work in that the patient is being asked to substitute loneliness for camaraderie. The more obvious solution, that the youngster get friends who don't drink, is not likely to be easily accomplished. First, it is probably the case that there are more adolescents who drink than there are those who don't. But there are certainly many adolescents who still do not drink, or do not drink excessively. The problem here, however, is that the nondrinkers may not want to have very much to do with the patient who is deeply involved in the drinking scene. They are different kinds of human beings, have different interests, are on different wave lengths, and are not likely to get along very well. Group therapy can sometimes be helpful to such youngsters in that it helps them acquire some of the social skills necessary for shifting into a healthier group.

The Comparison of the Therapist's Statements with the Parents' Statements

It is common for adolescents in treatment to say to the therapist: "That's exactly what my mother and father say. And that's one of the reasons I don't like you. What are they doing? Sending you letters?" My response to this usually goes along these lines: "Yes, you're right on that point. My view on that issue is identical with that of your parents. However, if you consider me to be their rubber stamp, you're wrong. If you'll think back, I'm sure you'll agree that there were times when I've criticized them and taken your side. I work on the principle that I call the shots as I see them. When I agree with them, I will state so; and when I agree with you, I'll say so as well. I'm nobody's parrot." There are therapists, unfortunately, who take care not to espouse the parents' position to the patient lest they be viewed by the youngster as being the ally of the parents. Such therapists are making an error. There are times when we should be the allies of the parents, and there are times when we should be the ally of the youngster. We should always be the ally of what we consider to be the healthy position. Some therapists believe that if they take the parents' position, under any circumstances, that they will be the target of the same hostility that the parent is receiving. This may very well be the case, but it is not a justifiable reason for lying low and hiding one's true position. There are therapists who believe that they will compromise the child's receptivity to their advice if they take the parents' position on a particular subject. This is an error. The youngster's receptivity is going to be based on the nature of the relationship that has evolved and relates to the multiplicity of factors contributing to the development of that relationship. And there are therapists who believe that strictly siding with the patient is necessary for the establishment of a good therapist-patient relationship and if they were to side with the parents, even once, then the relationship might be compromised, if not destroyed. This too is an error. A relationship is based on many factors. If it is a good one, the youngster will be able to tolerate benevolently motivated criticisms, which may at times be identical to those made by the parents. If it is a poor relationship, it is not going to be helped by strictly protecting the youngster from confrontations with the reality of his or her life.

One of the purposes of treatment is to open the patient's eyes and help the youngster deal more realistically with life's problems. Most adolescents in treatment live in a dream world. They have delusions of invulnerability and fantasies that are often grandiose. They are choosing unrealistic and self-destructive resolutions to their life's problems. Therapy must help them open their eyes and see the world more realistically. This is what the parents have generally been trying to do and, on most issues, it is likely that the therapist will be trying to accomplish the same thing with the patient. The youngster needs all the help he or she can get. The youngster needs input from many sources: parents, teachers, and the therapist. Shutting up because the youngster complains about the reiteration is not a reason for keeping quiet. It works against the principles of therapy. I am not suggesting that the therapist ignore the fact that reiteration may reach a point of diminishing returns. The therapist's droning on, in spite of the fact that the patient is tuning him or her out, is likely to be antitherapeutic. Rather, I am only saying that the therapist should not avoid reiteration because the patient accuses him or her of saying the same things that the parents have stated.

SEXUAL AND DATING PROBLEMS

I will use sexual and dating problems to serve as examples for some of the principles presented above. I have selected this area because it is one of the more common ones dealt with in the treatment of adolescents. As mentioned, it is not the purpose of this book to cover the treatment of the wide variety of adolescent disorders that the therapist may have to deal with. Rather, it is its purpose to present general principles of treatment of such youngsters and to provide clinical examples from the therapy of some of the more common problems. These principles, I believe, will serve the therapist well in the treatment of other disorders not specifically focused on in this book. Furthermore, one therapist can only have experience with a limited segment of the wide variety of psychopathological problems that these youngsters can exhibit. Because most psychopathological problems are derived in the attempt to deal with basic life issues, there is much overlap in the treatment of these disorders. Because sexual and dating problems are among the common difficulties that confront adolescents, knowledge of the treatment of these difficulties will often serve therapists well in the treatment of other disorders of youngsters in this age group.

The Therapist's Values Regarding Adolescent Sexual Activities

One cannot discuss dating and sex among adolescents without dealing with the issue of values. Accordingly, I will present at this point my own values regarding sex among teenagers. Some of this presentation is an elaboration of my discussion of sexual relationships in Vol. I (1999a). I recognize that my values in this area may not only be different from those of some readers but are different from those of patients I see as well. Youngsters and their parents are entitled to information regarding the therapist's values in this area before involving their youngster in treatment. As mentioned in Chapter One all therapy involves the imposition of the therapist's values on the patient. Most often, especially in the realm of antisocial behavior, the therapist and the parents share the same values. The subject of sexual values, however, is more often a "touchy subject," especially when the parents are strongly committed to conservative religious beliefs. Furthermore, the reader will be in a better position to appreciate my discussion of the treatment of adolescent sexual problems after a presentation of my own values in this realm.

I believe that it is psychologically healthy (a term that is a substitute for what *my* values are) for a youngster to engage in heterosexual caressing, kissing, and petting, on occasion in the early adolescent period. In the mid-adolescent period, I believe it is healthier for things to "steam up" to the point where the youngster enjoys orgasm. And by 17 or 18 I believe it is healthy for the youngster to have sexual intercourse. However, I believe that parents do well to impress upon their youngsters that the sexual experience is likely to be more gratifying if there is an ongoing intimate relationship with the sexual partner. Transient sex should be discouraged, with the parents' appreciation however that a certain amount of sex might still be engaged in. It is hoped that the youngster will have the *living experience* that sex in the context of an ongoing relationship is ultimately more gratifying. My values here are not that stringent to preclude entirely transient sexual experiences. At the same time, I believe that it is *crucial* that parents impress upon their youngsters the risks of pregnancy and the terrible drawbacks of out-of-wedlock teen pregnancies. In addition, they are grossly negligent if they do not warn their youngsters about the dangers of sexually transmitted diseases, especially AIDS. At the time of this writing (early 1988), the AIDS epidemic is becoming ever more frightening and the warnings for sexual selectivity and the use of condoms ever more compelling. Unfortunately, the oft-mentioned adolescent delusions of invulnerability may work against the youngster's heeding this warning.

Furthermore, parents do well to encourage masturbation as an acceptable release for sexual cravings. They do well to promulgate the notion that no human being need suffer sexual frustration and that when heterosexual opportunities are not available, masturbation is a perfectly acceptable and even desirable outlet. I have often said that the ideal birthday present for a 13-year-old boy would be a five-year subscription to Playboy magazine and a lock on his bedroom door. And the ideal gift for a 13-year-old girl would be a vibrator and a five-year subscription to a teenage romance magazine. (I believe that males are more likely to be "turned on" by stark visual-sexual representations, whereas females are more likely to be turned on by loving and romantic fantasies.)

In my value system I do not consider abortion to be a sin or an inappropriate way of dealing with an unwanted pregnancy. I recognize, however, that there are others who have very strong beliefs that abortion is merely another form of murder and that there is absolutely no situation under which it is justifiable. From the psychological point of view, I believe that the earlier the abortion is done the less the psychological trauma to the mother. Abortions during the first trimester can generally be accomplished through dilatation and curettage (D and C) and are less likely to be traumatic than a second trimester abortion in which labor is induced and an actual fetus comes forth.

In the initial interview the parents have every right to question the therapist about his or her position on these subjects. This does not preclude inquiries into the possible psychological implications of their questions, but they are still entitled to the therapist's direct answers on these subjects. Classical analysts would be unreceptive to such a conversation and would use each of these questions by the parents as a point of departure for psychoanalytic inquiry. I object to this approach in this situation. First, the parents are not analytic patients; they are the parents of the adolescent patient. Second, they are entitled to answers to these questions and the therapist should be willing to provide them. Again, this does not preclude additional discussions regarding the analytic implications of the questions.

I recall a situation in which parents, very religious Catholics, brought their 15-year-old daughter to me. In the first two-hour consultation they very firmly stated that they did not want me to talk about sex with their daughter. I told them that I would make no such promise and that if I am to conduct the therapy properly I must have the right to discuss any issue at all that I consider relevant to a youngster's problems. I told them, as well, that I would not force their daughter to talk about sex if she didn't want to, but that I cannot imagine my conducting a therapeutic program with a 15-year-old girl without the subject coming up at some time or other. I told them that if they felt that this answer was not acceptable to them that it would probably be better for them to seek treatment elsewhere. I informed them as well that I did not believe that any competent therapist would agree to such a restriction on the treatment and that if a therapist did agree to such a restriction they would do well to think about the qualifications of such a person. Although obviously unhappy with my response they agreed to go along with the treatment.

In the next session, the first with the patient alone, she told me that her parents told her that they would let her continue treatment (which she argued strongly for), but made her promise them that she would not talk about sex. I told her that she was free to talk about anything and everything she wanted to and if there was a subject that she did not want to talk about I was not going to coerce her. However, I informed her as well that my experience has been that the most important subjects to talk about in treatment are generally just those very topics that patients don't want to talk about. However, my bottom line statement was that it was her treatment and she was free to talk about anything she wanted to and free not to talk about things she didn't wish to. During the next four or five sessions, she carefully avoided talking about sex. She did get some definite therapeutic mileage out of these discussions of other issues, some of which were not related to sex at all and others only remotely so.

It was at this point that the patient came in with a dream that she herself easily recognized as having obvious sexual implications. She then informed me that her parents had questioned her after each session about whether or not she was discussing sex. Heretofore, she was able to honestly deny that she had and so felt comfortable with the treatment. Now she was faced with a dilemma. If she were to be honest and tell her parents that she discussed sex with me—even though it was she who brought in the dream and that it was she who first recognized its sexual implications—they would pull her out of treatment. If she told them that she did not discuss sex, she would be lying and she would feel guilty about that. In the course of the discussion I pointed out to her that since it was 99.9 percent predictable that her parents would discontinue her treatment if she mentioned the dream, she should consider the possibility that mentioning it might be a way for her to withdraw from the therapy and it would thereby serve as a resistance against the treatment. We discussed also the issue of the resistance not simply being over the discussion of sexual material but other anxiety-provoking issues that had been discussed in previous sessions. The session ended with her not knowing exactly what she would do. The following day I received a telephone call from the father informing me that he was withdrawing his daughter from treatment and that all future sessions were cancelled. He told me that his daughter had informed him that we had talked about sex and that he was going to find a therapist who agreed beforehand not to discuss any sexual issues whatsoever. I wished him luck and, needless to say, I have never heard from these people again.

Since the late 1960s we have experienced what is justifiably called a "sexual revolution." The most dramatic confirmation of this is the ever increasing rate of teenage pregnancies. Prior to the late 1960s, teenage girls generally were quite ashamed to admit that they had sexual intercourse or even sexual experiences. The pendulum has so shifted that many girls are ashamed to admit that they are virgins, especially after a year or two of college. Another reflection of this change is the greater freedom that women have to use profanity. When I was a teenager, in the 1940s, girls who used profanity were generally viewed as crude and even loose. This is no longer the case. A 13-year-old girl was brought by her mother recently at her request. She sought consultation to determine whether or not she had psychological problems because most of her girlfriends had already started to masturbate and she had no urge to engage in the practice at that point. Both the patient and her mother considered this a justifiable reason for seeking a consultation. The girl freely spoke about the subject without any embarrassment. I informed her that I did not consider her to be abnormal and that some people do have strong sexual urges by her age and some do not. From everything else I learned about her I considered it safe to predict that she would be starting to have stronger urges within the next couple of years and that at that time, if she felt the desire, I would consider it perfectly acceptable and normal for her to masturbate. However, I impressed upon her that she should not do it in order to keep up with her friends, but because she herself felt the desire and the need.

Such a consultation would have been unimaginable 20 years ago. And I say this for two reasons. First, the youngster would not have brought it up as a reason for consultation and, even if she did, I can't imagine a mother agreeing that her failure to masturbate at 13 might very well be a manifestation of psychiatric problems. Second, even if she did get to my office for this reason, it would be hard to imagine her speaking in such a relaxed fashion about the subject. In general, my experience has been that pubertal and post-pubertal girls are far less inhibited talking to me about their sexual feelings than they were in the past and therefore I am seeing more females in this age bracket in recent years than I did in past years. I consider this a good trend because many of these girls come from divorced homes in which they have little if any contact with their fathers.

Helping Reluctant Boys Make Their Initial Dating Overtures

Boys are generally quite fearful of "making the first move"—lest they be rejected. The recent sexual revolution and the modern-day notions of sexual egalitarianism notwithstanding, boys are still the ones who are expected to make the first overtures. (I am not saying that this is either good or bad; I am only stating what is the prevailing practice in our society.) Many boys are filled with various rationalizations for not making the first move. My general approach here is to utilize what I call the *door-to-door salesman principle*. I tell the boy about the experience of the door-to-door salesman who must have the guts (or "balls") to tolerate the frustrations and lowered feelings of self-worth that come with each rejection. They are willing to suffer these discomforts because of their awareness that a certain percentage (often predictable) will ultimately buy their wares. And this happy thought enables them to tolerate their inevitable rejections. Therapists do well to help the adolescent compare himself to such a salesman. They do well to reassure the boy that even if he is rejected by girl number one, and even if he is rejected by girl number two, there is certainly girl number three or four who will be more receptive. This does not preclude my looking into personality qualities of his that might be contributing to his rejection.

Some boys will rationalize their reticence to make overtures with comments such as "All the girls in my school are 'dogs' or 'ugly'." To this I may respond, "From what you describe it appears that sometime around 16 years ago someone put some poison in the town drinking water that brought about severe facial deformities in all the girls that were born at that time." The youngster usually gets my message. I also try to impress upon such boys that I am "100 percent convinced" that there are girls in his very high school who would be overjoyed at the prospect of having a date with him. I also try to impress upon such youngsters the fact that the girls are as "horny" as the boys and that they too are extremely desirous of forming relationships with them.

Next, we reach the point of the initial telephone conversation. Once again, I impress upon such youngsters that anxiety under these circumstances is normal, and that even overwhelming anxiety is normal. However, I inform them that the difference between the brave man and the coward is simply this: whereas both the brave man and the coward are basically afraid, the brave man swallows the lump in his throat and does the thing he's frightened of; the coward flees. I also impress upon the youngster the *nothing ventured nothing gained* principle. Right now he is lonely. If he doesn't make the call he'll remain lonely. If he makes the call there are two possibilities: 1) The girl will be receptive and he is likely to have an enjoyable experience and 2) The girl will reject him and he will once again be lonely. Although such advice may seem obvious, it is not so obvious to the adolescent youngster and he may need repeated proddings of this kind to get him to make the telephone call.

I also try to impress upon the youngster the fact that we cannot be uniformly loved by all people on earth. In fact, only an infinitesimal fraction of people are going to be strongly attracted to us. Accordingly, we cannot take it personally when we are rejected. Although there may be alienating personality qualities (which we certainly must look at in treatment) the rejection may have nothing to do with the rejected individual but simply related to the fact that the boy is not the girl's "type." I also impress upon the youngster that our discussion is actually the *lecture* part of the course and that more important is the *lab* part of the course in which he goes out, makes the call, and then comes back and tells me about what happened. If he doesn't have the gumption to make the call, then his treatment is likely to be sterile, intellectualized, and not go very far. In some cases I will even sternly tell the youngster that his making the call is a "homework assignment" and that I will be very disappointed in him if he comes back next time not having done his assignment.

I have found it useful to engage the youngster in a "practice" telephone call in which I play the role of the girl he is calling and he plays himself. We then enact various scenarios which involve both acceptance and rejection. Usually, I get significant input from him regarding what I should be saying and inform the youngster that because he knows the girl far better than I he is more likely to speculate what responses she might make. In the course of such a scenario I educate the youngster regarding the significance of the girl's responses. For example, I help him differentiate between the response "Sorry I'm busy" with nothing stated thereafter from "Sorry I'm busy" and an invitation to discuss alternative arrangements. If the youngster is placing himself in a humiliating position I will often point this out to him as a step toward helping him protect himself from future such embarrassment. For example, if the youngster reports to me that he had offered six different alternatives after the first telephone rejection, and was rejected on each, I will inform him that that was far too many. Two, or at most three, should be the upper limit—unless the girl provides convincing reasons why she cannot accept the invitation and suggests on her own an alternative time and place. I help the patient appreciate that such a response indicates that she is quite receptive to going out with him and her refusal to accept the first invitation is not a manifestation of disinterest. As will be discussed in Chapter Seven, the section on adolescent group therapy, such conversations may be particularly useful when the girls in the group provide their input. And the role-playing of such conversations may also be useful.

Sometimes a boy will complain to me that the girl's situation is the preferable one in dating because she doesn't have to suffer the fear of being rejected. She knows that once an overture is made the boy has singled her out from others and is demonstrating interest and attraction. I try to point out to such boys that they are taking a narrow view of the situation and that each sex has its advantages and disadvantages in the dating situation. Furthermore, it is difficult to say which one's position is the preferable one at that stage of life. Although the boy is correct here that, with regard to this aspect of dating, the girl does not have to suffer the fear of being rejected, she suffers the anxiety of not being chosen. Present mores strongly dictate that the boy be the assertive one and make the initial approach. The girls experience thereby a certain sense of impotency in that they may have little if any control over whether or not they will be selected. Of course, a certain amount of flirting and expression of interest in the boys may result in their "coming on," but such maneuvers may very well fail.

I try to engender in each sex a sense of sensitivity to the other. For example, a girl who is pretty, vivacious, and sought after by many boys may become insensitive in the way she rejects them or even taunt and tantalize them in a sadistic way. She has to be helped to appreciate how hostile her mechanisms for self-aggrandizement are and has to be helped to place herself in the position of the boys and appreciate how she would feel in their situation. Similarly, there are attractive boys who will be cruel in their rejection of girls who have demonstrated their interest.

I present now a clinical vignette that demonstrates well the approach to initiate dating I used with a sexually inhibited 14-year-old boy. Harry entered treatment because of poor school performance, in spite of extremely high intelligence, and profound shyness. Both his parents were professional scientists and highly unemotional and intellectualized. Their pressures on Harry to perform well in the academic area were formidable. Harry's poor school performance was, in part, a rebellion against his parents' coercions. In addition, they had a condescending attitude toward practically everyone and little meaningful involvement with anyone outside their family. Harry's shyness and uninvolvement with others was a reflection of his parents' attitudes about people. The family was Catholic, very religious, and puritanical in their attitudes about profanity, sex, and pleasurable activities.

After about a year of therapy, Harry joined his parochial school's computer club, where he immediately became recognized as the most knowledgeable and enthusiastic member. The activity suited him well because of his very high intelligence and his interest in activities that did not involve emotional expression. A few months after joining he began to report in session his club's new project: computerized matching of boys in his school with the girls of a nearby Catholic school. All students in both schools were to fill out a questionnaire describing various basic physical characteristics, interests, personality preferences in members of the opposite sex, etc. All these data were to be fed into a computer and every boy and girl would be matched to three others. A large dance was to be held, everyone was to be assigned a number, and at prescribed times each student would dance with the partner assigned by the computer.

For weeks Harry spoke excitedly of the details of this project. I was most pleased about it, not only because of his enthusiasm (a rare quality for Harry to exhibit) but because it would provide Harry with the opportunity to involve himself with girls in a way that would produce less anxiety than some of the more traditional methods of boy-girl meeting. When the week came for the students to fill out their questionnaires, Harry spoke animatedly about the large numbers of questionnaires being received and how happy he was that everything pointed to the program's being a success. In the context of this discussion I casually asked Harry what answers he had written on his questionnaire. Harry replied, "Oh, I'm not putting in any questionnaire. My job is to organize the whole thing and make sure that everything works well with the computer." I was astonished. For weeks we had spoken about this activity and not once did I ever consider the possibility that Harry himself would not enter. The session took place the day before the deadline for the submission of the questionnaires. There was little time to work things out, to help Harry assuage his anxieties, and to help him appreciate what he was doing.

Speaking more as a frustrated father than as a therapist, I told Harry that I was astonished that he wasn't submitting his own questionnaire. I told him he was making a grave error, that everybody gets nervous in such situations, and that he has to push through his fears if he is to enjoy the rewards of a new situation. I spoke quickly and somewhat heatedly—ending with the the warning that if he came back to the next session without having submitted his questionnaire I would not only be very disappointed in him but very irritated with him as well.

One could argue that my approach was extremely antitherapeutic. I was coercing this boy; I was pushing him into an anxiety-provoking situation; I would be producing unnecessary guilt and self-loathing if he did not comply with my request; and I was jeapordizing the therapeutic relationship by such coercive and antitherapeutic tactics. I agree completely with these criticisms and I was completely aware of these dangers as I spoke to Harry. My hope was that this risk would be more than counterbalanced by Harry's appreciation, at some level, that my frustration, anger, and coercion came from a deep sense of concern; that only an uninvolved therapist could sit calmly by and allow him to pass up this wonderful opportunity. (I am reminded at this point of a psychiatric ward nurse who once reported to me overhearing a conversation among three children. The first said, "My mother's a bitch." The second, "My father's always hitting me." And the third, "My father never even hits me!" Obviously the third's situation was the worst.

Having a father who never even bothers to discipline and even punish is a severe deprivation indeed.) I hoped also that the general strength of our relationship was such that he not only would comply, but that he would appreciate that I was being basically benevolent.

Harry did submit his questionnaire. On the night of the dance he "could not find" one of the girls with whom he was matched and the second "didn't show up." However, he did spend some time with the third. But because he didn't know how to dance (and forgot my suggestion that he ask her to teach him a few steps), they talked awhile and then went their separate ways. I was not surprised that no great romance developed from this first encounter with a female. One cannot expect a patient to overcome lifelong inhibitions in one evening. However, the ice was broken. Had I not reacted as I had, I believe that Harry would not have taken this step and I would have therefore been somewhat remiss in my obligation to him. I saw no evidence that Harry's relationship with me had in any way suffered because of my coercion; in fact, I believe that it was strengthened. However, this improvement could not have taken place if the coercion had not occurred at a time after a good relationship had already formed. To have used such an approach very early in treatment might very well have destroyed, or seriously compromised, our relationship.

Helping Sexually Inhibited Boys

Sometimes a sexually inhibited boy can be made to feel less guilty about his sexual desires by my demonstrating sexual interest of my own. For example, when a boy tells me that he feels somewhat guilty about the fact that he is interested in and turned on by girlie magazines such as *Playboy* I might say, somewhat sarcastically, "I think the best way I can help you with those feelings is to take a look at that magazine myself, especially the centerfold. It's only when we discuss this with an actual picture in hand that we will be in a good position to talk about your feelings. Of course, I'm doing this purely from a *clinical* point of view. (I may then start smiling.) It's not that I have any *personal* interest in seeing those pictures. It's purely for *your* therapy. If you think for one minute that I myself would be titillated by such pictures you would be entirely wrong." Almost invariably the patient gets my message which, I believe, helps assuage his guilt. Basically I am saying that I too find those pictures titillating and this helps the patient feel less loathsome for his own interest. I believe that this is one of the situations in treatment where sarcasm is warranted in that it enhances the efficacy of the therapeutic message. If a boy feels inhibited about masturbating over such pictures, I try to assuage his guilt and impress upon him that this is an extremely widespread phenomenon and that most boys, if they were to be honest, would admit that they engage in the practice. If he claims that most of his friends deny that they do so, I try to convince him of the fact that they are most likely lying. I may tell him, "There are two kinds of boys: those who jerk off over these pictures and *admit* that they do and those who jerk off over such pictures and *deny* that they do." If the youngster has any misguided or erroneous notions about the dangers of masturbation, I will try to correct these distortions. He may believe that masturbation causes sexually transmitted diseases, sterility, rings under the eyes, or other telltale signs. All these distortions must be corrected.

A 16-year-old boy once told me that he had read in the newspapers that some women in Washington D.C. were going to protest the city's law that women are not permitted to appear in public with their chests bare, whereas men can. They were going to protest en masse by appearing publicly, completely bare from the waist up. This was told to me by a boy who was quite inhibited in telling me about his own interests in girls. In response to his information about the Washingon demonstration I took my pen and pad and said, "That's very interesting. Where did you say that demonstration was going to be held? What city did you say? When did you say it was going to take place? I'm very interested in the exact day and the exact time. And I'd like to know *exactly* where they're going to be demonstrating. These are the kinds of demonstrations that *really* interest me." The patient quickly got my message. I too was telling him that I thought it was a turn-on. Of course, the patient appreciated that I was not actually going to make a trip to Washington, but my intense interest (exaggerated somewhat) transmitted to him the message that I found the prospect titillating. I continued then: "I'm fully sympathetic with what these women are doing. The law is inegalitarian and I'm 100 percent against it. I'm convinced the world would be a better place if women were free to walk around topless. These women have a definite *point* to make, or should I say *points*." By this time the patient was chuckling along with me. I was not only providing here a guilt-assuaging message in an enjoyable vehicle but, possibly more important, was adding a note of levity to the therapy—counterbalancing thereby what can often be a morbid and grim experience. This is likely to entrench our relationship and strengthen thereby the foundation of the therapeutic process.

It has been my purpose in this section to discuss primarily the approaches I utilize when helping youngsters become more comfortable in the dating situation. I will, however, present here one of the most important bits of advice I provide all men (adolescent or adult) when counseling them regarding their sexual involvement with women. I generally refer to this as the *"ladies first" principle.* All young men should be introduced to this principle in their adolescence and it is unfortunate (for both men and women) that too few adolescent boys are given this important advice. Once the youngster starts becoming engaged in sexual activities I tell him about some important biological differences between men and women regarding orgastic capacity. I advise him of the fact that there is great variation among women regarding the speed with which they become aroused—varying from those who take an extremely long time to those who may be aroused almost instantaneously. Accordingly, I advise patience and tenderness with those women who are slow to become aroused. I then move into the subject of orgasm and apprise the youngster of the fact that women are generally more capable of achieving multiple orgasms, often in rapid succession, than are men. Even women who are extremely slow to be aroused, once they reach orgasm, may be capable of achieving one after another. Men, in contrast, have varying degrees of what is known as a "refractory period." This is the time of loss of arousal that immediately follows ejaculation. Some men have a relatively short refractory period (a few minutes), but most men have longer refractory periods (as long as a few hours). The older the man the greater the likelihood of a longer refractory period. Also, during the refractory period the man is less likely to be able to maintain an erection and thereby satisfy the woman intravaginally.

Accordingly, if the man reaches his orgasm first he may not be in the mood to continue sexual involvement with the woman, whether with an erect penis or in any other way. This can leave the woman frustrated and resentful. If the man holds back, however, until the woman reaches her orgasm (or a few orgasms) and then has his discharge, his refractory period will not generally be a source of significant frustration and/or resentment to the woman. I tell him that the *method* by which the woman reaches orgasm is not crucial; it doesn't matter whether the stimulation be penile, oral, or manual (by the lover or the woman herself). Nor is it important whether the site of primary stimulation is clitoral or vaginal. What is important is that the the man be patient and sympathetic so that the woman can reach her orgasm first.

I inform the patient that one of the most common complaints that women have about their male lovers is their lack of appreciation of these facts and their insensitivity to the woman's frustration after the men have enjoyed sexual release and not considered the woman's needs. I go further and inform the youngster that there are many lesbians who state that one of the important reasons they have turned to women for sex is because women are more sensitive to them and are appreciative of these important facts. So important is this principle that I believe even the most staunch feminists will generally agree that men who subscribe to this type of "ladies first" behavior are not sexist and are not "male chauvinist pigs." So vital is this principle that it may be the most important advice I give my adolescent boy patients in the course of their treatment. If they get nothing else out of the therapy, they will at least have obtained some help in becoming better lovers—and this cannot but be therapeutic.

Helping Girls Who Feel Unattractive

A girl feels unattractive. In the course of her therapy I help her appreciate that there are a wide range of facial and body types and that no one can be uniformly attractive to everyone. Although her particular appearance may not be attractive to some boys, there is no question that her appearance is attractive to others. And I point out that this is the case for everyone, including myself. The fact that her therapist has had his share of rejections makes it easier for her to accept hers. However, I don't stop there. I try to look into anything she might be doing that might be detracting from good grooming and attractive appearance. If this is the case, I *benevolently* point out these oversights to her and do what I can to help her rectify the situation. Sometimes, as a man, I recognize that my ability to provide such information may be compromised and I thereby advise her to speak with her mother, other adolescent girls, a beautician, and those who are more knowledgeable than I in this area. This does not preclude my going into the question of *why* she has not done what other girls her age are routinely doing. The adolescent girl may be more receptive to a discussion of *what* she can do for herself and improve her appearance than the issue of *why* she is not concerned with her grooming. Both areas are important even though the youngster may be more receptive to information about grooming than analytic inquiry.

If the youngster then shows efforts to improve her appearance I make it a point to mention my awareness of the changes. But I do not do this simply at the intellectual level. When the changes are made, I don't wait (as many classical analysts would) until the youngster says something. And, when I do speak up it's not simply at the intellectual level, for example, "I see you've changed your hairstyle" or "I see you're more careful now with the clothes you are choosing to wear." Rather, I will say, "I want you to know that I noticed the change as soon as you came into the room. It's striking how pretty you look now. I'm sure the boys' heads turn when you walk into the room." My hope here is to get across the message that I find the girl attractive and *somewhat* titillating. Some classical analysts would say that my comments here are seductive and therefore a terrible therapeutic contaminant. I am in disagreement. I am not communicating to the youngster specific sexual fantasies that she might now be engendering. Rather, I am merely communicating a mild level of titillation that most men would have in her presence. D.J. Holmes (1964) discusses this point in his vignette about an adolescent girl who was making efforts to make herself more attractive. With regard to the issue of what comments, if any, the therapist should make Holmes states (p.277): "If she has put much honest labor into restyling her hair or making an attractive dress for herself, it would probably be more damaging to withhold comment. She might secretly wonder if her therapist has gone blind, but would be even more likely to marvel at the magnitude of his inhibitedness.... This open expression of appreciation on the part of the doctor naturally carries a hint of sexual interest. As such feelings are inevitable anyway, any effort to write them off entirely as 'countertransference' will be correctly interpreted by the patient as an act of emotional cowardice—an uneasy withdrawal from the very kinds of feelings which she finds so difficult to tolerate in herself."

Helping Promiscuous Girls

As mentioned, I consider a girl's having sexual intercourse in late adolescence to be normal and healthy. The ideal that I try to promulgate is the one that sex is most enjoyable in the context of an ongoing relationship, but an occasional experience outside of such a relationship can also be a source of pleasure. I emphasize also that such experiences outside of the relationship are likely to be a cause of pain and grief to one's special partner and that this must be taken into consideration before embarking on such additional experiences. I point out, as well, that in a marriage they are most often so devastating that they can contribute to the breakup of the marital relationship. I want to lay the groundwork here for dealing here with a future situation and/or conflict that the adolescent may very well ultimately have.

If a girl is promiscuous, i.e., she indiscriminately engages in sex with a large number of boys, there is generally a pathological problem operative. Often it relates to feelings of low self-worth, and the feeling that she could not attract boys without providing them with sex. I try to help such girls appreciate that they are humiliating themselves and that the lack of respect the boys have for them for their promiscuity is likely to lower even further their feelings of low self-worth. Some of these girls are so naive and gullible that they do not see the obvious fact that they are being exploited, so deep seated are their cravings for any manifestation of affection. I also look into other problems that may be contributing to the promiscuity. These may relate to family difficulties, deprivation of affection from mother and/or father, and various psychological traumas that may contribute to her looking for sexual gratification as an antidote to her grief, tensions, and frustrations. To the degree that one can help her work these out, to that degree will the therapist help her with her promiscuity problem.

CLINICAL EXAMPLE OF A THERAPEUTIC REPORT

Recently, with increasing frequency, I have found it useful to provide adolescents I see in consultation with clinical reports in the form of a letter written directly to the patient. Reproduced here verbatim (with minor changes to hide his identity) is an example of such a letter to a 21-year-old boy (psychologically still very much a mid-adolescent) who came to me for consultation from a distant city. He manifested mild symptoms of schizophrenia, abused drugs and alcohol, yet was functioning well in many areas.

February 28, 1988

Dear Robert:

This is the report I promised to send you regarding my consultation conducted on February 23, 1988. As you know, my opinions regarding your situation are based on the three hours of interviews I conducted with you, your mother, and father as well as my review of your records—especially those from the T. Hospital. I want you to know that I consider your decision to get a report a judicious one in that many people do not remember all the things I say during consultations such as yours. Having this letter will enable you to refresh your memory should you wish to in the future.

I think you do well to consider yourself to have a disorder that affects the proper functioning of the nerve cells and pathways in your brain. On the basis of the tests that were performed and my own evaluation of you, I think it is reasonable to conclude that only certain small sections of your brain are involved. The rest appears to be working quite normally. No one knows with certainty exactly what kinds of impairment are involved in your disorder. The disorder is probably related to chemical and/or electrical impairments in nerve cell functioning. It is not only the nerve cells and their fibers that are involved but probably the places where the nerve cells connect with one another. Considering the fact that a number of people in both of your parents' families, especially your father's, suffered with what sound like psychiatric disturbances, it may be that you too have inherited some genetic predisposition to psychiatric disturbance. It would be a serious error, however, for you to consider yourself incapable of doing anything about this situation. We are not dealing here with something like hair color or eye color, which is also genetically determined. In the course of this letter I will make reference to the things you can do to help yourself.

One way of looking at your condition is to consider yourself to have a disorder that is very similar to seizures. Seizures result from firing off or discharing of nerve cell fibers at times when they shouldn't be, and in ways which they should not be. At times some of your nerve cells work in improper ways and so you start having thoughts and feelings which you recognize are strange, unusual, and probably not accurate. Your thoughts about your knee accident somehow being planned by others and your thoughts about women's vaginal bleeding are in this category.

I mentioned to you at our meeting that I suffer with a similar phenomenon related to a disorder of internal brain functioning. Specifically, I have mild hearing loss associated with ringing in the ears (called tinnitus). However, the tinnitus does not arise in the ears primarily but in the brain stem. When I pay attention to it it sounds like crickets or buzzing sounds. When I do not pay attention to it, it is as if it were not there. I have had it for about 10 years now and I have learned to live with it. When it gets louder I don't pay attention to it, and just do other things.

You do well to treat your strange thoughts as I treat my tinnitus: something not to take too seriously. Many people with your condition will refer to these strange ideas as the "crazy thoughts" and try not to take them seriously and do not act out on them. It is to your credit that most often you do not. People with more severe cases of your condition take them seriously and then get into difficulty because they may even act out on their thoughts and feelings because of their belief that they are true. It is fortunate, as well, that your thoughts do not take malevolent forms, that is, cause you to believe that people wish you harm or want to hurt you. People with more severe cases of your condition commonly have such kinds of thinking.

Just as people with seizure disorders can obtain relief from anticonvulsant medication, which suppress the nerve cell activity that produces seizures, the Haldol you are taking can suppress some of these "crazy thoughts." Your doctors have tried a number of different medications, and I have good reason to believe that the medications you are presently taking are proper. These are powerful medicines and, like all powerful medicines, there are strong side effects. From what I can see the Cogentin is suppressing the abnormal involuntary movements often produced by the Haldol. You describe yourself as somewhat fatigued by the Haldol, and I myself observed this during our interview. You mentioned that Dr. R.S. spoke of raising your Haldol from 5 mg. to 10 mg., but that you were reluctant to do so because of the lethargic side effect. I suspect that you are right on this point.

Because you are depressed your doctors have put you on the antidepressant amitriptyline. Although your depression may also be related to impairments in nerve cell functioning, I am convinced that other things that have gone on in your life have contributed to the depression. To the degree that you can improve these (to be discussed below), to that degree can you hope to discontinue the antidepressant medication. It may be, however, that you will have to be on the Haldol (or similar drug) for a long time.

Unfortunately, your lifestyle has been one in which you have worsened the condition of your brain cells. This is especially the case for the LSD, which is not only a very powerful stimulant of nerve cells but also damages them. It will very quickly produce a state of toxic psychosis, a severe form of the kind of disorder with which you are suffering. One could say that it was just about the worst possible substance you could take.

Furthermore, the marijuana you have smoked, unlike

alcohol, gets stored in the protective covering (insulation) of nerve cell fibers and just sits there interfering with nerve cell functioning. The body has to work to pump out marijuana. It can take a long time for this to happen. I understand also that you have been smoking hashish, a more powerful form of marijuana. I hope you appreciate that hashish's capacity to damage the nerve cells in your brain is even more powerful than that of standard pot.

I understand, also, that you have used cocaine and opium. I hope you appreciate that when a person becomes addicted to these substances they become incorporated into the body chemistry. The intense craving that the addict has for these drugs relates to the biological need for them created by the addiction. These substances lock into places on nerve cells that are supposed to be occupied by normal body substances. Obviously, they do not help normal nerve cell functioning; rather they compromise the functioning of the nerve cells and this cannot but do you harm.

All the drugs you have been abusing not only interfere with nerve cell functioning but can *destroy* nerve cells as well. As I mentioned to you during our meeting, once a nerve cell is destroyed it never grows back. It is replaced by what is called connective tissue, which fills up the space where the disintegrated nerve cell was but does not function as a nerve cell. People who are alcoholics also do damage to the nerve cells of their brain. A small amount of alcohol, taken once or twice a week, would probably not do you any harm. Even alcohol, however, impairs judgment—even one drink. What happens, then, is that the individual who promises him- or herself to stop after one drink then loses good judgment and continues drinking—sometimes to toxic levels. The owners of the gambling casinos in Las Vegas and Atlantic City know this phenomenon well. They give free drinks to all people who sit at the gambling tables. They know quite well that once a person has one or two drinks, the individual is more likely to lose good judgment and gamble away his or her money. One could argue that the gambling houses should *pay* the gamblers to drink, because the owners ultimately earn so much more from customers who are inebriated. I hope you will think about the potential of alcohol to impair your judgment when you do decide to have one drink only and promise yourself that you will not drink more. Furthermore, the women who serve drinks at gambling casinos are often scantily dressed, exposing much of their breasts. This too distracts the men who are gambling, causes them to stay longer at the gambling tables, interferes with their sober judgment, and causes them to lose more money.

You have gone beyond judicious levels of alcohol consumption. It is clear, as well, that one factor involved in this is your excessive dependence on your peers and your strong need to "keep up with the others." It is unfortunate that you feel embarrassed telling your friends that you don't wish to drink. If you cannot overcome this problem, then you should make a promise to yourself that you will drink only one drink in the evening, and then "nurse it" as long as you can. It is no crime, either, to say you like ice cubes in your beer. This will keep it cool longer and also water it down so you'll get more mileage out of the drink. I hope you will promise to limit yourself to no more than one or two drinks a week. You may not be able to improve the functioning of the impaired nerve cells you were born with, but you certainly have full control over whether or not you will make them worse. You have been damaging your nerve cells voluntarily and you have thereby worsened your condition.

Now to your habit of smoking 1–1/2 packages of cigarettes a day. I will not dwell upon the fact that smoking is a terrible irritant to your lungs, so much so that it can produce lung cancer, emphysema (a disease of the lungs which results in severe interference with breathing and even death), and other lung disorders. Nor will I talk about the effects of smoking on your circulatory system and its contribution to strokes and heart attacks. Nor will I focus on the fact that nicotine is an addicting substance. Rather, I want to focus on the effects of smoking on your brain cells and not in some distant, remote time but each time you smoke a cigarette *now*. The hemoglobin molecules in your blood stream pick up oxygen from the alveoli, little air sacks in your lungs. There is a place on the hemoglobin molecule in your red blood cells where the oxygen gets attached. The smoke you inhale is very rich in carbon monoxide. The carbon monoxide molecule fits perfectly into that spot on the hemoglobin molecule where the oxygen should be. Once the carbon monoxide molecule is there the oxygen cannot attach. Accordingly, you are carrying large amounts of carbon monoxide to your brain when you smoke. The brain cannot use carbon monoxide and so you are voluntarily depriving your brain cells of oxygen. This has to impair your thinking. You should think about that when you smoke.

Psychological and environmental stresses can also worsen your condition. The more you get your life in order, the more you handle yourself in a mature, adult way, the better will your nerve cells function. The happier and more secure you are, the less attention you will pay to your "crazy thoughts." With regard to these environmental influences, I believe you were quite lucky with regard to your parents. As you know, I know your parents well from my previous evaluation of your family a few years ago. I consider your parents to be loyal, dedicated, and most loving of you and your brother. Their dedication during your formative years helped protect you from the kind of worsening of the problem that many people with your genetic predisposition suffer. In addition, although there were some problems in their relationship with one another, from what I can see, they have been dedicated to you and have not exposed you to any significant detrimental environmental influences. Your genetic predisposition makes you more susceptible to developing severe psychiatric illness than those who do not have such genetic programming.

I did not get to know you well enough during our consultation to explore in depth the various psychological problems that you have. Your parents consider you to be functioning at the 17-year level. I am in agreement with them on this point. I do not think you have come to the realization that you are now almost 22, an adult by most people's standards. You have yet to buckle down and take life seriously. Although your involvement with peers is a good sign, your involvements are too much at the teenage level. My hope is that when you go to college in September you will take your education very seriously and work toward your career goal. I believe that your decision to major in business is a reasonable one for you and I wish you luck in it. You also have a problem in being accident prone and this is clearly related to many difficulties, both physical and psychological. The stresses associated with your accidents can only worsen your brain cell condition.

As you know, the name of the disorder that you have is schizophrenia. Like all disorders, there is a range from those with very mild cases, to those who have very severe cases. I consider you to have a very mild case, but a case of it nevertheless. Your main symptoms are the "crazy thoughts" that we have spoken about. I consider your case mild for a number of reasons. First, you are most often able to look at your inappropriate thoughts and recognize them as improper. As mentioned, many people with your disorder are not able to do this and they not only believe their thoughts, but act out on them. In addition, many people with schizophrenia have severe impairments in their relationships with others. This is not your situation. From what I can see, you have very good relationships with your brother and friends outside the home. Many people with schizophrenia are immediately labeled as odd by those who come in contact with them. Fortunately for you, this is not your situation. Many people with schizophrenia withdraw from life; it is as if they have given up. You are out there plugging and involving yourself. Many people with schizophrenia have significant sexual problems. From what I understand, you have functioned fairly well in this area and are in the normal range. A sexual relationship—with someone with whom you have a close, tender relationship—can be one of the greatest pleasures in life. So enjoy it.

It is to your credit that when you broke up with your old girlfriend you started to look for a new one. That is a sign of health. Some people would just bemoan their fate and wallow in self-pity. I believe that a healthy, loving relationship with a girl can be one of the most potent antidepressants. And when you have established such a relationship it might even work to the point where it might lessen your need for antidepressant medication. Although your depressive states may have biological factors involved, there is no question that environmental and psychological factors operate as well. The more you do to make your life happier, the less you will need to rely upon antidepressant medication. Many people with schizophrenia draw very bizarre pictures of other people when asked to do so. Your drawings are in the normal range, although somewhat on the immature side. This is consistent with what I said earlier about your functioning more on the 17-year level than on the 22-year level.

At this point I would like to comment on your feelings that there are "bugs" crawling through your hair and flying around your face. The dermatologists have found no evidence for any disease of your scalp. This symptom is called for*m*ication. Do not confuse it with "for*n*ication." (They are very different things.) It may be that this is a symptom of your nerve cell impairment. It may be a result of the irritation and destruction of nerve cells that was brought about by your taking drugs, especially LSD. Perhaps it is purely psychological, although I do believe it has some kind of a physical basis in nerve cell functioning. I think you do well to view it as one of your "crazy symptoms" and try to go about your business like I suggested you do with the other "crazy thoughts." The more you get your life in order the less you will think about these things.

You mention that you have been working with Dr. R.S. for about two years and that you recently decided to drop from a frequency of once a week down to a frequency of once every other week. From what you tell me you appear to have a good therapeutic relationship with him. It sounds like you are talking to him about the things that are important for you to discuss. I believe it would be an error for you to cut down to less than once a week at this point. When you are on drugs, you get less out of psychotherapy. When a person is stoned, he is not going to accomplish much in a therapeutic session. When a person's brain has residua of drugs taken previously, that individual is also going to be compromised in what can be accomplished in a psychotherapeutic session. I hope this will serve as another motivation for you to *stop taking drugs*.

I hope you find this letter useful. I am also sending a copy to your parents and an extra copy for you to give to your doctor. Last, I have one request of you. And that is that you either drop me a note or give me a ring in about six months. I would like to find out how you are doing.

Sincerely,
Richard A. Gardner, M.D.

I believe the letter speaks for itself. The patient and his parents considered the letter to be quite useful and he frequently made reference to it in his treatment. Although I had verbally presented him with just about all of the information and advice contained in the letter, writing it down provided a permanence to my comments that enhanced the likelihood that my advice would be remembered and reviewed. Furthermore, the written word has a power that the spoken word does not. Although it is probably not justified, most people show greater respect for that which is written than that which is spoken. Letters such as these take advantage of this phenomenon. The letter has also been reproduced because it incorporates some of the therapeutic messages I impart to adolescents in the course of my individual work with them.

FIVE

THE TALKING, FEELING, AND DOING GAME

I have mentioned in passing *The Talking, Feeling, and Doing Game* as an instrument that may be useful in the treatment of adolescents. Here I will present the game in detail and discuss its utilization in adolescent therapy. As mentioned, it is likely to prove more useful with younger adolescents (ages 13–15) than those who are 16 and older. However, one can use it occasionally with these older youngsters as well. Because younger adolescents are often uncomfortable in the direct face-to-face therapeutic situation, the game may be valuable in providing them with issues for conversation. In fact, many adolescents in this age group will state openly that the game gives them ideas to talk about.

THE BASIC FORMAT OF THE TALKING, FEELING, AND DOING GAME

The game is similar in appearance to the typical board games with which most children are familiar (Figure 5-1). It includes a playing board, dice, playing pawns, a spinner, a path along which the pawns are moved, reward chips, and cards that are drawn from the center of the game board. This familiarity, as well as the fact that it is a *game,* reduces initial anxieties and attracts the patient to the therapeutic instrument.

To begin the game both therapist and patient place their colored pawns at the START position. Alternately, they throw the dice and move their pawns along a curved path of squares which lead to the FINISH position. A pawn can land on one of a number of squares: white, red, yellow, SPIN, GO FORWARD (a specific number of squares), and GO BACKWARD (again, a specific number of squares). If the pawn lands on a white square, the player takes a Talking Card; on a yellow square, a Feeling Card; and on a red square, a Doing Card. If the pawn lands on SPIN, the player spins the spinner and follows the directions. Generally, these provide gain and loss of chips, or forward and backward movement of the playing pawn. Similarly, landing on GO FORWARD or GO BACKWARD squares results in movement of the pawn. The spinner and movement squares are of little, if any, psychological significance. They are included to ensure the youngster's fun and relieve some of the pressure associated with a high frequency of drawing only the aforementioned three types of cards.

Of course the core of the game is in the directions and questions on each of the cards. As their titles imply, the Talking Cards instruct the player to make comments that are primarily in the cognitive area. The Feeling Cards focus primarily on affective issues. The Doing Cards usually involve play acting and/or some kind of physical activity. The child is given a reward chip for responding to each of the cards. Although a token reinforcement is provided, the game is by no means a form of behavior modification. Positive reinforcement is not being given for behavioral change at the manifest level. Rather, the patient is being reinforced for providing psychodynamically meaningful material for psychotherapeutic utilization. The patient's and the therapist's responses are used as points of departure for therapeutic interchanges.

There is no actual time limit for the game. Both the therapist and the patient play similarly, and each responds to the cards. The first player to reach the FINISH position receives five extra reward chips. The other player continues until he or she also reaches

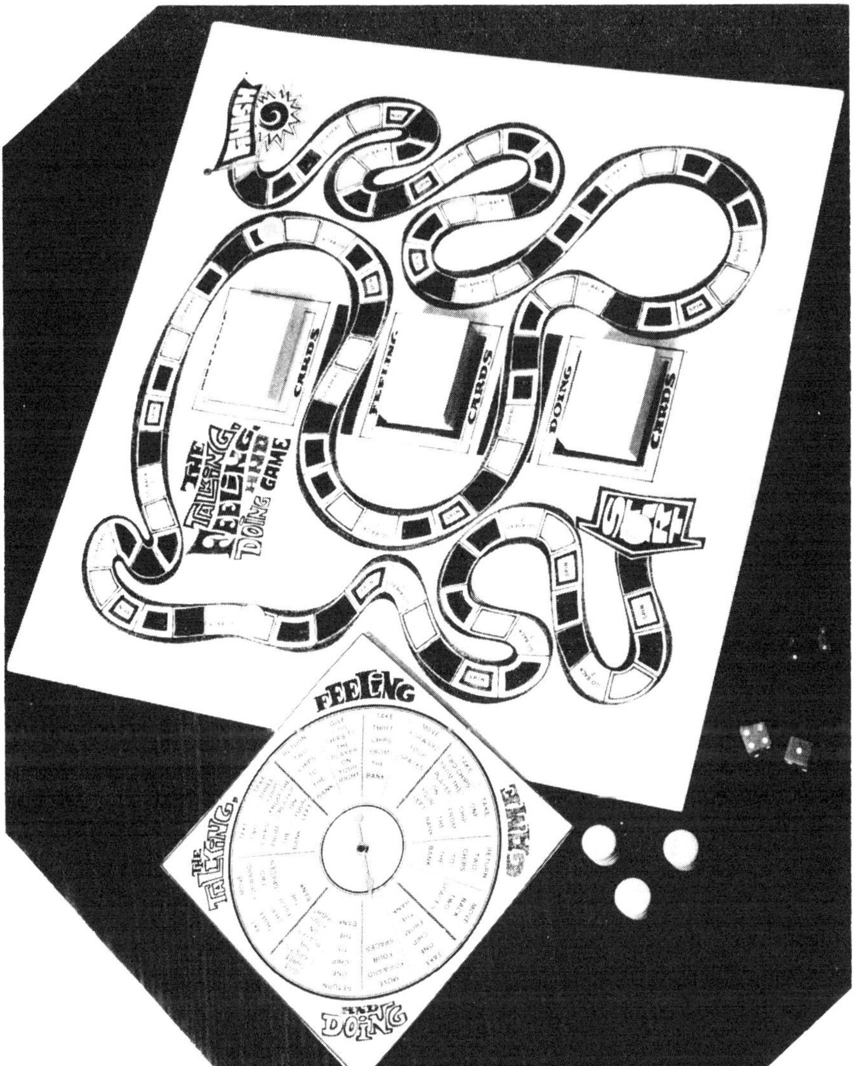
FINISH
THE TALKING, FEELING, AND DOING GAME
CARDS
FEELING CARDS
DOING CARDS
FEELING
DOING

FIGURE 5-1

FINISH. If the game is interrupted prior to one player's reaching the FINISH position, the one who is closest to that position receives three extra reward chips. The therapist should discourage active competition on the patient's part for the acquisition of chips. The game should be played at a slow pace, and each response should serve as a point of departure for psychotherapeutic interchange.

There are 104 cards in each stack. I always randomize them and have never "stacked the deck" with specific cards that I hope the child will draw. The cards are so designed that any card will be relevant to any player. About five percent of the cards in each stack are so simple and nonthreatening that just about any patient will respond. Basically these are placed there for the extremely fragile patient who would be threatened by the cards that might touch on basic problems of living. These simpler cards ensure that the patient will get chips and thereby remain motivated to participate in the game. The most liberal criteria are used when deciding whether or not the patient should be given a chip for responding. Again, the therapist wants to do everything possible to draw the youngster in and maintain his or her interest. Some typical low-anxiety cards: "How old is your father?"; "What's your lucky number? Why?"; "What is your telephone number?"; "What is your address?"; "What's your favorite flavor ice cream?"; "What present would you like to get for your next birthday?"; "What's your favorite smell?"; "Make believe you're blowing out the candles on your birthday cake."; and "Make a funny sound with your mouth. If you spit, you don't get a chip."

The remaining questions and directions are far richer psychologically and are at the "heart" of the game. These are not as anxiety provoking as a request to make up a story that will reveal free fantasies; however, they provide highly meaningful therapeutic material. Some typical cards: "All the girls in the class were invited to a birthday party except one. How did she feel? Why wasn't she invited?"; "Everybody in the class was laughing at a girl. What had happened?"; "A boy has something on his mind that he's afraid to tell his father. What is it that he's scared about?"; "What's the worst thing a boy can say to his mother?"; "Suppose two people were talking about you, and they didn't know you were listening. What do you think you would hear them saying?"; "What things come into your mind when you can't fall asleep?"; "If the walls of your house could talk, what would they say about your family?"; "Tell about something you did that made you proud."; and "What's the worst thing that ever happened to you in your whole life?".

The patient's responses are usually revealing of the psychological issues most relevant to him or her at that point. The questions and instructions cover the wide range of human experiences. The material elicited is likely to be relevant to the underlying causes of the patient's disturbance. The questions are designed to direct the patient's attention to the basic life conflicts which are being resolved in inappropriate and maladaptive ways by the symptomatology. They direct the patient's attention to the issues that I referred to previously, that is, the basic life conflicts that are at the foundation of psychopathological processes. As mentioned, each response serves as a point of departure for therapeutic interchanges. The therapist does not merely provide the patient with a chip and then race on with the game to see who can reach FINISH first. Rather, the therapist tries to get "as much mileage" as possible from each response, using his or her discretion in deciding how much discussion is warranted for each patient. Highly defensive and resistant youngsters will not be able to tolerate the kind of in-depth discussion in which the healthier child can readily participate.

The therapist answers the same questions as the patient. The greater the therapist's knowledge of the youngster's problems, the more judicious will be his or her responses. Obviously, it is not the therapist's role to provide answers relevant to his or her *own* life problems. Rather the responses should be designed to provide therapeutic messages pertinent to the patient's difficulties. I always respond honestly. Often I will provide a response that will relate to an experience of mine in childhood that is relevant to the patient's problems. Children generally enjoy hearing about the events of their parent's lives that occurred at that time in the parent's childhood that corresponds to the age of the child at the time of the conversation. Such discussions draw children closer to their parents. The same principle holds in therapy. Such revelations, then, can contribute to a deepening of the therapist-patient relationship. As mentioned, a good relationship is crucial if therapy is to be successful. Without it, there will be little receptivity to the therapist's messages and practically no identification with him or her.

Many therapists, especially those with a classical psychoanalytic orientation, may take issue with the freedom with which I reveal myself. They would argue that I am contaminating terribly the therapeutic field and making the patient's free associations practically useless. I am in full agreement that such revelations contaminate the patient's free associations. However, the classical approach is not without its drawbacks. It does indeed provide the so-called "blank screen" for the purest projections. However, the acquisition of such information is done in a setting which, I believe, is antitherapeutic. It creates a distance between the therapist and the patient that compromises the development of a good therapist-patient relationship. The patient's thoughts and feelings about the therapist become distorted and divorced from reality. The situation increases the likelihood that the patient will develop delusions about the therapist and will idealize him or her. It will widen the gap between them as the patient comes to view the therapist as perfect. We can love most those whom we know nothing about—but such love is more delusional than real, based as it is on a paucity of information. What is gained in the way of pure free associations is more than counterbalanced, I believe, by a compromise of the therapist-patient relationship and the antitherapeutic experience of the patient's comparing him- or herself unfavorably with the therapist. *The Talking, Feeling, and Doing Game* provides the therapist with the opportunity to reveal defects in a noncontrived and nonartificial setting. He or she thereby becomes more human to the patient, and this is generally salutary for their relationship. In addition, my revelations are not those that would compromise my own privacy and that of my family. Even with these restrictions, there is enough that has gone on in my life to provide me with a wealth of potential revelations.

I answer all questions. Some highly defensive patients, however, may find it difficult to do so. Sometimes, I will inform such youngsters that failure to answer the question will result in their not getting a reward chip, and this will lessen the likelihood that they will win the game. Some patients are motivated by this "threat" and try to respond to the card. On occasion, a patient will refrain from answering most cards but still involve him- or herself in the game. Many of these children listen attentively to my responses and, I believe, gain thereby from the game. Although I am working here in a partial vacuum, because I am not getting as much information from the patient as is desirable, my knowledge of the youngster's history and background provides me with enough information to give responses to the cards that are meaningful to the patient and pertinent to his or her problems.

The question is sometimes raised about winning and losing when playing therapeutic games with children. *The Talking, Feeling, and Doing Game* obviates this problem. It may not be immediately apparent to the reader that the main determinant of who wins the game is *luck*. If each player answers each card, the determinant of who wins the game is the dice. If a player obtains many high throws, then he or she will reach FINISH earlier and thereby acquire fewer chips. If a player obtains a larger number of low throws, more chips will be acquired when going from START to FINISH. Because low and high throws average out for each player, the number of wins and losses also average out over the course of treatment.

Although *The Talking, Feeling, and Doing Game* was originally devised to engage resistant children in therapy, it has proved useful for less defended children as well. In fact, it has proved to be the favorite therapeutic activity of the children in my practice. Many other therapists have informed me that this has been their experience as well. This therapeutic boon is not without its drawbacks, however. One danger of the game is that it will lure the patient (and, unfortunately, the therapist) away from utilizing techniques that are more likely to elicit "deeper" psychodynamic material. Dealing with this material is also important in therapy. Accordingly, the therapist should not injudiciously "respect" the patient's wishes to devote the entire therapeutic experience to this technique.

EXAMPLES OF CARD RESPONSES

Talking Cards

Human behavior lends itself well to being divided into thoughts, feelings, and actions. It was from this observation that I decided to name this game *The Talking, Feeling, and Doing Game*. Furthermore, the sequence here is also important. Thoughts generally precede feelings, and feelings precede actions. Certainly, the sequence is applicable for fight-flight reactions. One sees a danger. A possible emotional reaction is fear. In response to the fear one flees. The fear emotion enhances one's efficiency in fleeing. One runs faster when one is afraid. Another possible emotional reaction is anger. When one fights, the anger enhances one's efficiency in protecting oneself from the attacker. For emotions such as sexual arousal and hunger, feelings may precede thoughts. One feels hungry, then one experiences thoughts related to food acquisition. Then one takes action and attempts to obtain food. Because therapy is more likely to deal more with fight-flight emotions than those related to eating and sexual arousal (not that these aren't involved in treatment at all), I decided to place *Talking* before *Feeling* in the name of the game.

The Talking Cards encourage the patient to speak about his or her opinions on a wide variety of subjects. The questions are designed to elicit information related to the fundamental problems of life which confront all children. As discussed in Chapter Five the solutions to these problems can either be adaptive or maladapttive. We refer to a maladaptive solution as *symptomatic*. The game is designed to elicit discussion of these issues in the hope that the patient will learn how to deal better with these problems of life and thereby not have to resort as frequently to the pathological adaptations.

It is vital for the therapist to appreciate that *there are no standard answers for the therapist to provide*. Rather, each response must be tailored to the particular youngster with whom the therapist is playing the game. Accordingly, it would be an error to use the responses I provide here as models for the therapist's answers. Rather, they should be viewed as selected examples of the *kinds* of responses that I might provide and as guidelines for the therapist's own responses. The therapist's answers in this game should be designed to fit the patient's needs. Now to examples of Talking Card questions and the types of responses I provide.

Question: What sport are you worst at?

Response: I never really was very good at sports. So there are a lots of sports I am pretty bad at. Of the sports that were commonly played in my neighborhood when I was a kid, I would say that the one that I was worst at was basketball. I guess that I didn't try hard enough. It's not that I was born a klutz; I just think that I didn't work at it enough. I used to feel pretty bad when kids would choose up sides and I was the last one to be chosen. Had I worked harder at it, it probably wouldn't have felt bad when others played better.

The card "What sport are you worst at?" essentially forces the therapist to reveal an area of weakness. Even if the therapist were an olympic decathalon champion, he or she would still be provided with the opportunity to talk about a sport in which there is weakness. Besides providing the aforementioned benefits of such revelation, I use the response to put in a plug for the work ethic. The response also provides the patient with the knowledge that I too had my rejections and that I too was not chosen for involvement in various activities when I was a child. This is a universal phenomenon, and it is helpful for the patient to know that the therapist too suffered such rejections. It contributes to a sense of communion with the therapist and this cannot but be therapeutic.

Question: What things come into your mind when you can't fall asleep?

Response: If I had let someone take advantage of me during the day and didn't do anything about it, it would tend to linger on my mind. I would keep thinking of the thing over and over again–especially how I might have said something or done something, but I didn't say or do anything at the time. I'm sorry then that I didn't speak up or do something. But later, it was too late. And there may be nothing that I can then do about it. So I have trouble falling asleep because I keep thinking about what I should have done. Sometimes, however, there is something I can do about it, and then I do it at the time. Then I get it off my chest. Then I feel better. Then I can fall asleep more easily. I did the thing that I was supposed to do.

For example, something happened when I was a kid that caused me to lose a lot of sleep for a few nights. I was in junior high school at the time. I was walking out of a classroom. Some kids in the class made some kind of a smoke bomb and threw it into one of the desks. The teacher wasn't there and as they left the room the smoke started to pour out of the desk. I was scared that the desk would catch on fire. I wanted to run over and pull everything out of the desk because I was so scared that the whole school might burn down, but I was afraid that the other kids would call me "chicken." So I walked out of the classroom with the others. About five minutes later, I heard a fire alarm bell and I wasn't surprised. It was a big school with almost 1000 kids. And we all quickly left the building. As we got outside I could see the smoke coming out of the classroom. The fire engines came and put out the fire. Fortunately, it was caught in time and no one was hurt. Also, the fire didn't spread too far. The kids who lit the smoke bomb were kicked out of school.

I was really sorry that I hadn't had the guts to pull the stuff out of that desk and stomp on it. I think there were other kids in the classroom who wanted to do the same thing, but none of us had the guts. For the next three nights I kept thinking about how much trouble I would have saved everybody—especially those boys—if only I had done what I knew was the right thing. I know some kids probably would have laughed at me, but I would have known I was doing the right thing. It was a big mistake. And I still remember it after all these years, even though I only lost some sleep for a few nights.

Although my response at the beginning is designed to be general, the example I give makes particular reference to self-assertion. In particular, I focus on the importance of doing what one considers to be "right," even though it may be the unpopular thing. This message is especially important for adolescents who typically are slavishly dependent on peers, even when antisocial. I try thereby to encourage self-assertion, independent thinking, and action. Otherwise the pent-up resentments that such patients cause themselves can distract them from learning in school. It also contributes to their becoming targets for bullies and scapegoaters.

Question: What's the best story you ever heard or read? Why?

Response: Of all the books that I ever read when I was young, the one that I remember to have been the best was the one describing the life of Thomas A. Edison. As you probably

> know, Thomas A. Edison was one of the greatest inventors who ever lived. Although he wasn't the only man to work on these things, his inventions were important–giving us the electric light bulb, the phonograph, and the moving picture camera. He was a poor boy who grew up in Ohio. He was a very hard worker and was an extremely curious person. He was immensely interested in how things work.
>
> He had a laboratory near his home in New Jersey and it is said that he would sometimes work most of the night on his inventions. He loved learning about how things work, and he loved trying to figure out better ways of doing things. To this day, people all over the world use his inventions. To this day, he is remembered as having given mankind some of its greatest inventions. He must have really felt great about himself because of all the good he did for mankind. It was mainly his curiosity and hard work that did these things both for himself and for others. It was Thomas A. Edison who said: "Genius is 1 percent inspiration and 99 percent perspiration." Do you know what that means?

Edison epitomized the gratification and fame that can come to someone who is strongly committed to the work ethic. I emphasize here the great benefit that can come to others from the efforts of a strongly motivated person. My aim is to engender some desire on the youngster's part to view Edison as an admirable figure worthy of emulation and inspiration. Obviously, one such message is not going to achieve this goal. However, the seed is planted and with reiteration over time it is quite possible that Edison will become incorporated into the youngster's psychic structure and join with other introjects to serve as a model for identification and emulation.

> *Question*: Suppose two people you knew were talking about you and they didn't know you were listening. What do you think you would hear them saying?
>
> *Response*: I might hear the people saying that I'm the kind of a person who is direct and honest. Although people might disagree at times with what I've said, they would agree that I am direct about what my opinions are and don't pussyfoot about them. They know that when they ask me a question,

they'll get an honest and direct answer with no hedging, beating-around-the-bush, or saying things that I don't believe to be true. I am not saying that they would say that I never lied in my whole life and that I never will, only that they are pretty confident that I'll be honest with them.

You see, I believe that there is truth and wisdom to the old saying that "honesty is the best policy." If you tell a lie, you have to go around worrying that people will find out that you've lied. Also, lots of people feel bad about themselves when they lie. They feel guilty about it. And when people find out that you've lied, then they don't trust you even when you've told the truth. So these are the main reaons why I find it better to tell the truth rather than to lie. What's your opinion on this subject?

Identification with the therapist and modeling oneself after him or her is an important part of the therapeutic process. This is very similar to the educational model in which the child learns, in part, because of identification with the teacher and the desire to gain the same gratifications that the teacher enjoys from learning. The therapist not only serves as a model for learning, but should be serving as a model for other desirable attributes as well, e.g., healthy self-assertion, sensitivity to the feelings of others, feelings of benevolence toward those who are in pain, and handling oneself with dignity and honesty. This card enables the therapist to provide examples of such traits. However, the therapist should select traits that are particularly relevant to the patient's problems. Furthermore, the therapist must avoid presenting these with a flaunting or holier-than-thou attitude.

Question: Tell about something you did that you are ashamed about?

Response: I had an experience many years ago when I was a medical intern, that was very embarrassing. It was so embarrassing that I still remember it clearly to this day. An intern is a young doctor just out of medical school. Well, one Friday morning the resident, the doctor who was my boss, told me that I should prepare a speech about one of the patients that I was treating. He told me that I was to give it the first thing the following Monday morning. He told me to look over the patient's present and past charts as well as to study all the old X-rays. The patient had been sick for many years, and there was a lot of material to cover. He told me that if was important that I do a good job because this was the biggest conference of the month and that all the doctors in the hospital would be there. The hospital had over 200 doctors and it was a very important conference.

Anyway, Monday morning I got to the hospital and started to work with my patients. I noticed that none of the other doctors were there and wondered where everyone was. Suddenly, the telephone rang and I answered. It was the resident. He was very upset and he asked me why I wasn't at the conference. I was so surprised and shocked that I almost fainted. I realized that I had totally forgotten about the conference. I had prepared nothing! I was sick to my stomach. I immediately grabbed the patient's chart, the two X-rays that I could find, and rushed to the conference room.

What I should have done was to publicly announce that I was unprepared and to express my apologies. However, I tried to get away with it. I tried to go through the chart and give a speech about the patient, when I had very little information. I didn't lie or anything like that. I just tried to take a little information from one place and a little from the next but it didn't hang together. Finally, one of the older doctors who organized the conference interrupted me and suggested that we discontinue the conference. I was humiliated. But I was also relieved. I certainly learned an important lesson that day. And I have never again forgotten to prepare a speech. That event took place many years ago, and although it was painful and embarrassing, I learned an important lesson.

The request to "Tell about something you did that you are ashamed about" again requires the therapist to reveal an area of deficiency. In the vignette that I selected, I also provide a message about preparing things in advance, thinking ahead, and thereby protecting oneself from humiliation. This message is likely to be of some relevance to most youngsters in treatment.

Question: If you became mayor of your city, what would you do to change things?

Response: If I became mayor of my city, I would do everything in my power to bring about the passage of two laws. One would prohibit smoking in public places and the other would fine people large amounts of money for letting their dogs crap in the streets. Let me tell you my reasons for saying this.

I, personally, find cigarette smoking disgusting. I'm not saying this because smoking causes cancer of the lungs. I'd say this even if smoking *cured* cancer of the lungs. I'm just saying it because I find smoking nauseating. I think that if anyone is stupid enough to smoke, that person should be required to do it privately, in his or her own home. Many people who smoke don't care about other people's feelings. As far as they're concerned, other people can choke or even croak on their smoke. They don't think about the feelings of the people who are suffering because of their smoking. Unfortunately, a lot of people don't speak up and say how the smoke bothers them. But more and more people are doing this.

The other law, about there being big fines for people who let their dogs crap on the streets, would be for the same purposes. People who let their dogs do this don't think about how disgusted others feel when they step in the dog shit. It's really a disgusting thing to have to wipe dog shit off your shoes. It's too bad there are so many people in this world who don't think about other people's feelings.

What do *you* think about people who smoke and people who let their dogs crap on the streets?

The major thrust of my responses here is to help an insensitive patient appreciate how one's acts can affect others and that those who don't think about how they are affecting others are generally scorned.

Question: If a fly followed you around for a day and could then talk about you, what would it say?

Response: I followed Dr. Gardner around all day and I noticed that the people he's with hardly ever have any doubt in their minds about what he thinks. He's not afraid to tell people what's on his mind and to express his thoughts and feelings. He avoids a lot of trouble this way. If people had to wonder what he thought, there would be a lot of confusion and trouble. He also gets many things accomplished that he wouldn't have if he didn't speak up.

For example, during his lunch break one day, he went to a restaurant with a friend. He asked to be seated in the *No Smoking* section. After they were there awhile, a man sat down at the next table and started to smoke. Dr. Gardner immediately complained to the waiter and the man was asked to either put out the cigarette or sit in the *Smoking* section. The man quickly apologized and put out the cigarette. Some people probably would have sat there and said nothing. However, Dr. Gardner didn't. By speaking up, he stopped a person from doing something that was making him uncomfortable.

During the evening he went to the movies with his wife. The sound was on much too loud and lots of people were bothered. However, no one was doing anything about it. Dr. Gardner got up, went out to the lobby, and asked for the manager. He asked the manager to lower the volume of the sound. At first, the manager didn't believe him, so he asked the manager to go into the theater and hear for himself. The manager did so and realized that Dr. Gardner was right. He then lowered the volume and everyone was more comfortable. Again, he saved himself and other people a lot of trouble by politely and firmly expressing his thoughts and feelings. Of course, every once in a while, he may not express his thoughts and feelings and this usually causes some trouble. This helps him remember that the best thing, most often, is to tell people about things that bother you—but to do so in a polite way.

This is another example of my view that it is useful for therapy to help the patient learn important principles in living, which can be applied to specific situations as they arise. Clearly, my hope here is that this description will impress upon the patient the value of self-assertion. My hope also is that my own ways of dealing with these problems will served as a model for the youngster.

Feeling Cards

The Feeling Cards, as their name indicates, encourage primarily the expression of feelings. Many therapists view such expression to be the primary goal of the therapeutic process. These therapists will frequently ask such questions as: "How did you feel about that?" and "That must have made you feel very angry (sad, happy, etc.)." Others speak of therapy primarily as a place where the child can let out or get in touch with his or her feelings. Some pride themselves on their skill when, for example, they get a boy to express the anger he feels toward his father by hitting the head of the father doll with a toy hammer. I believe that this view of therapy is naive. I consider the expression of feelings to be a first step toward the alleviation of difficulties. Feelings serve in part to enhance one's efficiency toward reaching a goal. When frightened, we run faster; when angry, we fight harder and more effectively. When sexually excited we make love more ardently. When hungry we eat, sometimes voraciously. And when tired we sleep more deeply.

The therapist's goal should be that of helping patients express their thoughts and feelings at the earliest possible time that is reasonable and appropriate. At such times, the feelings are generally at a low level and can be used most effectively. When feelings build up to high levels they are likely to interfere with their effective utilization. When we are irritated we can use our irritation to attempt to remove the noxious stimulus that is evoking our frustration. If, however, we do not express outselves early, the angry feelings build up to levels of rage and even fury. When expressed under these circumstances the anger is not likely to be focused on the particular source of frustration. When it is expressed in a wild and even chaotic fashion, we are not likely to remove expediently the source of irritation. Furthermore, when feelings reach an extremely high level their gratification may become an end in itself, with little further purpose. A murderer, for example, will generally accomplish his of her goal with one or two stabs in the chest. The murderer who continues to stab the victim is no longer using the anger in the service of killing the victim. The same phenomenon applies to sexual gratification, eating, sleeping, and drinking.

As is true of the other cards, the patient's reactions should serve as a point of departure for therapeutic interchanges. The examples given here do not present such discussions. Again, there are no "right" answers to the questions and instructions on the Feeling Cards. Rather, my responses presented here may serve as guidelines for the therapist's responses when playing the game.

Question: What do you think happens to people after they die?

Response: No one knows for sure. Some people think that there is some kind of life or existence after death. Some believe that there is a soul or ghost that remains after we die. Some people believe that we actually come back to life in another form. And some people believe that there is absolutely nothing that happens after you're dead. They believe that your body just rots away in the ground and that there is no such thing as a soul or ghost or spirit or anything else. They believe that that's just the end of it all forever. That's my personal opinion as well. I don't believe that there is any kind of life or existence after you die. I'm not 100 percent sure, but it's the theory that seems most reasonable to me.

Therefore, because I believe that I only have one life, I try to make it the best life possible. I try not to do things that will foul me up. I work hard so that I'll be able to get the things I want in life. This doesn't mean that I don't take out time to have fun. I do that as well. I try to balance them out and spend time both at work and at fun. However, some of my work is also fun. And some of my fun is also work. The two tend to get mixed up at times. For example, writing books is work, but it's also fun for me. Hiking is fun for me, but it also involves some effort and work.

I think one of the worst things that can happen to a person is to reach the end of his or her life and look back and realize that most of it has been wasted. To avoid this, it is important for people to do those things each day that make life as good as possible. No matter what people believe about what happens after death, most of them agree that it's important to make the one life they have the best possible one. Do you think you're doing this for yourself?

Like many of the questions, the brighter the patient, the greater the likelihood the post-response discussion will be rich and meaningful. Although we may enter into a somewhat philosophical discussion, my main purpose here is to help the youngster gain a sense of the sanctity of life and the importance of doing the best one can for oneself at any point along the way. I believe that people who have a greater appreciation of this unhappy fact are more likely to be motivated to make the most of the relatively short time we have here.

> *Question*: What's the happiest thing that ever happened to you?
>
> *Response*: I've had many happy days in my life. Three of the happiest were the three days on which each of my children were born. Of course, that happened many years ago, but I still remember each of the days clearly. I was so happy on each of those days that I cried. They were tears of joy. I still have those warm feelings when I see little babies. It's hard for me not to touch them and sometimes I'll even ask the mother to let me hold the baby so I can cuddle and kiss the child. Although my children, like all children, may give me trouble at times, they also give me great pleasures. And the pleasures are certainly greater than the pains.

We speak often of the importance of the therapist-patient relationship in therapy. However, the factors that contribute to the development of a good relationship in this area have not been well delineated. This question can be used to help foster a good patient-therapist relationship. My hope here is that the patient's relationship with me might improve (admittedly in a small way) by the recognition that children produce warm responses in me. The response conveys the notion that I have the capacity for such pleasure with children in general and this response is not simply confined to my own children.

> *Question*: What's something you could say that could make a person feel good?
>
> *Response*: One thing you could say that could make a person feel good is to compliment the person on an accomplishment, that is, on something he or she did very well. For example, if a boy worked very hard making a model airplane, and it turned out very well and looked very good, then I'd say to him, "That's a beautiful job you did!" That would make him feel very good about himself. Or, for example, if a girl started the school year as a very poor student and then improved

significantly, she would also feel very good if someone complimented her on her accomplishment. If, for example, she was spending a lot of time in the early part of the year goofing off and fooling around, then she wouldn't feel very good about herself. Let's say that she then begins to study much harder. After a lot of work over a period of time, the teacher might say on her report card: "Congratulations, Sarah, you have really improved. Whereas you were once a pain in the neck because you never tried hard or did your homework, now it's a pleasure to have you in the classroom. It's a pleasure to be your teacher. You've really come a long way. Keep up the good work." Now that's the kind of thing that would make the girl feel good about herself. What do you think about what I've said?

When I congratulate a patient on an accomplishment, I generally focus my attention primarily on the deed or the act and direct the youngster's attention to the good feeling he or she must experience over the accomplishment. I secondarily mention other people who may be pleased over the patient's accomplishment and/or external rewards such as high grades, certificates, awards, etc. Also included here is the notion that hard work is necessary if one is to enjoy these benefits.

Question: What is the best kind of job a person can have? Why? Make believe you're doing that job.

Response: I think the best job a person can have is one in which that person earns money doing something that he or she finds enjoyable. Normally, the more education a person has, the greater the likelihood he or she will be able to get such a job. People who don't have much education, or who drop out of school early, are not likely to have such jobs. It's more likely that they'll have a miserable or lousy job that they hate.

Less important than the fact that they'll earn less money than the more educated person, is the fact that they hate what they're doing. And this is a bad way to spend one's life. It's much better to get education and training. Then, it's more likely that the person will be able to earn money doing something that he or she enjoys. Therefore, my answer to this question is that there is no one best job. My answer then is that it's any job that the person enjoys doing. And there are hundreds of different kinds of jobs different people can enjoy doing. What kind of job do you want to have when you grow up?

My hope is that my response will contribute to the patient's appreciation that what he or she is doing now is going to play an important role in his or her future life. In addition, my hope is that the response will contribute (admittedly in a small way) to the youngster's motivation to think about the future and to expend some effort toward gaining greater knowledge and skill.

Question: What do you think is the most beautiful thing in the whole world?

Response: Watching a beautiful sunset, whether it be from the top of a mountain or at the seashore, is to me one of the most beautiful things in the world. It makes me feel relaxed and happy to be alive. Sometimes I read poetry while watching such a scene. And the poems also make me think of beautiful things that help me appreciate how beautiful the world can be if one is willing to stop and enjoy them. Sometimes I will bring along a tape recorder and play a tape of some calm, beautiful music while watching such a scene. This is indeed one of the great pleasures of life.

Healthy pleasure is well viewed to be a general antidote for just about all forms of psychogenic psychopathology. When one is enjoying oneself in a healthy way, one is at that time not suffering the psychological pain attendant to psychiatric disorder. In addition, the pleasurable feelings are esteem enhancing. Because feelings of low self-worth are often involved in bringing about psychopathological reactions, any experience that can enhance self-worth can be salutary. And aesthetic pleasures are in this category. Accordingly, anything a therapist can do to enhance a patient's appreciation of beauty is likely to be therapeutic.

Question: What do you think about a boy who sometimes plays with his penis when he's alone?

Response: I think that it's perfectly normal—as long as he does it when he's alone. Of course, there would be something wrong with him if he did that in the open, in public; but as a private thing I think it's normal. In fact most teenage boys do it a lot, and many kids play with their penises when they're younger as well. There are some kids, however, who think that playing with their penises is a terrible thing. They think it's sinful, or wrong, or dirty. I completely disagree. Those kids are the ones that have a problem, and not the ones who play with their penises once in a while in private. What's your opinion on what I've just said?

Question: What do you think about a girl who sometimes plays with or rubs her vagina when she's alone?

Response: I think it's perfectly normal for her to do that when she's alone. Of course, that's not the kind of thing that one would generally do in front of other people. It's a private matter. What do you think?

For the sexually inhibited youngster these responses enable the examiner to approach a forbidden subject in a noncontrived way. Discussing the subject in itself is therapeutic as it provides the child with the living experience that such discussions do not result in dire consequences. That which is unmentionable is far more anxiety- and guilt-provoking than that which is spoken about. The child whose parents never speak about sex will generally become far more inhibited than the child whose parents preach often about the sins and evils of sex. Of course, the latter approach is likely to produce guilt as well, but probably not so much as the guilt produced by the situation in which the subject is unmentionable. For the child who is excessively guilty, I might add:

> There are some children who think that touching themselves is a terrible sin or crime. They think it's the worst thing a person can do. This is a strange idea because touching oneself is perfectly natural and normal. It only becomes a problem if the person does it most of the time and then doesn't do other things, or if the person feels very bad or guilty about it. Feeling that it's a terrible sin or crime is then the problem, not doing it. What are your opinions on this subject?

Question: Make believe you're reading a magazine showing pictures of nude ladies. What do you think about such magazines?

Response: Boy, there really are some exciting looking women in some of those magazines. I think they're great to look at once in a while. They have some of the most beautiful and luscious women in those magazines. Some people are ashamed to admit that they're interested in looking at those women. I don't think it is wrong, bad, or sinful to look at those pictures. I don't agree with those people. I think it's natural and healthy. It's only a problem if the person doesn't want to have anything to do with real people and wants to spend a lot of time looking at those pictures. What is your opinion on this subject?

This response is the one I provide for boys who are uncomfortable expressing sexual interest. Obviously, I attempt here to convey some of the excitement that most boys and men have when looking at pictures of nude women. I also attempt to lessen any guilt the patient may have over such interest. My hope is that the youngster will be receptive to my opinions on the subject and will identify with my attitude.

Question: A boy was laughing. What was he laughing about?

Response: This boy was not only laughing, but he was cheering. He was just jumping up and down with joy. He had just gotten his eighth grade report card and learned that he had gotten into three honors classes in the ninth grade. He was very happy. He had worked very hard in order to make the honors classes and had hoped that he might make one or two of them. But he didn't think that he would get into *all three*. He was very proud of himself and couldn't wait to get home and tell his parents. His teacher had written a note on the report card that said: "Robert, I am very proud of you. Good luck in high school." He was also very happy that he knew that, when he applied to college, having been in three honors classes would look very good on his record and this would help him get into the college of his choice. And so he ran home from school laughing and singing all the way. It was really a happy day for him. What do you think about what I said about that boy?

This is the kind of response I provide for youngsters with low academic motivation. My purpose here is to enhance their school interest by demonstrating the joys and ego-enhancement that are the potential benefits of such commitment to the educational process.

Question: Tell about an act of kindness.

Response: A good example of an act of kindness would be visiting someone who is sick in the hospital and giving up a fun thing that you'd prefer to do. Let's say that a boy was in an automobile accident, injured his leg, and had to be in the hospital for six weeks. Even though his mother and father visited him often, he was still very lonely. His really good friends were those who were willing to give up fun things like playing baseball, watching their favorite television programs, or just hanging around and relaxing. Instead they went to visit him in the hospital. He was very grateful when they came to see him. And they felt good about themselves for their sacrifices. Visiting the friend was an act of kindness. Do you know what the word sacrifice means?

This is the type of response I provide self-centered patients, those who have difficulty putting themselves in the positions of others. In the ensuing discussion, I try to help the egocentric patient appreciate the feelings of loneliness suffered by the hospitalized child. I also try to engender in the patient the feelings of self-satisfaction and enhanced self-worth that come from benevolent acts.

Question: Was there ever a person whom you wished to be dead? If so, who was that person? Why did you wish that person to be dead?

Response: During my childhood and early teens there lived a man in Germany named Adolph Hitler. He was a madman. He was insane. He was the leader of Germany during World War II and was personally responsible for the deaths of millions of people. He was one of the greatest criminals in the history of the world. He used to murder people whose opinions, skin color, or religion differed from his. He not only had them shot but he gassed them to death and burned their bodies in ovens. Millions of people died this way.

When I was a boy, I used to wish that he would die. I wished that someone would kill him. I hoped then that maybe all this crazy murdering would stop. To this day, I and many other people in the world feel sorry for the millions of people he killed and all the millions of friends and relatives who also suffered because of his murders. Even though the war ended in 1945, there are still millions of people who are suffering because of the terrible things Adolph Hitler did. These are the people who were put in his prisons and concentration camps and escaped, or were fortunate enough not to have been killed. And these are also the people who are the friends, relatives, children, and grandchildren of those who died there. He was a very cruel man. I really hated him, and I often wished he would die or be killed. Finally, in 1945 he committed suicide. If he hadn't killed himself, he would have been captured and executed for his terrible crimes.

This question can be particularly useful for children with antisocial behavior disorders who have little sensitivity to the pains they inflict on others. My hope here, by elaborating on Hitler's atrocities, is to engender in the antisocial patient a feeling for the pain that criminal behavior causes others. It is important for the reader to appreciate that when responding to Feeling Cards the therapist does well to try to dramatize as much as possible his or her responses in order to bring about a kind of resonating emotional response in the patient. To engender these feelings in the patient who is out of touch with them or who has not experienced them to a significant degree is one of the goals of treatment.

Question: Say something funny.

Response: Okay, I heard a funny riddle. "What's invisible and smells like worms?" (Generally, the patient does not know the answer. In such cases, I will give it.) "A bird's fart!"

This joke generally goes over quite well, except among the most inhibited. Incidentally, it is a statement of the low levels to which the child and adolescent therapist may have to stoop in the service of his or her calling. The joke, however, may be useful as an icebreaker for the patient with sexual-inhibition problems. Sexual and scatological issues often get fused and inhibitions in the sexual area often extend to this area as well. By telling the joke the therapist serves as a model for what I consider to be healthy, normal sublimation. It may contribute to a lessening of sexual inhibitions. The child may reason: "If it's okay for him to talk this way, it's okay for me." In addition, the introduction of some levity into the therapeutic experience is also useful. It lightens the session, makes the therapist more human, and increases the likelihood that the child will become involved. It is part of the seductive process, so important in child and adolescent therapy.

Doing Cards

The Doing Cards involve physical activity in association with the child's responses. These cards, more than the Talking Cards and Feeling Cards, involve a fun element, and this serves to make the session more enjoyable. My purpose here is to counterbalance some of the less pleasurable aspects of therapy that are likely to reduce the motivation for treatment of even the most highly involved patient. Some of the Doing Cards involve modeling and this can also be therapeutic. There are some therapists who consider role modeling and physical activity to be a central part of therapeutic process. I am not in agreement. Often, there is an artificial quality to role modeling, and this makes it less therapeutic than actual experiences or imitations that are spontaneously derived from a situation that arises naturally in the course of the therapeutic session. Accordingly, I most often use the Doing Cards as a point of departure for direct discussion. My hope is that in the course of such discussions the patient will have emotional reactions and experiences that will contribute directly to therapeutic change.

Question: What is the most selfish thing you ever did? Make believe you're doing that thing now.

Response: Well, the most selfish thing I ever did was a long time ago—it was right after the Second World War—it was in 1946 or 1947. I was looking for a way to earn money to pay for my education in college. It was very hard to get jobs after the Second World War. All the war factories were closing down, and people were fired from their jobs. They didn't need so many people anymore to make tanks and guns and things like that. And all the soldiers were getting out of the Army. And everybody was also getting out of the Navy and Air Force. There were millions of people trying to get jobs. Well, I finally got a job selling magazines to the wives and mothers of soldiers who had been in the war. I told the people how important it was to buy the magazine because it would help the veterans, the people who fought in the war. After working a few days I found out that this magazine was kind of phony. A lot of people weren't getting the subscriptions they were paying for, and I felt very guilty about what I was doing.

I was preying on people's sympathy. I was saying that this was very important for the parents and the wives of the soldiers who were killed or who had fought in the war, and it was a kind of phony organization. I didn't realize it when I got the job, but after I started working I realized it, and I soon quit. But I felt very guilty, and I think I worked a day or two too much because I needed the money so badly that I stuck with it awhile, but then my guilt overcame me and I quit the job. It had been a selfish thing to do. Sometimes when people are hungry, when they need money a lot, then they do things that they would never want to do. I was ashamed of myself when I did that. Do you want to say anything about that?

As mentioned, *The Talking, Feeling, and Doing Game* provides therapists with the opportunity to reveal their own deficiencies in a noncontrived and natural way. This lessens the likelihood that the patient will idealize the therapist. It makes the therapist a more real human being. It lessens the likelihood of the development of the unfavorable comparison in which the patient views the therapist as perfect, and views him or herself as a bundle of psychopathology. The particular incident was chosen because it demonstrates how guilt can be useful in preventing a person from engaging in antisocial behavior. This is the kind of response I provide for patients who do not have enough guilt over their antisocial behavior. My hope is that the vignette will contribute to the development of a slightly stronger superego.

> *Question*: You're standing in line to buy something and a child pushes in front of you. Show what you would do.
>
> *Response*: Let's say I'm a kid and I'm standing here in line and some kid pushes himself in front of me. A part of me might want to push him away and even hit him. But another part of me knows that that wouldn't be such a good idea. I might get into trouble or he might hit me back and then I might get hurt. So the first thing I would do would be to say something to him like, "Hey, I was here first. Why don't you go back to the end of the line and wait your turn like everybody else." If that didn't work I might threaten to call some person like a parent, teacher, or someone else around who is in charge. But sometimes there are no other people around to call, so I might just say that it's not worth all the trouble and that all it's causing me is the loss of another minute or two. If, however, the person starts to push me, then I might fight back. But that would be the last thing I would try. Some people might think that I'm "chicken" for not hitting him in the first place. I don't agree with them. I think that hitting should be the last thing you should do, not the first. I don't think that people who hit first are particularly wise or brave; rather, I think they're kind of stupid. So in this sitation I'd talk first and try to solve the problem. If that didn't work, I'd drop the whole thing. It's not worth fighting about.

This is the type of response I am likely to provide the antisocial patient. As is obvious here, I am trying to educate the antisocial youngster to the more civilized option that individuals have learned to use in order to bring about a more relaxed and less threatening society. These options may not have been part of the antisocial patient's repertoire. Whatever the underlying factors are in such a patient's antisocial behavior (and these, of course, must be dealt with in the treatment), such education is also a part of the therapy.

Question: Make believe you're smoking a cigarette. What do you think about people who smoke?

Response: First of all, I want to say that I have not once in my whole life ever smoked a single cigarette. I remember when I was about 14 years old I went to a party. Some of the kids there were smoking. One kid gave me a cigarette. I really didn't want to smoke it, but I felt that if I didn't take it, all the kids would think that I was "chicken." So I took the cigarette, and I lit it, and I took one puff. I then gasped and started to choke. It really make me sick to my stomach. I then put out the cigarette and said to the guy that had given it to me, "I can't really believe that anybody can like this shit. The only reason that you guys are smoking is because you want to look like big shots. It must take a long time to get used to smoking this filthy weed." And that was the first and last time I smoked a cigarette in my whole life.

Now, if I'm to get a chip, I've got to make believe that I'm smoking a cigarette. Okay, here I go! (I imitate cigarette smoking.) Ugh, is this terrible. (I start coughing heavily.) This is disgusting. This is nauseating (more heavy coughing). Ugh, I can't stand this any longer. I hope I've done enough of this to get my chip. It's a heavy price to pay for a chip. People who smoke cigarettes must be crazy. Not only is it a disgusting habit but it can give you all kinds of terrible diseases like lung cancer, heart disease, and diseases of your blood vessels.

I think kids start to smoke because they want to act like big shots. It makes them feel like adults. Then they get hooked on cigarettes and they can't stop. When they get older, and begin to appreciate how really terrible it is, they still can't stop. It's a heavy price to pay for looking like a big shot. Also, it's no great stunt to smoke. If you really want to feel big you have to do things, over a period, that make you feel good about yourself. Thinking that you're going to feel good about yourself by putting a cigarette in your mouth is simple minded. It just doesn't work that way. What do you think about what I've just said?

The response, of course, touches on the most common pathological mechanisms that contribute to adolescents' beginning to smoke. It is quite likely that the antisocial patient subscribes strongly and somewhat blindly to these sick values. Not having basic competence in meaningful areas, he or she is likely to embrace quick and superficial methods for enhancing self-esteem. Of course, the utilization of smoking in this regard is strongly promulgated by the advertising of the cigarette industry. Cigarette manufacturers know well that they will increase sales if they associate cigarette smoking with sexual attractiveness and adult "maturity." My response also directs itself to the peer-pressure element in the initiation of cigarette smoking. As mentioned, I do not create stories when responding to the cards in *The Talking, Feeling, and Doing Game*. The experiences I relate in my response actually occurred and my reasons for not smoking are those that I genuinely hold.

> *Question*: Make believe someone grabbed something of yours. Show what you would do.
>
> *Response*: I would first try to use talk before using action. I'd tell the child to give it back and threaten to grab it back if he or she doesn't return it. If the child was my size or a little taller, I'd try to grab it back, providing it wasn't something that could break. If it was something that could break and/or the person was bigger, I would threaten to call the teacher or my parent(s) if it wasn't given back immediately. I might ask a friend or two to help me get it back. But I wouldn't just stand there, say nothing, and let the person get away with it.

This response is designed for youngsters with self-assertion problems. My response provides advice regarding the sequence of steps one does well to follow when one's rights are being infringed upon.

> *Question*: Make believe you're playing a dirty trick on someone.
>
> *Response*: I don't think I'm going to get a chip on this one. I don't like playing dirty tricks on people. I remember when I was a kid how badly I felt if someone played a dirty trick on me. And I used to feel sorry for those kids who had dirty tricks played on them. I remember once a kid in my class used to like stealing other children's books and hiding them. He thought it

was very funny. Actually, it was cruel. Then the kid whose book was stolen would go home and not have a book to do his or her homework. He or she would have to go to a lot of trouble to borrow someone else's book or go over to someone else's house. Sometimes the kid wouldn't even find the book and then the person whose book was stolen would have to pay for it. Sometimes dirty tricks can be dangerous. I remember once a boy in my class thought it was funny to trip another kid in the classroom. Well the boy that was tripped fell down and banged his head against the desk. He hit his head right above his eye and his eye almost got knocked out. He got a big cut over his eye and it was bleeding terribly. I really felt sorry for him and everybody was angry at the kid who tripped him. That kid, of course, got into a lot of trouble. The kid who got hurt had to go to the hospital for stitches and for treatment of his eye. His parents threatened to sue the other parents. However, the parents of the boy who tripped the kid agreed to pay for all the medical expenses. So at least they both didn't have to pay for lawyers. These are just some of the reasons why I don't like playing dirty tricks on anyone. How do you feel about playing dirty tricks on people?

In an attempt to strengthen the antisocial patient's superego I elaborate upon the pains that can be caused by those who hurt others. Youngsters with superego deficiencies, who act out their hostility, generally do not think about the discomforts and pains they cause others.

CONCLUDING COMMENTS

The popularity of *The Talking, Feeling, and Doing Game* has been a great source of gratification. It has become standard equipment for the child and adolescent psychotherapist, and many therapists consider it vital in their work with youngsters. Over the years I have received many letters in which the therapist has expressed gratitude for my introduction of the game. I have even had the dubious compliment on a few occasions of plagiarized versions being introduced. These, to the best of my knowledge, have never enjoyed similar popularity. (One such plagiarizer lost motivation to continue marketing the game after a letter from my attorney "reminding him" of the consequences if he did not cease and desist.)

Although the game was originally devised in an attempt to engage children who were not free enough to provide self-created stories when utilizing the mutual storytelling technique and its derivative games, it has proven useful for more cooperative and insightful children as well. In fact, I would say that it is a rare child who will not get involved in the game.

The game can also be useful in selected family therapy situations. Generally, unsophisticated and/or uneducated parents may welcome the game as a catalyst for family discussion; more sophisticated and/or educated parents will generally not need such assistance in their family therapy work.

The Talking, Feeling, and Doing Game is not without its disadvantages. All good drugs have their side effects. In fact, it is often the case that the more powerful the drug the greater the side effects. One of the main drawbacks of *The Talking, Feeling, and Doing Game* is that it may be *too* enticing to both the patient and the therapist. It is seemingly an easy therapeutic modality. Many therapists, I am certain, play it without fully appreciating its complexities and how difficult it can often be to utilize it properly for therapeutic purposes. The patient, too, may find it attractive because it seemingly protects him or her from talking about more painful subjects directly. It should not be used as the only therapeutic modality because it will deprive the therapist of some of the deeper unconscious material that can more readily be obtained from dreams and discussions. In short, therapists should not be tempted into using the game throughout every session; they should do their utmost to balance the therapeutic activities with other modalities.

SIX

PSYCHOANALYTIC INQUIRY AND DREAM PSYCHOANALYSIS

The younger the child, the less the youngster is cognitively capable of psychoanalytic inquiry. In the early adolescent period there are occasional youngsters interested in this kind of endeavor; my experience has been that most are not. For younger adolescents, those who generally will play *The Talking, Feeling, and Doing Game,* there are certain questions that may be useful in increasing the likelihood of the youngster's involving him or herself in more introspective discussions. In the first section of this chapter I present some vignettes that demonstrate the utilization of these game cards for this purpose. In the next section I will present my views on dreams and their analysis. Finally I will present a clinical example that demonstrates psychoanalytic inquiry via the analysis of a dream. Dream analyses serve as excellent vehicles for demonstrating psychoanalytic theory and technique. Although I am often quite critical of many aspects of psychoanalysis, it would be an error for the reader to conclude that I disagree entirely with all aspects of the theory and its utilization. I consider myself to be judiciously selective, taking those aspects of the theory and its implementation that appear reasonable and useful and rejecting those that do not.

THE USE OF THE TALKING, FEELING, AND DOING GAME IN FACILITATING PSYCHOANALYTIC INQUIRY

As mentioned, there are rare children who can make use of analytic inquiry. I am not against children's doing so. I am only against the attempt to apply the technique to the vast majority of children and adolescents. *The Talking, Feeling, and Doing Game* often has value in facilitating inquiry in youngsters who are possible candidates for such an introspective approach to the alleviation of their problems.

> *Question*: Of all the things you own, what do you enjoy the most? Make believe you're doing something with that thing.
>
> *Response*: Of all the things I own, one of the things I enjoy the most is my video cassette recorder and camera. I like making television programs of myself and the people whom I treat. It's even better now since I bought a color TV system, because now we can see it in color rather than black and white. It not only helps me learn things about the people who come to see me, but it helps me learn things about myself. The TV system gives people a chance to see themselves the way others see them. It's very hard for most people to look at themselves clearly. The TV system helps people do this. Even though some of the things that people learn from it may not be pleasant, the information can be useful. I'm very interested in understanding why people do the things they do, and the television system helps me learn these things. I'm very curious about how the human mind works. I find it an interesting and fascinating subject to learn about. And that information can help me be of help to other people, and the television set helps me to learn these things.

My hope here is that some of my own enthusiasm for psychological inquiry will engender a similar interest in the patient.

> *Question*: What is one of the stupidest things a person can do? Show someone doing that thing.
>
> *Response*: One of the stupidest things a person can do is to make believe there is no problem when there really is. The person who does that is not going to do anything to solve the problem. So it's going to continue to exist and may even get worse.

At this point I might ask the patient if he or she can think of an example of someone who does this, that is, someone who has a problem and makes believe that there is no problem. My hope is that the patient will provide an example that relates to his or her own situation. If not, I might provide the following example of the youngster who is unmotivated in school and denies the problem.

> *Response*: Well, one example would be a girl who is doing very poorly in school and is making believe that she has no problem. She just thinks about other things. When others try to tell her that she's having a problem in school, she doesn't want to listen. Then she doesn't do anything to correct the problem or to solve it. Then things will probably just get worse and at the end of the year she may find that she'll have to repeat the grade. Or, even if she gets promoted, she may find that she gets very embarrassed in school because most of the others know the answers and she doesn't.

I might at this point discuss with the patient my story "Oliver and the Ostrich" from *Dr. Gardner's Stories About the Real World* (1972b). The story deals with the issue of the denial mechanism in the context of a discussion of the ostrich. In the story it becomes apparent that the ostrich does not hide its head in the sand in times of danger ("The ostrich wouldn't do such a foolish thing"). It focuses on the adaptive mechanisms (primarily involved in flight or fight) that ostriches actually do utilize in dangerous situations. (They do not differ from the rest of the animal kingdom in this regard.) This story has proven popular among my patients, and it can contribute, I believe, to a reduction in the utilization of denial mechanisms.

> *Question*: What is the worst problem a person can have?
>
> *Response*: I think one of the worst problems a person can

have is to make believe that there are no problems when there really are. Such people don't do anything about the problems they have. By making believe there are no problems, they continue to ignore them; but problems don't just go away. Because these people make believe there are no troubles, they don't do anything to solve their problems.

A boy, for example, might be doing very poorly in school, but might not wish to think about it. When his parents try to tell him about the trouble, he might stick his fingers in his ears so that he can't hear them, or he might close his eyes so that he can't see them waving his poor report card at him. This may make him feel better at the time because he then doesn't have to think about his terrible report card. However, he might end up with having to repeat the grade. By then, it would have been too late to do anything about the problem. Perhaps then he'll learn his lesson. Perhaps then he'll start thinking about *why* he has this problem. That's why I say that making believe there's no problem when there really is can be one of the worst problems a person can have.

Question: Who was the best teacher you ever had? Why?

Response: The best teacher I ever had was a man named Dr. Geoffrey Osler. He was a neurologist. A neurologist is a kind of doctor who specializes in diseases of the nerves. He really loved being a teacher. He was very excited about what he taught. When he taught, everybody in the class got excited about the subject matter as well. Enthusiasm spread throughout the whole class. In his class, learning was fun. In addition, he had a tremendous amount of knowledge and everyone respected him for it. Although it's been over twenty years since I took his course, I still remember many of the things he said. In addition, he started me thinking about a lot of things I hadn't thought about before and I still find myself trying to learn more about those things. He increased my curiosity. He increased my desire to find out the answers to interesting questions. I feel very lucky to have had such a teacher.

Dr. Osler was also interested in understanding how the human mind worked. He was also a psychiatrist, but he was primarily a neurologist. He liked to understand why people did

> the things they did. I, of course, am a psychiatrist, and I want to learn even more about the reasons why people do the things they do. And I try to get my patients to be curious about that as well. It's sometimes amazing to find out the reasons why a person does what he or she does. Often, people don't understand why they do something and, when they come to understand why they do things, they are really amazed. Also, when they do understand these things, it can often help them prevent or avoid trouble.

My aim here, clearly, is to sweep the child up in the same enthusiasm that I had, and still have, about Dr. Geoffrey Osler. My hope here also is that the child may develop some curiosity about finding out about the inner workings of his or her own mind.

> *Question*: What turns you on, that is, what excites you?
>
> *Response*: One of the things that excites me is puzzles and games in which you have to try to figure out answers. I remember when I was a kid I used to love playing checkers and chess. I also used to like doing puzzles in children's books. Later on I used to like doing crossword puzzles in newspapers. When I was in junior high school, and started to learn algebra, I used to love to figure out mathematical problems, especially those that were very hard to figure out the answer. I remember when I was a teenager there was a program on the radio called *The Quiz Kids*. They used to take the best students from the various high schools and ask them very hard questions. I wasn't smart enough to be a quiz kid, but I used to love listening to that program. I used to love trying to figure out the answers to the questions and once or twice I even got an answer when none of the quiz kids did. I really felt good about myself then. But more important I found it a lot of fun to try to figure out the answers to difficult questions. That's the kind of thing that really turns me on. It also turns me on to understand why people do the things they do. That can help people stop doing those things.

Here I attempt to engender in the patient the same kind of excitement I have about learning. My hope is that the reponse will enhance the patient's curiosity and motivation to learn, both about things in general and about his or her own mental processes.

> *Question*: Make believe you've just opened a letter you've received from someone. What does this letter say?
>
> *Response*: Let's say it's a letter from a former patient. I'll read the letter:
>
> Dear Dr. Gardner:
>
> I am writing to you from college. I appreciate very much your therapy. Before I came to treatment, I was not doing very well in school. In treatment I learned some of the reasons why I was having trouble in school, and I solved some of these problems so that I now have been able to go to college. When I first came to you, I didn't want to think about the reasons why I was doing certain things. But after I started thinking about them, I realized that I could learn some important things about myself. And that helped me get better. Thank you for all your help.
>
> Your friend,
> Bob
>
> Anything you want to say about that?

My hope here is that the patient might be motivated for self-inquiry in order to enjoy the benefits derived by Bob.

DREAM PSYCHOANALYSIS

The best way to demonstrate psychoanalytic technique is via the analysis of dreams. I am in full agreement with Freud who held that the dream is the "royal road to the unconscious." Because the same principles are applicable to the analysis of other material as well, I will use dream analysis to present my view on this treatment modality. The same principles that I utilize with adults are applicable to adolescents; however, as will be seen, I must modify these when working with younger patients.

The Purposes of Dreams

It is reasonable to speculate that human beings have wondered about the meaning of dreams as far back as there were people dreaming. Wise men and seers have often been viewed as particularly astute in ascertaining the meaning of dreams. Joseph's dreams in the Bible are well known. I have many criticisms of psychoanalytic theory and technique, but I still consider certain elements in psychoanalysis to be extremely useful. One of these is its contribution to dream analysis. Although I am not in agreement with the reflex way in which many analysts see oral, anal, and oedipal themes in them, I am in agreement with some of the basic theories of Sigmund Freud regarding the meaning of dreams. Particularly I believe that the emergence of unconscious material is more likely to take place at night. During the day the necessary involvements and distractions of real living do not allow us much time to attend to potentially emerging unconscious material. At night, when external stimuli are reduced significantly, unconscious material becomes freer to enter into conscious awareness. However, because of guilt and/or anxiety attendant to the emergence of such material, the individual disguises it. The dream is a product of such disguised emerged material. I consider it to be one of the richest (if not the most rich) source of information about unconscious processes. It is also a testimony to the creativity of the human being (even that of a child and adolescent) because of the ingenuity that is sometimes utilized in its formation. I present here what I consider to be some of the most reasonable theories regarding the meaning of dreams. I do not claim that this is an exhaustive statement, only that these theories appear most reasonable to me. Our paucity of knowledge about the meaning of dreams also compromises our ability to provide a comprehensive statement about their meaning at this point.

The Dream as a Vehicle for Wish Fulfillment The theory that the dream serves the purpose of wish fulfillment is ancient. Many dreams are obvious examples of this mechanism. The hungry person dreams of food. The thirsty individual dreams of drink. The sexually frustrated person dreams of sexual gratification. And the angry person dreams of wreaking vengeance. Freud too considered wish fulfillment to be one of the dream's primary purposes. Freud went further, however, in describing dreams to have a *latent* and a *manifest* content. The latent material resides within the unconscious because its emergence into conscious awareness produces guilt and/or anxiety. However, so strong are the forces pressing for release of unconscious material that its emergence into conscious awareness cannot be long prevented. Accordingly, an internal psychological compromise is devised in which the repressed material is permitted access to conscious awareness, but in a disguised form. By using such disguise mechanisms as *symbolization* and *condensation*, the individual essentially fools him or herself into not recognizing the true nature of the material that has now entered conscious awareness. It is as if the right hand has fooled the left hand. In addition, the individual utilizes the mechanism of *secondary elaboration* in which the dream is given an organization that it does not intrinsically possess. Such organization enables the individual to feel more comfortable with the dream because it now follows some traditional sequence. Secondary elaboration also serves the purposes of self-deception in that the reorganization process disguises the dream even more.

Associated with the dream's wish-fulfillment function Freud also believed that one of the dream's purposes was to preserve sleep. For example, a hungry person might be awakened by hunger pangs that threaten to interrupt the vital sleep process. By dreaming of eating, the individual again "fools" the hunger pangs, fantasizes satiety, and thereby preserves sleep. Another example provided by Freud of the dream's sleep-preserving function is that of the person who, while dreaming, hears loud environmental noises. In order to prevent the noise from awakening the dreamer, the fracas is incorporated into the dream. In this way, the dream satisfies its sleep-preservation function. However, Freud had difficulty fitting the nightmare into this theory in that this kind of dream usually ends with the person's awakening. This exception did not cause him to abandon the general theory of sleep preservation; rather, he concluded that the nightmare was an exception to this principle and when an individual had a nightmare the dream process was considered to have broken down and failed in its primary function of sleep preservation. Although I am in agreement with Freud that one of the purposes of the dream is to provide wish fulfillment, I believe Freud put too much emphasis on this dream function, to the neglect of others. I consider the wish-fulfillment function to apply only to one possible category of dream. As I will discuss, I consider there to be other functions unrelated to wish fulfillment. And the nightmare, which I will discuss below, is an example of one of these functions.

Freud ascribed many sexual meanings to dreams, interpretations that I would be less prone to consider sexual. In particular, many of the symbols found in dreams were considered by him to be phallic or vaginal. However, Freud also emphasized the importance of utilizing the patient's own free associations in order to ascertain what the symbols meant for that particular patient. He presents, thereby, a somewhat contradictory theory about the symbols. He considered certain symbols to be universal, especially in the phallic/vaginal realm. Yet he viewed other symbols to be idiosyncratic and devised by the patient. I have little conviction for the notion of universal symbols that are somehow inherited from the unconscious minds of one's parents and ancestors. (Carl Jung was especially committed to this notion.) Rather, I believe that environmental influences (familial, social, and cultural) are the most important (if not exclusive) determinants of what a symbol (dream or otherwise) will mean. In addition, I am far less likely to ascribe sexual meanings to many of the symbols that Freud and his followers so quickly assumed to have such significance. These criticisms notwithstanding, I consider Freud's *The Interpretation of Dreams* (1900) to be a monumental contribution and recommend it to all those who are interested in learning about the classical psychoanalytic theory of dreams.

There are some dreams in which there is simple release of pent-up thoughts and feelings which might also be considered a kind of wish-fulfillment dream. I am referring here to sexual dreams in which the individual gains sexual gratification as a way of providing release for pent-up and frustrated sexual feelings. The adolescent boy's "wet dream" would be an example. As the youngster grows older and has greater opportunities for sexual fulfillment, he experiences a diminution in the frequency of such dreams. The association of the dream with ejaculation raises some interesting questions. Does the dream fantasy precede the sexual excitation and resultant ejaculation, or does the hormonally induced genital arousal stimulate the production of the dream fantasy? Another type of simple release dream would be one in which an individual fantasizes harm befalling some individual toward whom intense angry feelings are felt. In these simple release types of wish-fulfillment dreams, there is little, if any, disguise. The individual is generally quite clear about the basic function of the dream. However, if there is guilt and/or anxiety over the release of these feelings, then some disguise elements may be introduced, such as substituting the identity of the object of the sexual or hostile feelings.

The Dream as a Vehicle for Alerting the Individual to Danger This is an extremely important function of the dream, which I believe was not given proper attention by Freud. In fact, I believe that the dream may more commonly serve the alerting role than the role of simple wish-fulfillment. Most dangers are not repressed. The individual looks at them squarely and then reacts appropriately, generally either by fight or flight. However, there are certain situations in which an individual may wish to ignore the fact that a danger exists because to appreciate it might result in guilt, anxiety, or other untoward reactions. Under such circumstances the information about the danger is relegated to unconscious awareness. An internal psychological conflict then arises. On the one hand, thoughts of the danger press for release into conscious awareness in order to alert the individual to its existence. On the other hand, such appreciation may result in a variety of unpleasant and even painful psychological reactions. Again, the dream compromise is brought into play. The danger emerges into conscious awareness in disguised form, satisfying thereby both arms of the conflict.

Let us take a theoretical example of this kind of dream: a situation in which a personnel manager in a large corporation has an appointment with a prospective employee. About an hour prior to the interview with the job candidate, he receives a call from a senior official in his organization telling him that the interviewee is a relative of his wife's and that he should be given special consideration. During the interview the personnel manager scans briefly the man's application, but does not give it the detailed perusal that he normally does. Following the interview the personnel manager decides that he is going to recommend the applicant for a position and hopes that this decision will place him in a favorable position with the senior official who recommended that he give the man every opportunity. That night the personnel manager has a dream in which the applicant that he saw that day, now an employee in the company, stealthily enters the company vault and successfully absconds with a huge sum of money. Then, after the theft is discovered, the personnel manager finds himself under serious criticism – even to the point where his job is in jeopardy – because he has hired the man. He wakes up, horrified over the prospect of losing his job.

Let us carry the example further and place this man in psychoanalytic treatment. The analyst encourages the patient to think about any possible clues he was given that the man might have had criminal tendencies, or even a record. The patient states that he had absolutely no awareness of such. However, when reviewing carefully the details of the interview, the analyst learns that the patient rapidly looked over the application. Recognizing this as atypical behavior, the analyst suggests that the patient review again – but this time very carefully – the application. The patient then returns to his office, reviews the material very carefully, and notes that there was a two-year period which appears to be completely unaccounted for. This occurred when the interviewee was between 19 and 21 years of age. Immediately, he calls back the applicant and, in the course of the interview, asks him about the gap in his school and work history. At this point, the applicant, somewhat apologetically, states that he was in jail during that period, but dismisses it as the result of a series of "adolescent indiscretions" that were not even worth mentioning. He goes on to reassure the personnel manager that these incidents are "water under the bridge," that he has learned his lesson, "paid his debt to society," and can be relied upon to be a "solid citizen." The personnel manager returns to his next analytic session and, in the discussion of what has transpired, comes to the realization that the applicant is *still* somewhat psychopathic, in that he initially withheld the information rather than disclose it, and that such deceptive tendencies not only existed in the past but exist at the present time as well.

He now finds himself presented with a new problem. Does he hire the man in order to keep himself in favor with the senior company official or does he reject the applicant and risk thereby the disfavor of his superior? As a result of further analytic work he decides that this dilemma is not a burden he need assume himself; rather, he can present all the information (pro and con) to the senior official and let *him* decide what to do. This is not an option that he had previously considered, but it emerged from the analytic interchange. It is an example of the way in which therapy opens up new options, options that may not have been considered previously by the patient, options that are often preferable to those already operating in the patient's repertoire. If he follows this course, he need not feel responsible for any untoward consequences of hiring this individual. Now it becomes the senior official's responsibility if the applicant does not prove trustworthy.

This example has been presented because it demonstrates well how the dream can serve to alert an individual to a danger that he or she might not previously have been aware of. In this case, the man had to repress from conscious awareness his recognition of the gap in the application to avoid risking the displeasure of a senior official. There was a danger, however, and it pressed for release into conscious awareness. A dream compromise was made, one that satisfied both unconscious and conscious processes. Had the man not been in treatment he might not have appreciated the significance of the dream and might thereby have suffered significant untoward repercussions for his oversight. Furthermore, and unrelated to this discussion of dreams, the vignette demonstrates how therapy, by opening up new options, can help individuals deal better with the fundamental problems of life in ways that they might not have previously considered.

At this point, I will present a dream that I myself had about a patient. It serves as an excellent example of the dream's value as an alerting mechanism. Many years ago a man of 25 requested treatment for homosexual difficulties. He considered his homosexuality to be psychogenic and hoped that therapy would help him achieve a heterosexual life pattern. The patient was born and raised in New England and had attended a prestigious boarding school and Ivy League college. His father had died when he was three and he had absolutely no recollection of him. He was raised with his mother and three older sisters, all of whom doted over him. His mother often undressed in front of him, even into the teen period. He first began having homosexual experiences in boarding school, but did describe some successful heterosexual experiences as well. However, his homosexual experiences were much more gratifying to him. In his early twenties he married in the hope that this might bring about a heterosexual orientation. He had not told his wife about his homosexuality at the time of his marriage. After about a year she became aware of his activities and at first hoped that she might be able to salvage the marriage. When I saw him, she had decided upon divorce and he went into therapy, hoping that he could avoid future similar consequences of his homosexuality. At the time he entered treatment, he was also in difficulty in the firm where he worked. He was employed by an investment banking firm, and it was becoming increasingly clear to him that he was being passed over for promotions because of suspicions of his homosexual lifestyle.

During the first two months of treatment, the patient appeared to be involving himself well in the therapy. He was a mild-mannered man who was quite polite and formal. His relationships, however, were invariably tempestuous, especially his homosexual relationships, in which there was significant jealous rivalry. In association with the stresses of these relationships, he would often drink heavily and sometimes become quite depressed.

Consciously, I did not consider the patient to be significantly different from other patients I was seeing with regard to any particular thoughts and/or emotional reactions that I might be having about them. One night, however, after about two months of treatment, I had a dream in which the patient was pursuing me with a knife in an attempt to murder me. Although I fled in terror, he was gaining on me and I awakened just at the point where he was about to stab me. The pursuit seemed endless. When I awakened, it was with a sigh of relief when I appreciated that it was only a dream. I was in analytic training at the time and so I began to think seriously about what the possible meaning of the dream could be. I had to consider the most obvious explanation, namely, that my dream was a reflection of unconscious homosexual desires toward my patient (his putting a knife = penis into me). Because I have never had any particular inclinations in this direction, I found it difficult to accept this as a possible explanation. However, I also had to accept reluctantly the latent homosexual explanation because of the way unconscious processes operate. I was also taught in analytic training that when a therapist has a dream about a patient, it invariably indicates inappropriate countertransferential reactions. I was not too comfortable with this unflattering explanation either. I could not recall having had any dreams previously about my patients (nor have I had any since), but I did, on occasion, exhibit what I had to accept were inappropriate countertransferential reactions. Accordingly, I was left with the feeling that the dream was important but without any particular explanation for its meaning. (At that time, I was not appreciative of the alerting value of dreams.)

About two weeks after the dream, the patient entered the session in an agitated state. Although I do not have verbatim notes on the interchange that ensued during that session, the following is essentially what took place:

> *Patient* (quite tense): I'm very upset. I can't take it any longer. I can't continue this way.
>
> *Therapist*: Tell me.
>
> *Patient*: This is very difficult to talk about.
>
> *Therapist*: I suspect that it will be, but I know you appreciate that it's important for you to discuss those things here that you are hesitant to speak about.
>
> *Patient*: Yes, I know I have to tell you but it's difficult.
>
> *Therapist*: I'm listening.
>
> *Patient*: I can't stand it any longer. I've got to tell you. I'm in love with you. And I've been in love with you since the first session. I can't stand it any longer. While I'm talking to you about my problems, I keep thinking about how much I love you.
>
> *Therapist*: You know, the word *love* can mean many things. It would be helpful to us if you could tell me the *exact* kinds of thoughts and feelings you've been having when you say that you love me.
>
> *Patient*: That's even harder.
>
> *Therapist*: I can appreciate that; however, if we're to fully understand what's happening, it's important that you try to tell me.
>
> *Patient*: If you really want to know, I want to have sex with you.
>
> *Therapist*: Even there, having sex with someone is a statement that covers a lot of ground. I'd like you to try to be more specific about the particular kinds of thoughts and feelings you're having when you say that you want to have sex with me.

Patient (hesitantly): Well, I just wouldn't want to start having sex right away. I'd want there to be some overtures on your part, some advances by you.

Therapist: I'm starting to get the picture. Now what specifically would you want me to say and do.

Patient: Well, I just wouldn't want you to simply ask me. I'd want you to plead.

Therapist: What would you want me to say specifically?

Patient: I'd want you to beg me. I'd want you to get down on your knees and beg me to have sex with you. (Patient now becoming agitated.) I'd want you to be extremely frustrated, to be very horny. I'd want you to be on the floor kissing my feet, begging me over and over again to have sex with you.

Therapist: What then?

Patient: Well, I wouldn't just have sex with you then. I'd want you to beg more. I'd want you to kiss my feet. I'd want you to promise to do anything at all to get me to have sex with you. You'd be on the floor crying and pleading. But I still wouldn't gratify you. I'd let you squirm. I'd let you plead. (Patient now becoming enraged.)

Therapist: What then?

Patient: Finally, when I felt you had enough punishment, I'd make you get undressed and then I'd make you lie down on the ground on your belly. Then I'd fuck you in the asshole and reduce you to my level. I'd humiliate you and gratify you at the same time.

Therapist: Is that the end of the fantasy or is there more?

Patient: Oh, there's more; I just wouldn't stop at that. First, I'd call your wife. I know you're married; you have that ring on your finger. And I saw those pictures on your desk; I assume those are your kids. Anyway, what I'd do then would be to call your wife. I'd tell her that you're a fag. And I'd tell her that you have sex with your patients.

Therapist: What do you think would happen then?

Patient: Then she'd divorce you. What woman would want to live with a fag?

Therapist: Anything else?

Patient: Yeah, I wouldn't stop there. I'd call the people who are in charge at the Columbia Medical School, the dean or whoever it is. I'd tell him that they have someone on the faculty there who fucks his patients. I'd also tell them you're gay. And I'd tell them that you had sex with me. Then they'd kick you off the faculty.

Therapist: Anything else?

Patient: Yeah, one more thing. I'd call the medical society and tell them what you really are, a fag, a gay doctor who fucks with patients. And they'd take away your license.

Therapist: Anything else?

Patient: No, that's it.

Therapist: You know, you started this session by telling me that you "love" me. Is this your concept of love?

Patient: Well, maybe it's not love, but it's the way I feel. Maybe it's the way I feel because I know that you don't love me the way I love you.

Therapist: Here you tell me you love me and then you tell me how you want to humiliate me, expose me as a doctor who has sex with patients. Then you tell me that you would like to have my wife divorce me and then I'd be kicked off the faculty at the medical school and then lose my medical license. It sounds to me like you want to destroy me. It doesn't sound very much like love to me. It sounds to me like the opposite, like hate.

In the ensuing discussion, the patient was too upset to be able to gain any insight into what was going on. His treatment did not last much longer. He left about two weeks later, claiming that I really did not have very much affection for him. If I genuinely wanted to show my affection, I would have sex with him.

Although the vignette demonstrates well an important psychodynamic mechanism operative in some patients with male homosexuality, namely, the use of love as a reaction formation to hate, it is not presented here for that purpose. Rather, it is presented as an example of an alerting dream. It is reasonable to speculate that at the time of the dream I was already receiving subtle signals of the patient's hostility. I was not aware of these consciously and may have been threatened by them. However, the awareness of the hostility built up in my unconscious and finally erupted into conscious awareness via the alerting dream. Had the man continued in therapy I would have used the dream to help me make decisions regarding hospitalization. The dream suggested that this was indeed a dangerous man. Of course, one would not and should not use one's own dream as an important criterion for deciding whether or not to hospitalize a patient. The clinical behavior must be paramount; however, the dream should not be ignored either. As I hope the reader agrees, the dream can be a powerful source of information about dimly sensed but not overtly recognized dangers.

The Dream as a Method of Desensitization to a Trauma This is another function of the dream that has nothing to do with wish fulfillment. Here the individual has been exposed to a severe psychological trauma and the dream serves the process of desensitization. Following the trauma the individual is not only consciously preoccupied with thoughts and feelings associated with the trauma but is so overwhelmed by it that many of the psychological reactions associated with it become relegated to the unconscious awareness as well. This is not specifically related to the fact that the individual feels guilt and/or anxiety over thinking about the trauma; rather, the trauma is so overwhelming that sleep time must also be utilized if one is to effectively accomplish the purposes of desensitization. The principle of desensitization is basically this: Each time the individual reexperiences the trauma it becomes a little more bearable. And, over time, with repeated reliving of the trauma, even though only in fantasy, the individual adjusts to it.

A situation in which desensitization dreams are common is the one in which a soldier has been exposed to uninterrupted battlefield condtions over an extended period. He may have been injured and observed friends to have been injured and even killed. Under these circumstances he may have suffered a severe enough stress reaction to the combat that hospitalization may prove necessary because he has become ineffective in his capacity to function adequately on the battlefield. In the hospital the soldier has repetitious dreams in which the battlefield conditions are being reexperienced. In the dream he may hear shells blasting around him and even may respond with the same fright reaction that was present during combat. So powerful may be the need to relive the experience that the dreams themselves may not appear to be enough and he may actually hallucinate the same experiences, again in the service of densensitization. Whereas the dreams occur at night, the hallucinations take place in the waking state. The dreams and hallucinations may not be the only vehicles for sensitization. The soldier becomes obsessed as well with thoughts of the battlefield conditions. And each time they are relived mentally, some adjustment takes place. Last, he is likely to be talking about his experiences frequently and such discussions serve as a desensitization mechanism as well.

The Nightmare In the typical nightmare the child is fearful that some malevolent figure will cause him or her terrible harm. Typically, the figure is a monster, other frightening creature, or sometimes even a nebulous blob or point that is approaching the child menacingly. Usually, the figure comes into the child's room from a window, or out of a closet, or out from under the child's bed. The closer the malevolent fantasy gets to the child, the more frightened the child becomes. And the child generally awakens just at the point when the malevolent creature is about to touch or envelop the child. At the point of awakening, the child is generally quite frightened, is often crying, and is usually consoled by parents who reassure the child that there are no such things as monsters, creatures, etc. The creatures in nightmares have a way of evaporating completely when lights are turned on and do not appear in broad daylight. Like vampires, they abhor the rays of the sun.

In my residency days I was taught that the malevolent figures in a child's nightmare represent one or both parents. In order to ascertain whether the creature is symbolic of mother or father, the examiner was advised to question the child in order to elicit information about the sex of the interloper. If male, then father was viewed to be the hostile parent; if female, then mother got accused. The child who dreamed of witches was to be viewed as one whose mother was inordinately hostile to him or her, and the child who dreamed of monsters (usually identified as male) had the misfortune of being brought up in a home where father was hostile. Even then, I was uncomfortable with this explanation and suspected that I was falsely accusing parents of being hostile when there was no signficant evidence for more than the normal amount of irritation and impatience that any parent will exhibit from time to time in the child-rearing process.

It was with these considerations that I began to formulate

another concept of the meaning of the nightmare. Specifically, I came to believe that the interloper is better understood as the incarnation of the child's own unacceptable angry impulses that have been relegated to the unconscious. Nightmares begin when children are about two to three years of age. This is a time when they are continually being frustrated by parents who must–if they are worthy of the name *parents*–inhibit and restrict the child continually throughout the course of the day: "Don't go into that cabinet," "Don't stick your hand up on top of the stove," "Stay away from the baby," "Big boys don't wet their pants," "Don't run out in the street," etc. There is hardly a five-minute period when children of this age are not restrained, constricted, and warned about some catastrophe that will befall them if they're allowed to go their merry way. The resentments engendered by such frustrations are enormous, yet they cannot be expressed overtly because of the fear the children have that they may lose the affection of significant figures who are vital for their well-being and even survival. Also, there are many other stimuli impinging upon the child during the day that distract him or her from the pent-up anger. At night, when these other distracting stimuli are removed, the pent-up hostilities of the day, which are continually pressing for expression, are allowed release. Daytime activities such as sports, sibling fights, and television–which have provided some release of hostility–are no longer available. At night, residual hostility from unresolved daytime frustrations is then freer to press for release.

In the nightmare, the symbolic derivatives of the child's anger (the robber, monster, terrible creature, etc.) press for expression into the child's conscious awareness (symbolized, I believe, by the child's room). The child disowns the angry feelings that are his or her own by projecting them outward. They are viewed as coming from outside the house, the closet, or from under the bed. Accordingly, the child utilizes two mechanisms for reducing guilt and/or anxiety over the expression of anger: symbolization and projection. Via symbolization, the anger is not viewed as anger; rather, it is viewed as some malevolent creature. And via projection, the anger is not viewed as the child's own; rather, it is projected outward in the form of a creature that comes toward the child from without. The child wakes when the anger is about to enter the child's own space, at the point where there is the risk that it will be recognized as coming from within. The malevolent figure may (as I was taught in residency) symbolize hostile elements within significant figures (such as parents). I believe, however, that this explanation should not be given first priority. It is the child's *own* anger that is basically feared. When the frightening figures threaten to abduct or kidnap the child, then the dream may reflect separation anxieties.

In my theory of the meaning of a child's nightmares, I generally do not consider them to be an abnormal phenomenon between the ages of two and seven or eight, unless they occur with a frequency greater than three or four times a week. I consider them to be a normal way of dealing with the inevitable frustrations and resentments that arise during the course of the child's life in this phase of development. Accordingly, I do not consider them pathological, nor do I consider them worthy of psychoanalytic inquiry. If they are occurring more frequently than a few times a week, then one must look for some problems in the child's life that may be contributing to their intensification. Generally, this would involve looking for abnormal degrees of anger-engendering experiences, such as harsh treatment by parents, neglect, and rigid, and/or punitive teachers.

Last, it is important that the examiner differentiate the nightmare from the *sleep terror disorder*. I generally view the former as a psychological phenomenon which may reach pathological proportions. Most psychiatrists today agree that the latter is a physiological disorder associated with very specific EEG changes. Phenomenologically the sleep terror disorder is quite different from the nightmare in that during the nightmare the child is lying in bed with eyes closed and some restlessness may be observed. In the sleep terror disorder the child's eyes are open and the child may even be running around the house—even though in an altered state of consciousness. In addition, when the nightmare is over the child generally remembers most, if not all, of what he or she has dreamt. When the child is awakened or wakes up spontaneously from the sleep terror disorder, there is generally amnesia for the event. Viewing as I do sleep terror disorders to be of neurophysiological origin, I do not consider them worthy of psychoanalytic inquiry.

The Panic Dream On occasion I have seen patients who have dreams in which there is no recollection at all of any cognitive material. They wake up panicky and, as hard as they try, they cannot think of any associated fantasies. Many psychoanalysts hold that such dreams are a manifestation of the threatened eruption into conscious awareness of unconscious thoughts and feelings over which the individual feels formidable guilt and/or anxiety. Whereas some individuals are able to allow themselves release of such material via symbolization, condensation, projection, and a variety of other disguise mechanisms, these individuals are so fearful of release of these thoughts and feelings that even the disguised representations are not permitted eruption into conscious awareness.

A number of years ago I had such a patient, a young woman of about 21. She was clearly a very tense and inhibited individual, who not only did not allow herself to enjoy sexual experiences, but even denied having sexual urges. I suspected that her panic dreams related to the threatened eruption into conscious awareness of sexual feelings over which she was so guilty that she could not even allow their expression through dreams at night. I theorized that her dreams produced awakening just at the point where some kind of symbolic release might materialize. A friend and colleague of mine at the time was actively involved in sleep research and we both agreed that she might be a good candidate for study. Specifically, the plan was that we would monitor her sleep in the sleep lab, awaken her immediately after she had dreamt, and then learn the nature of her dream fantasies.

Although this occurred about 25 years ago, I still remember the night quite clearly. The patient went to sleep in one room and was wired up to my friend's equipment in the adjacent room, where we could observe her and review the recordings of her sleep patterns. Because of his sleep research, my friend had already adjusted well to being a night person. Because I was very much a traditional day person, it was decided that I would sleep as much as possible, only to be awakened when my patient showed evidence of dreaming. There being no bed in the monitoring room, I had to sleep on the floor. On five or six occasions throughout the course of the night my friend awakened me and whispered excitedly that my patient was now dreaming. However, after a few seconds, she would spontaneously awaken—at which point she denied any recall of any dreams. This was not surprising because there were only a few seconds of dream activity recorded. Finally, around six in the morning, my colleague informed me that she was now having what appared to be a lengthy dream. At the end of this dream we awakened her to have her record her dream verbally on an audio tape recorder. Her response: "I dreamed that I was with these two men. I don't know who they were. They were strangers. They kept asking me to go on a picnic with them, but I wouldn't. They kept asking me to go on the picnic and I kept telling them no. That's all I can remember, but I know that I never went to a picnic with them." The only conclusion that one can definitely draw from this experience is that a patient's resistances can be so formidable that they can prevent the revelation of anything the patient really doesn't want to reveal—no matter how intrusive the examiner's tools of investigation. I cannot say whether the "picnic" the patient envisioned my friend and I to be taking her to involved sexual activities. I could only say that whatever its purpose, she was going to have no part of it.

In recent years, most psychiatrists would consider this kind of dream to be the nighttime equivalent of the panic attack. It would be interpreted simply as some kind of cerebral discharge, analogous to a seizure. I believe that this explanation has some merit. I believe that there are some people with very low threshholds for flight reactions, with the result that these reactions may be triggered by inconsequential stimuli. The panic attack, then, may be a manifestation of such a reaction. I would not, however, completely discount the psychoanalytic explanation as being totally inapplicable to all patients. I still hold that the aforementioned patient's attacks were more likely related to the threatened eruption into conscious awareness of unconscious material (in this case sexual) over which she felt guilty. She never had any similar attacks during the day. This, of course, does not disprove my explanation but it certainly may lend some support to it. At night, without the distracting stimuli of the day, the repressed sexual urges were more likely to pressure for release and attention and produce the panic (anxiety) attack (dream).

The Dream as a Mechanism for Providing Brain Cell Stimulation I do not believe that the aforementioned categories cover all the different types of dreams. They cover the main kinds of dreams that I have had experience with in my work with patients. There are many dreams that I do not understand. Even after eliciting the patient's associations, I am still left without the faintest idea about the dream's meaning. I suspect that for some of these dreams, there may not be a meaning and that they may simply be a manifestation of nocturnal cerebral activity. Just as muscle cells need to be constantly stimulated to remain strong and viable, so do nerve cells. Tonic contractions of muscle cells keep them "in shape"; perhaps nerve cells in the brain need cognitive stimulation to keep them in shape. Such nerve cell stimulation may be provided in the daytime by cognitive rambling and daydreams, and during the nighttime by dreams that may have no additional meaning other than to provide such stimulation. This notion, of course, is one that many psychoanalysts would have difficulty with in that they would argue that the contents of a dream are selected from a universe of possible combinations of thoughts, feelings, and imagery, and that it must be highly meaningful. Although I approach dream work with the goal of analyzing and with the belief that most are analyzable, I am still left with the lingering feeling that my failure to analyze some (but not all) of them has less to do with inadequacies on my part (certainly possible) and more to do with the fact that the dream may not be analyzable. And the reason is that there is nothing to analyze. The dream is merely a manifestation of some kind of cognitive brain activity taking place throughout the course of the night. Last, I recognize that there may be other categories of dreams that I am not appreciative of, and so I do not consider these additional possible explanations when attempting to understand a patient's dream.

Teaching Adolescents How to Psychoanalyze Dreams

Adolescents Who Are Candidates for Dream Analysis The older the youngster the greater the likelihood he or she will be able to profit from a psychoanalytic inquiry into a dream's meaning. Also, the more intelligent the patient the more receptive will he or she be to the therapist's suggestion to try to understand the meaning of the dream. Introspective patients are more likely to be receptive to such endeavors than those who tend to act out their thoughts and feelings. Youngsters whose parents are introspective, especially if they have had psychoanalytic experiences themselves, are more likely to involve themselves in the endeavor of analyzing a dream. Another factor is intellectual curiosity. Youngsters who are good students are more likely to be good dream analyzers. They are interested in expanding their horizons and learning new things. They enjoy learning for learning's sake. And learning about the meaning of a dream is just another example of an opportunity to satisfy one's intellectual curiosity.

If the therapist has had a successful dream experience with the patient, then the likelihood of the youngster's involving him or herself meaningfully and enthusiastically in further dream analysis is enhanced. Such a successful analytic experience would be one in which the patient and the therapist together have successfully analyzed a dream with the result that the youngster has had the *experience* that such inquiries provide interesting and useful information. This experience is hard to define. It is one in which the patient essentially says "Ah ha, now it all fits together," or "That's right," or "What do you know?". There is a kind of "eureka" response. Not only is there an intellectual understanding, in which everything seems to fall into place, but an associated emotional reaction of having made a wonderful discovery. This is an important goal to be worked toward. If this aim is realized, then one is more likely to have a patient who will be receptive to dream analysis (regardless of age); and if one does not reach this goal, then one is not likely to have a patient who will commit him- or herself in a meaningful way to dream analysis. Obviously, the older the patient, the greater the possibility that the therapist will be successful in reaching this goal.

If, during my initial two-hour consultation, I consider the patient to be a possible candidate for dream analysis, I will recommend that the youngster place a paper and pencil at the bedside and jot down any dreams that occurred during the previous night. I suggest that the youngster make a deliberate and conscious attempt to try to recall *any* dreams that occurred during the night. I emphasize that there is no dream that is so short, silly, or embarrassing that it doesn't warrant my attention. I try to impress upon the patient the fact that dreams have a way of evaporating and that even the most brilliant person with the most prodigious memory is likely to forget just about all of his or her dreams within a short period. I also impress upon the patient that merely writing the dream down does not suffice; rather, it is important that the dream be brought to me so that I can peruse it while we are analyzing the dream. I believe that it is reasonable to state that 95 percent of all the patients I see (including the most seemingly motivated adults) do not recall this whole message. Any part of it is generally forgotten, whether it be to write down the dream or, if written down, to bring it to the office. Most commonly, people will state: "It's so vivid I didn't think I had to write it down" or "I wrote it down, but I didn't think it was necessary to bring it to the office." Such failure to recall my statement is clearly in the service of the disguising mechanisms of the dream and is a true testimony to their power. Whereas some adults will obstruct the dream analytic process by "forgetting" to write them down, adolescents are more likely to flatly refuse to go to the trouble and will state so.

Fundamental Principles of Dream Analysis As a foundation for my discussion on teaching adolescents how to understand the formation of dreams and techniques for analyzing them, I present here what I consider to be the basic theory of dream formation by unconscious processes. This is not intended to be a comprehensive theory of dream formation. As the reader can already appreciate, my discussion above of the various types of dreams can only lead one to the conclusion that they are quite complex and that there is still much that we have to learn. These qualifications notwithstanding, I believe that the principles outlined here can serve well to help adolescents analyze their dreams. Their repertoire of knowledge is smaller than adults' and the information they can draw upon to form dreams is less comprehensive. In addition, the processes of symbolization, condensation, and projection tend to be less complex and sophisticated than those utilized by adults. The dreams of adolescents are generally more complex than those of younger children but less sophisticated than those of adults.

One does well to view the dream setting as a theatrical production. The dreamer not only writes the script, but is also the choreographer and dictates the movements, gestures, and behavior of all the protagonists. The dreamer also sets the stage and decides what props shall be brought in, where they shall be placed on the stage, and when they shall be utilized. The individuals who appear in the dream may be drawn from the whole gamut of humanity: real and fictional, past and present, well known and unknown. The props can be selected from the infinite variety of things, scenes, and objects. Animals may be used and even composites of a wide variety of animate and inanimate objects. Traditional rules of logic, movement, and sequence need not be respected.

The protagonists of the dream generally represent the dreamer and/or individuals who are of significance to the dreamer at the time. An individual may divide him- or herself into two or more parts, with each part representing one or more aspects of the dreamer's personality. For example, a very religious adolescent girl, who is guilty over her emerging sexual feelings, may have a dream in which she is observing the Virgin Mary reprimanding a prostitute. It is reasonable to conclude that the girl is symbolizing herself here in three separate forms: 1) the Virgin Mary, a symbol of her desire to be pure, 2) the prostitute, who symbolizes her emerging sexual inclinations, and 3) the observer, the girl herself who is witness to her conflict. The dream is also a demonstration of her guilt over sex and her view that people who do not engage in such activities are pure and innocent and those who do are no better than whores.

Another rule that is useful to follow in understanding dreams is that the individuals who appear in the dream who are ostensibly of trivial or inconsequential significance are generally not so. If, for example, an adult woman of 50 has a dream in which she is walking with another woman whom she has not seen since childhood, then one does well to conclude that the friend is being brought into the dream as a symbol of some quality that exists in the dreamer herself. They were both childhood friends and therefore the two lend themselves well to serving as alter egos of one another. The examiner does well to ask the woman what thoughts come to mind regarding the old friend whom she has not seen for many years. With rare exception, the qualities that she recalls the friend to have had during childhood are likely to be qualities of her own that are of some concern to her (the dreamer) at the time of the dream. The old friend is not being brought in for the friend's benefit. Rather, she is being brought in for the dreamer's benefit. Our dreams are very egotistical, and we do not waste our valuable time for the benefit of others, especially people we haven't seen in 40 years. Although adolescents obviously have less past time into which they can dip, the same principle holds.

It is also reasonable to assume that the dream is dealing with issues related to events that occurred within the day or two prior to the dream's occurrence. Each night, the dream deals with the "unfinished business" of the day. Most people's lives are so filled with various kinds of recent "unfinished business" that we do not dip back in time to weeks or months before the dream to work through older problems that may not have been resolved. Generally, the unresolved problems of the day are dealt with the same night or the next night. Then, even though older business may be "unfinished," there are newer events that take priority over older unresolved issues. The "old stuff" appears to pass into oblivion and is superseded by material that now commands our attention. We cannot go around endlessly nursing old wounds or continually trying to resolve every problem that confronts us.

Our minds tend to work on the same principle as that used by the administrator who files away reports of problems without the need to resolve them. The difference, however, is that the administrator may never deal with any problem and file them all away. We may try to deal with each problem each day and try to deal, as well, with problems that may have taken place the day before. However, the attempt to do so is complicated by the fact that we continually have to deal with new problems that confront us and command our more immediate attention. It is hoped that the dreams will at least solve some of these problems so that our minds do not end up like the filing cabinets of the administrator. It would be an error for the reader to conclude that the older material *never* is dealt with in dreams. If the older material relates to severe psychological traumas, especially those that have persisted over time, then the dream may be utilized in the service of dealing with these. An example of this would be the desensitization kind of dream that is used to deal with the psychological traumas attendant to prolonged exposure to military combat. Under these circumstances, the older material takes priority over newer; however, it does so because it has remained a present-day concern as well.

Consistent with this notion of the higher priority that dreams give recent material, the props that have been brought in are more likely to be related to recent events, especially the previous days' experiences. Whatever the object that the patient selects to put on the stage—and these are selected from a universe of possible objects—it generally has some relevance to events that were taking place during the day or two prior to the dream's occurrence. Also, one must consider the general ambiance of the dream. Does it take place in the frozen snow or the hot jungle? Are there grey clouds or bright sunshine and a clear sky? Is it underground in a cave or above ground on top of a mountain? All these aspects of the environment are of meaning in the dream because they have been selected from the infinite variety of possible milieus.

As mentioned, I do not believe that a particular symbol necessarily has the same meaning for everyone. Freud was especially prone to ascribe sexual meaning to many dream symbols. A snake, for example, may very well symbolize a penis. But it can also symbolize feelings of low self-worth and surreptitiousness. Snakes crawl on the ground and are quite "sneaky" in the way they approach us. However, snakes are also poisonous and they may, therefore, symbolize hostility and murderous wishes. One cannot know what the snake means to any particular person unless one elicits that individual's free associations to it. There are individuals for whom a snake may have some special significance, unrelated to the aforementioned more common possible meanings. The examiner who approaches dream analysis with the assumption that the snake has some particular meaning is likely to lead the patient into incorrect interpretations of the dream. Furthermore, even traditional sexual symbols may stand for other things. A phallic symbol may not simply stand for a penis but for power and strength—traditional associations to the penis in our society. A vaginal symbol may not simply stand for the vagina but for femininity, passivity, and child rearing. These, too, are traditional associations to the female in our society. (I am making no statements here as to whether or not these associations are "good" or "bad." I am merely stating that they are common associations in our society at this time, although things may be changing somewhat.) A common dream experience is one in which the individual feels like he or she is being overwhelmed by bugs, insects, or other noxious vermin. These often represent threatened eruption into conscious awareness of a variety of unacceptable thoughts, feelings, and impulses. One must try to ascertain from the dreamer's associations what these noxious intruders might symbolize.

Explaining the Theory of Dream Formation and Analysis to an Adolescent With the aforementioned principles as background, the examiner is in a better position to explain the principles of dream formation and interpretation to the patient who is a potential candidate for dream analysis. I generally begin in the following way: "Did you know that the mind has two parts, a conscious part and an unconscious part?" (The reader may wonder here whether I have forgotten about the superego. Of course, I have not. I simply use this oversimplified dichotomy for the purposes of helping a patient learn the basic principles of dream analysis.) I then try to get the patient to appreciate that in the *conscious mind* are facts that people are generally aware of, for example, age, address, name of school, name of teacher, favorite flavor ice cream, etc. I will then discuss the kinds of things to be found in the *unconscious mind*. Here are thoughts and feelings which the youngster may feel guilty about and may think are wrong. For example, a youngster may think that it is very bad to have an occasional wish that a brother or sister might get hit by a car. To such a patient I might say, "That boy (girl) doesn't realize that to have a thought like that *once in a while* is *normal* and that it doesn't really mean that the person wishes the brother or sister *really* to be hit by a car. It only means that the person is angry at that brother or sister at that point. Anyway, if the person feels very bad about such a thought and thinks that only the worst kinds of people have such a thought, then that person is going to push that thought out of his or her mind and push it into the unconscious part of the mind so that he or she doesn't have to think about it at all."

I then engage the youngster in a discussion of the kinds of thoughts and feelings that might be relegated to the unconscious and those that a person might comfortably accept as conscious. When the patient provides examples of thoughts and feelings that might be relegated to the unconscious, I may learn something about the things that that particular youngster is guilty about.

Once the concept of conscious/unconscious has been understood, I proceed to a discussion of the process of dream symbolism. One technique that I have found useful in helping adolescents understand this concept is that of the "secret code." I ask the patient if he or she has ever seen a James Bond movie. I generally receive an answer in the affirmative. I try to help the youngster recall some secret agent therein who used a secret code. We then discuss the formation of secret codes, for example a code in which the number 1 stands for A, 2 for B, 3 for C, etc. When one "cracks" the code, one merely tries to figure out which letter stands for which number. In this way the code is "decoded." I will generally use the terms "crack the code" or "decode the code" to refer to the process of analyzing the symbol. Once this concept is understood, I explain to the patient that dreams also make up their own codes. I explain that the unconscious mind changes information into code form before the information is released into the conscious mind. In this way the person may not feel so bad or ashamed about the thoughts and feelings involved.

I will then ask the patient to see if he or she can decode or crack the code of a dream that I will now present. I have found this example to be useful:

> A little girl is walking down the street. She sees a boy her own age making wee-wee. In her home she was taught that it's naughty to look at a little boy doing that. She wanted to look at the boy, but she felt very bad and guilty because she wanted to look at him. So she turned away and didn't look. But she was still very curious to see what his penis looked like. That night she had a dream. In that dream she saw that *very same* little boy watering the grass with a hose. He was holding the hose in his hands and a stream of water was coming out of the hose. The water curved out from the hose down to the grass. What do you think the hose stands for? What do you think the water stands for? Do you think that dream had anything to do with what happened that afternoon when she saw the boy making wee-wee and wished that she could see his penis?

The overwhelming majority of youngsters will generally "figure out" the meaning of this dream. When they do, I try to emphasize the point that the dream satisfies a wish: "The little girl wished that she could see the boy make wee-wee, but felt that it was wrong or bad and so could not satisfy her wish. At night, she gratified the wish to see his penis. However, because she felt this was the wrong thing to do she had to put it into a code form."

To emphasize further the wish-fulfillment function of the dream, I will generally provide questions to the youngster that provide practice with the use of the dream for this purpose. For example, I might give this question:

> A boy's father comes home one day and tells him that he has tickets for a football game that weekend. He's very happy. He's very excited about the fact that he'll be going to a football game in a few days. In fact, he tells all his friends about the fact that that Saturday he's going to a football game. Unfortunately, on Friday the boy gets sick. He's so sick that he has to stay in bed and he can't go to school. He has a high fever and a headache and he's nauseated and he vomits. The doctor says that he'll have to stay home and will have to remain in bed for at least three days. The boy is very sad. He wishes that he could go to the football game. What do you think he dreams of that night?

Again, it is a rare patient who does not get the correct answer to this question. I then take the wish fulfillment issue further. I may discuss the kinds of dreams a poor boy may have, a boy who has no money. Or the kinds of dreams a very hungry girl might have, a girl who hasn't eaten or drunk anything for many days. I will then follow these relatively simple dreams with dreams in which there is a combination of both wish fulfillment and symbol formation. For example:

> A boy named Tom started a fight with his younger brother Bill, and Bill went crying to their father and told him what Tom had done. The father got very angry and punished Tom. He told him that he could not watch his favorite television program that night. Tom was *very sad* that he couldn't watch his television program. He was also *very angry*, so angry that he felt like doing something very mean and cruel to his father. But he quickly put that thought out of his mind because he realized that if he were to do something mean or cruel to his father that he might even get a worse punishment. That night Tom had a

> dream about his father in which the angry feelings came out. Can you make up a dream showing how the angry feelings came out?

If the patient tells a dream in which the anger is acted out overtly, I may accept that as an answer. However, I may also say, "Well, that's one possible dream. However, this particular boy felt very bad about such angry thoughts. He felt so bad and guilty about having such thoughts that he could not let them into his conscious mind. He had to make up a code. He had to disguise the angry thoughts before he could let them come into his conscious mind." I will then ask the youngster to make up a dream in which the anger is released in coded form. If the patient cannot do so, I may suggest a dream in which the boy's *friend* hits the father with a baseball bat. Or, the boy might have a dream in which he is hitting a policeman. Or the father, while driving his car, has an accident. In this way I help the patient appreciate the concept of wish fulfillment by symbolic processes.

With this introduction into the theory of dream formation and analysis, I may then turn to the patient's dream and ask him or her to try to figure out what it means. A good principle to follow is that the element that is most likely to produce useful information is the most idiosyncratic or atypical one. These are the more highly individualized symbols and are more likely to provide useful leads regarding the dream's meaning. The therapist must keep in mind the fact that his or her suggestions regarding the meaning of a particular element in the dream are always speculations. The therapist should do everything to get the patient to present his or her own guesses and hunches regarding a symbol's meaning before the therapist offers any speculations. Even the patient's "wild guesses" may be more on point than the therapist's carefully considered explanations. The patient's guesses are more likely to be related to the unconscious issues that have brought about the dream's formation.

One device that I have found useful in getting youngsters to free associate to a dream entity is to utilize what I call the "foreign boy" question. Let us say, for example, a patient has a dream in which a shoe appears. One could simply ask the youngster what comes to mind in association with the word *shoe*. If the patient appears to have difficulty providing associations I might ask this question: "Suppose a foreign boy moved into your neighborhood and he didn't know very much English. Suppose he asked you what the word *shoe* means. What would you say?" I have found this question to provide a much higher percentage of useful associations than the more general question, "What comes to mind about the word *shoe*?"

It is only after the patient has exhausted all possible associations and explanations that the therapist should offer his or her interpretations or hunches for the patient's consideration. The hope here is that the patient will latch on to the explanation and have the aforementioned feeling that "It fits," "You're right," or "That's it." When the therapist observes this response, then he or she knows that the interpretation is likely to be valid. But if the patient just merely says, "Yes, that sounds right," without the feeling that the explanation "clicks" or is on target, then one cannot be sure that the interpretation was indeed valid. Last, one does not merely analyze dreams as an intellectual game. The purpose is to utilize what is learned in the service of the therapeutic goals.

CLINICAL EXAMPLE OF DREAM PSYCHOANALYSIS

George entered treatment at the age of 15 because of difficulties in forming relationships with friends. Clearly of superior intelligence, in terms of academic abilities, he had a brain like a sponge and sopped up knowledge from a wide variety of sources. It appeared that he never forgot any fact that related to expansion of useful knowledge. But he did not absorb information indiscriminately; rather, he had a keen interest in what was going on in the world and did not concern himself with frivolous and useless bits of information. However, from kindergarten days he was different from the others, primarily because of his intellectual precocity. Although some youngsters with George's genetic endowment might still relate well to others, George did not. It was not that he flaunted his knowledge; rather, he seemed to engender jealousy from his peers. Over the years of his elementary education he became increasingly isolated from others, mainly because he withdrew from taunts rather than deal with them more directly.

When the patient was about 12 years old and began to exhibit his pubertal growth spurt, the parents noted a slight limp. On neurological examination it was found that there was asymmetry between his left and right side. The consulting neurologist considered this to be a residuum of slight cerebral palsy, related to mild trauma to the brain incurred during birth. Apparently, the damage was extremely slight, affected only certain motor pathway functioning and obviously did not in any way interfere with intellectual functioning. The asymmetry was accentuated by his pubertal growth spurt but gradually reduced itself spontaneously. George's psychological reactions to the disorder were greater than the physical impairments engendered by it. In fact, it did not interfere with his going into track as his favorite sport during the junior-high- and senior-high-school periods.

By the junior-high-school level George was involving himself to a significant degree in his own fantasies. However, I did not consider him to be schizophrenic. Instead, I considered him to have a somewhat schizoid personality disorder. During that period he began involving himself with boys who spent hours playing *Dungeons and Dragons*. For the reader not familiar with this game, it is primarily a fantasy game in which the players weave stories around a wide variety of medieval figures. The game generally goes on for a few hours and sometimes all-night marathon sessions. There are rare instances in which youngsters have been so swept up in the game that a wide variety of pathological acts have ensued, including murder. On the one hand, I considered the game to be psychologically detrimental to George and advised him of my opinion in this regard. On the other hand, it did serve as a vehicle for his involving himself with peers. I presented George with both arguments and told him that he must make the final decision about his involvement. Not surprisingly, George decided to continue playing the game although he would not let himself get swept up into all-night marathons.

George's mother was a somewhat cold and restrictive woman, but a good mother nevertheless. His father was a more outgoing person. Both parents dedicated themselves to bringing up George and his sister in as healthy a way as possible. There were no significant marital difficulties. George's sister was a more outgoing person and had no significant psychiatric difficulties. At 13 she was starting to become interested in boys. In contrast, George at 15 still showed absolutely no interest in involving himself with girls. In fact, he even denied any feelings of sexual excitation. I suspected that powerful psychological forces had suppressed significantly his normal sexual urges.

During his first session I told George that I would like him to place a pencil and pad at his bedside and, each morning, think about any dreams he had. I told him that I would like him to write down his dreams and that he should not assume in advance that a dream was too short, simple, obvious, or inconsequential to be so recorded. I emphasized that even the most miniscule dream, even one word, may be a rich source of information for our work. I impressed upon him that there should be absolutely no excuse for not writing down a dream and that if he found himself giving himself excuses he should recognize that he was rationalizing. I also impressed upon him that it was important that he bring the written dream to me so that I could read it and that merely writing it down and leaving it elsewhere would compromise significantly our utilization of it. Furthermore, I emphasized that it was important to write the dream down *immediately* because they have a way of evaporating and no one, no matter how brilliant and no matter how good his or her memory, is going to remember a dream for long. Last, I also advised him that if he didn't write it down, I would have to waste time in the session writing it down and the later rendition might not be as accurate as the original.

It may be of interest to the reader that I have been presenting this spiel to patients for over 30 years. It is a rare patient who will then bring in a dream in accordance with the aforementioned instructions. In fact, I cannot recall a patient who has done so. Every possible excuse is provided, e.g., "It was so obvious and clear in my memory that I knew I would remember it," "I wrote it down but I didn't know that you wanted me to bring in the paper," "It was very short, only a sentence, so I didn't write it down," and "I know what it means so I didn't write it down." So common are the rationalizations and so frequent is the forgetfulness regarding these instructions that I can safely say that I cannot remember one patient who has ever come in the session after my initial instructions and followed every single one of them. Rather, for most it may take weeks and even months to get them to do so. And there are some who do not follow through with these instructions throughout the full course of their treatment. The consistency with which patients do not "remember" these instructions is a strong statement about the power of psychological defense mechanisms and the threat that dream analysis poses to patients. As will soon be seen in the transcript below George was no exception and he too provided a rationalization for not recording his dreams.

In the session during which I discussed with George the writing down of his dreams, we also discussed our making a video cassette tape of each of our sessions. In recent years I have been encouraging all my patients to make video cassette tapes of their complete sessions, from the beginning to the end. They then watch the tape at home between sessions. I have found this an extremely helpful therapeutic modality and cannot recommend it highly enough. Elsewhere (1989) I have described in detail this valuable utilization of the video cassette tape in treatment. The clinical vignette presented below was being videotaped and the dream George discussed incorporated the video equipment into it. Presented below, verbatim, is a transcript from George's tenth session. The discussion of the dream is presented in toto, but I will periodically interrupt with descriptive and analytic commentary.

Therapist: So what's doing?

Patient: Really, nothing much has been happening in the past two days. No exceptional dreams or anything, I haven't written down...

Therapist: No dreams at all?

Patient: There was this one dream. I don't remember the end of it when I woke up.

Therapist: Okay. What did I tell you about dreams?

Patient: Write them down.

Therapist: Did I tell you no matter how short, no matter how fragmented, no matter how silly? No matter how inconsequential they may appear?

Patient: Yes.

Therapist: Very important. No matter how simple and

obvious it is, write it down and don't trust to memory, okay? So when did you have this dream?

Patient: Last night.

Therapist: Let's hear what you remember of it. We may not be able to make anything of it, but we may. But if you don't bring it in...

Patient: It was simply that we were taking my dog Charlie to some show or something...

Therapist: To a show. What kind of a show? Like a dog show?

Patient: A talk show.

Therapist: Like a TV talk show?

Patient: Yeah.

Therapist: Okay. And what was his participation?

Patient: He was basically there on a talk show...for some reason I can never understand.

Therapist: But he was going on a show?

Patient: No, I was taking him on a show.

Therapist: And he was going to be the guest?

Patient: I guess so, yeah.

Therapist: He was going to be the guest. Anything more in the dream?

Patient: No...I woke up...

Therapist: Okay, tell me about your dog Charlie. What can you tell me about him?

Patient: He's a golden retriever. He's an adult. We got him from my uncle when they had to move to Sweden. He sometimes runs away but he always comes back. He likes to be petted. He likes attention. He's really not mean to anything, except our cat. He's terrified ...

Therapist: He's scared of the cat?

Patient: No, the cat is scared of him.

Therapist: What does he do to the cat?

Patient: Chases him.

Therapist: Does he ever harm her?

Patient: I don't know if he means to harm her. The cat just runs up a tree. Then the cat comes down and looks one way and looks the other way...

Therapist: So he kind of bullies the cat, huh?

Patient: Yeah. Also, he likes to get his cookie at night—a dog biscuit. After we let him out for the night we give him his cookie and we give him his worm pill. He doesn't do tricks or anything like that. He just likes a lot of attention, and if you're mad at him he knows he's done something wrong. He sleeps in the house. He eats about anything.

Therapist: He eats anything?

Patient: Anything edible.

Therapist: If you were asked the question—I'm asking the question—are there any similar traits that you and Charlie have in common? It's a difficult question to ask, but sometimes people can answer quite easily. Would you say there are any traits you and Charlie have in common?

Patient: I guess I like attention now and he likes it too. I like to be petted a lot like Charlie. A lot of time I seem to understand a little bit what he wants or what my cat wants ...

Therapist: Let's look at the question of similar traits. They like attention. They like to be petted. Any other similar qualities you and Charlie share?

Patient: We like the family. I think that's about it. I usually don't get hyper over a cookie or anything like that.

Therapist: Let's go back to the dream now. Do you have any idea what the dream means?

Patient: No.

Therapist: What could the talk show stand for?

Patient: I don't know.

Therapist: Okay, look. How does this sound? The talk show might have something to do with your therapy. How is this like a talk show?

Patient: You've got microphones. You turn on a VCR. You've got the George/Dr. Gardner show ...

Therapist: We've got a camera there. We've got a television camera, right? We've got microphones and what do we do?

Patient: We talk.

Therapist: Right. And it's kind of a show because we use the tape. We can show it and look at it later.

Patient: Of course, we don't nationally televise.

Therapist (humorously): Well, if you want to do that, we'll see what we can arrange. We've got some very interesting sessions ...Okay, so we think it's reasonable to think the talk show might represent therapy?

Patient: Yeah, it might.

Therapist: And we're having a chat like you would in a talk show. I'm the host, you're the guest. Right?

Patient: Yeah.

Therapist: Okay. So let's say that the talk show in your dreams represents what we're doing here. So what else?

Patient: Why does Charlie represent me? I don't know. Charlie is someone I really like. I really like Charlie.

Therapist: Okay. How does this fit in? He was to be the guest on the talk show. There's a special switcheroo here. So what about Charlie?

Patient: Charlie is something very special to me, for one thing. I don't know exactly what Charlie represents. He's not an exceptional dog in any way.

Therapist: So why do you have *him* coming to be the guest?

Patient: And me just bringing him? That's another one that I can't understand.

Therapist: What's your guess?

Patient: Not to play a mean trick on you. Would it?

Therapist: A trick? Okay, let's follow that up.

Patient: But you were not expecting a dog though. Not you. But the talk show was expecting Charlie though.

Therapist: Okay, it's a trick on me. You want to play a trick on me.

Patient: The uncomfortableness, with the psychiatry thing.

Therapist: Okay, uncomfortable with psychiatry. So how did the trick of Charlie work?

Patient: To give you a hyper dog to talk with!

Therapist: Is he a hyper dog?

Patient: Half the time he's not, half the time he's asleep.

Therapist: So you've given me a hyper dog to talk with. What would happen?

Patient: He'd jump around all over the place.

Therapist: Yeah. And what would happen then? You said

something about discomfort with psychiatry? A little while ago? So how does the dog fit in there with discomfort with psychiatry?

Patient: Like dog-day afternoons or something?

Therrapist: What does that have to do with discomfort with psychiatry? You said discomfort with psychiatry didn't you?

Patient: Yeah, as a possible subconscious discomfort.

Therapist: Okay, how would having Charlie come here as the guest relate to discomfort with psychiatry?

Patient: He would replace me. And I would be safe?

Therapist: You would be safe. Why?

Patient: You would be filming my dog instead.

Therapist: How do you feel about that in terms of your treatment? How much would I learn from him? In terms of going to a talk show, how much is he going to talk?

Patient: Not too much. I got him there, and I got him on stage and stuff.

Therapist: Okay. So what is the dream saying then?

Patient: I still like to elude you every now and then.

Therapist: Uh huh. So by substituting your dog you are protecting yourself from revealing certain things, right?

Patient: Yeah.

At that point I believed that George and I had basically analyzed the dream. However, an important determinant regarding whether or not a dream interpretation "sinks in" is the patient's reaction to it. Ideally, the therapist wants the patient to reach the point where there is a deep sense of appreciation that the interpretation "fits." More valuable is the patient's having the experience that can be best stated with the words "Eureka! That's it, of course!" Most patients are dubious about the value of dream analysis, especially early in treatment. If the therapist can bring about a situation in which the patient, after analyzing a dream, has the aforementioned eureka experience, then it is more likely that more dreams will be forthcoming because the patient will have had the living experience that dreams can be useful. This conviction for dream analysis can then spread into the conviction for other kinds of analytic inquiry.

Therapist: Okay. I'm going to ask you this question. Do you think that our interpretation that we have derived is a valid one? Does it grab you?

Patient: It does sort of grab me, yeah.

Therapist: Does it add to your conviction that dreams, even fragmented ones, even the little seemingly silly, ...

Patient: As a reflection of the subconscious to the conscious ...

Therapist: Does this analysis add to your conviction as to the use of these dreams in understanding what's going on here?

Patient: Yeah, I think it does.

Therapist: Because I hoped that it would, in the hope that it might motivate you to write them down. Now I don't think we're finished with this, I'm just saying this to you now in the hope that it will spur you on to see what else we can derive from this dream. The big question is what are the things that you are hiding from me that you are using Charlie to help you hide? That's the question.

The transcript cannot convey the degree of conviction associated with the patient's words. The tonal quality of his voice and his gestures led me to the conclusion that George indeed did have a mild kind of eureka experience. But George was not the kind of boy who exuded enthusiasm about anything. His relating more dreams in the future was the best evidence that the dream analysis had "grabbed him." I then began an inquiry that would enable us to get more mileage out of the dream. These derivative discussions are an important part of dream analysis. The therapist should not simply be content with a simple analysis of the dream. One wants to take the material revealed and extract from it as much therapeutic mileage as possible. Therefore, I asked George what things he might be hiding from me, things not alluded to, except indirectly, in the dream.

Patient: That too is in my subconscious.

Therapist: Just guess, whatever comes into your mind.

Patient: Like how we never really talk about the cerebral palsy and stuff, maybe.

Therapist: Okay. Let's talk about that. What things about that do you want to say?

Patient: Well, I didn't really tell anybody about it, not that I think about it half the time, if not three-quarters of it. Because I feel that it is irrelevant, or has very little relevance, or very little impact on my life, it really doesn't affect it.

Therapist: So you don't think there's much to talk about that?

Patient: No. I never felt it was a *strong* hamper on my life.

Therapist: Have you ever felt it was a *weak* hamper on your life?

Patient: The one time it really affected me was when I had the little vein problem, or tendon problem, or whatever it was. Where I really grew too fast for myself.

Therapist: Okay. Is there anything else you want to say about that?

Patient: Well I do work here on the mental dysfunction and stuff, right?

Therapist: Yes.

Patient: Yeah, and the effect on the brain. You said in the first meeting that it might have some effect on my friendship relationships.

Therapist: Okay, and how did I say it might have some effect?

Patient: Certain processes of my brain are weakened like putting myself in other people's fears and stuff.

The patient is referring here to remarks I made near the end of our first two-hour consultation. I was commenting on his impairments in putting himself in other people's positions. I mentioned that this might have a neurological substrate, especially considering that there was some brain dysfunction associated with brain trauma. However, I also pointed out that environmental and psychological factors played a more important role and related to his withdrawal from involvement with others.

Therapist: Okay. What are some of your thoughts on that now? Is there anything about that issue of putting yourself in other's people's position you are afraid to talk about or hesitant to talk about?

Patient: No, not usually, I just don't really talk about it.

Therapist: So that isn't something that you're hesitant to discuss with me? I would be more interested in things that have gone on, thoughts and feelings you've had which you have said to yourself, "Oh, I wouldn't want to talk to him about that" or "That makes me very shy, I prefer not to discuss that." By the way, you are free to reveal, or not to reveal, any parts of these tapes. In terms of watching them, you can say to your parents, "I prefer not to have you see this," or you can even say,"I prefer not to have anybody view any part of that tape." That tape is yours, and you can show or not show it. You can obliterate it all by going over it with some other material. So, getting back to the question: is there anything that's happened to you where you would say, "Oh, I'd rather not discuss that"?

Patient: Yeah, sometimes some of my dreams and hopes and stuff like that. Like I usually used to daydream and I didn't like to tell people.

Therapist: What are the things done in your daydreams?

Patient: I find myself daydreaming less and less now, but...like I said, the daydreaming has to do partially with my retreats from myself that we talked about Monday.

Therapist: Monday—to do with what?

Patient: The retreats from reality, and being George.

Therapist: Okay, where are you at, at this point, with these daydreams?

Patient: Like I said I'm doing it less.

Therapist: Why do you think you're doing it less?

Patient: Because I'm trying to do it less.

Therapist: And why are you trying to do it less?

Patient: Because you and my parents and everybody has pretty much shown that the less I do it the more receptive to real people and the better I become.

Therapist: What are you substituting for it? What are you doing instead?

Patient: What I'm planning to do partially is, trying to write some stuff. I've been thinking about it. A lot of my retreats are stuff that I think could be good for maybe writing down one day and make into stories and stuff.

It certainly would have been nice if the patient had said that he was substituting human involvements for his daydreams. However, that would have been too much to ask at that point. Such a great leap forward in therapy would not likely have taken place and, if he professed such interest, I would be a little dubious. His substitution of writing for fantasizing is certainly desirable, but it is only a small step forward in that it is too solitary an experience.

Therapist: Okay, so you're writing material for stories?

Patient: Yeah.

Therapist: What kind of stories. Let's hear about those.

Patient: I usually write down how people would react to exceptionally crazy stuff, to an exceptionally crazy situation.

As mentioned so many times in this book, abstractions and generalizations are of little therapeutic value. The therapist does well to get specific examples of the issues patients are talking about. These concrete examples are the therapist's handle for grabbing on to an issue that can be discussed meaningfully. Maintaining the discussion at the abstract level is likely to be a complete waste of time from the therapeutic point of view.

Therapist: For example?

Patient: How do aliens come down, pick up TV waves, and send clones of The Three Stooges down for observation?

Therapist: Go ahead. What else, what other kind of stuff?

Patient: And from there I pick up like how the Defense Department would react after they got these pictures of three big fat guys. And what the generals would do. And like tanks coming out against The Three Stooges and they think like they're very evil. Strange aliens with sonic weapons and it just goes on like that...

Therapist: So the main thing is that evil, strange, aliens...

Patient: Not evil or strange...

Therapist: Did you say *evil* before?

Patient: Now, you've got these aliens, right? From outer space, and they are observing things here on Earth. And they pick up TV waves, right? Because they're sent here from outer space. Okay. An Earth spaceship picks it up and sees The Three Stooges. The aliens figure Earth is very violent, but they want to send down observers. The aliens see only three people around to do the observing. The three people they've got on their video tape. So they clone them, in order to be inconspicuous. The only people the aliens saw were The Three Stooges. So they cloned them. So they sent these clones down and they're discovered. Word was sent to the army about the three clones.

This general, now he's playing Battleship for the admiral on the big computer board. He picks this up: "We're being invaded." First thing he says, "by Russians or some others?" Then he goes, "not by Russians." Then he goes, "by the Chinese," and he's going down all this list. He's not letting his subordinate really break in. And then his subordinate says "aliens." And the general says, "You mean from Mexico?" And he just says, "No, from outer space." And there is very little description, what do the aliens look like? Green-eyed, tentacled, no, there are The Three Stooges. And he says like, "Oh well, we better just stay quiet about it." And he's asking, "Who knows what, does the KGB know about it?" "No." "Does the FBI know about it?" "No." "Okay, fine. Worst thing: Does the press know about it?" "Yes." "Yeah...watch the press... watch the press." And they're just running from the army and the press and everybody and it's really crazy after a while.

Therapist: So everybody's kind of persecuting them?

Patient: Uh, yeah.

Therapist: Why are they persecuting them?

Patient: Why, because they're aliens. It's not persecution. The press just wants to talk to them, but the army doesn't want to get shown up by three aliens who look like Larry, Curly and Mo. I guess some people help them every now and then. The army is chasing them because they're aliens.

Therapist: So the army doesn't want to get shown up? I'm not clear about that.

Patient: What happens is that the army doesn't really want to be looked on as a fool. We have to stop and catch these three aliens. You know Larry, Curly, and Mo look really stupid. The army couldn't do that.

Therapist: The army would be fools if they couldn't capture them, but they are trying to capture them and everybody else views them as kind of atypical and oddballs and crazy.

Patient: They're aliens.

Therapist: And what is the main goal once caught? What will they do with them?

Patient: Well I guess a view would be to really capture or kill, because they're figuring armies of real mean green men could follow afterwards ...

Therapist: Okay, so that's the kind of fantasy you're putting down into a story?

Patient: Yeah.

Therapist: How does it end?

Patient: Eventually they're taken back up into the spaceship.

Therapist: And then what happens?

Patient: And then they're replaced with two different replacement aliens that may be a little more inconspicuous.

Therapist: Okay, what do they look like?

Patient: Normal people. And then he closed the curtains.

Therapist: Okay, this is a self-created story? You didn't get this from anything did you?

Patient: No, this is my own story. It does have some definite references to other stories. This is one of a kind by itself, though.

Therapist: You know, a story is like a dream, in a way. It tells something about the personality of the person who makes it up, and it can be analyzed like a dream. Do you understand that, do you appreciate that?

Patient: Yeah.

Therapist: How would you analyze this "dream"?

Patient: Maybe The Three Stooges represent my own alienation?

Therapist: Okay, how? The stooges represent how you feel about yourself, as an alien?

Patient: Yeah, I guess so.

Therapist: And who are the army people?

Patient: They are the people who want to ostracize me from the community or something.

Therapist: Yeah. Does that grab you?

Patient: Yeah, I thought of it more as a good story. I really like it. I was telling it to one or two of my friends some of the stuff I was going to put in and he really liked it so I think I'm going to eventually write it down.

Therapist: Okay, let's talk about it from the analytic point of view, okay? So here we have a story in which you see yourself as an alien, as being different and as being persecuted, pursued, and they want to get rid of you. Does this say something about how you see yourself?

Patient: Yes.

Therapist: The important question is what are you doing that is contributing toward this alienation from others?

Patient: Well the stooges are running because the army has tanks, and guns, and stuff like that. And they're running and hiding.

Therapist: Okay, I understand that, that is part of the persecution. The question I'm asking you is with regard to yourself as contributing to your own alienation. What are you doing in reality to contribute to your own alienation from others?

Patient: Like you know, not being assertive or anything.

Therapist: Yes, that's certainly true. Okay, what else?

Patient: The retreats, and withdrawal, and stuff.

Therapist: What else?

Patient: My passivity, my sometimes...with regard to the helping complex and stuff. My doing things for people that I really don't want to.

Therapist: Say that again?

Patient: The helping complex sometimes hurts when I go overboard or something? It's basically like you said, a lot of it is self-esteem. Like you said loss of self-esteem, self-confidence,

Therapist: Okay. Any recent examples of lack of self-assertion?

Patient: Not really too much.

Therapist: Any experiences recently where you asserted

yourself in situations in which you wouldn't have done so in the past?

Patient: Like basically the lack of assertiveness is a passiveness like my mother is. Like with Larry and the refrigerator.

The patient is making reference here to a problem he was having with a friend, Larry. Specifically, Larry was quite insensitive to the patient's feelings and acted in George's house as if he were in his own. For example he would repeatedly go to the refrigerator in George's home and eat enormous quantities of food without asking permission. At first, the patient was squelching his resentment over Larry's behavior in his home. As a result of my conversations with him, George asserted himself with Larry and confronted him with his insensitive behavior. In response, Larry "laid a guilt trip" on the patient. His essential message was that he (Larry) was a very depressed and disturbed boy and that if George were to restrict him from going to the refrigerator that Larry might become more depressed and even commit suicide. He even got the patient to believe that if he did commit suicide it would be George's responsibility. And this resulted in George's pulling back and suppressing all self-assertion lest he be responsible for Larry's death. Here again, I impressed upon George that he was being manipulated and there was absolutely nothing about Larry's behavior that suggested to me that he was significantly depressed or that suicide was a genuine risk.

Therapist: Where do things stand on that? That was the friend who you didn't want to go into your refrigerator.

Patient: Yeah.

Therapist: Okay. And he was making you feel responsible for his depression and suicidal thoughts.

Patient: As I said last Monday, for some reason, he plays upon my feeling of responsibility for him.

Therapist: In what particular area, for example.

Patient: Like if he says, "I'm going to commit suicide" or "I'm going to write a suicidal letter," I feel responsible for it even though I shouldn't.

Therapist: Where do things stand on that right now?

Patient: Like I said we haven't seen each other any more since Monday because Mom doesn't let him over.

Therapist: Has anything happened since then? Have you heard about anything?

Patient: No.

Therapist: Okay, so how do you feel about that whole thing at this point?

Patient: I used to feel okay about it, because I did assert myself, didn't let Larry play on my guilt or anything.

Therapist: Any other examples of self-assertiveness?

Patient: Not recently.

Therapist: Because if you are passive and submissive and you let people take advantage of you, then you contribute to that view of yourself as an oddball. Well, look, we have to close. I think that we have to talk more about this view of yourself as an oddball, as an alien. I think that you have to realize that these stories you write may give us useful information in therapy. But they could, at the same time, be a substitute for fantasizing and another form of withdrawal. You have to recognize this.

Patient: I do think a lot about the stories.

Therapist: But there's a certain danger to them.

Patient: Yes, when you get into the stories, but they can help also, because I can write a story down and maybe it serves my creative juices by writing down...

Therapist: Yes, there's a positive element in it. I'm not denying it, but then again too much time with them takes you away from reality.

At the time of this writing, about 20 months later, George is in his last year in high school. He is still in therapy. He has become much more assertive and outgoing but still is (and probably always will be) a somewhat uptight and intellectualized person. His knowledge of the world is sometimes astounding. He is a good example of the kind of patient who can definitely teach me things from time to time and I sometimes have to stop our discussions because I recognize there is the danger I might be exploiting him by tapping his knowledge to a significant degree. All (yes, all) his SAT scores and achievement tests were in the high 700 range. He was immediately accepted to his first-choice college. Unfortunately, I was not able to make much headway with his fear of girls. At the time I write this he has still not had his first date. Nor has group therapy helped him very much in this area. I just can't seem to get his sexual hormones secreted into his bloodstream. George has come to recognize, however, that he does have a problem in this area. My hope is that in the more sexually stimulating atmosphere of a college co-ed dorm, his juices will finally start to flow. There is no question that he would make a fascinating boyfriend for a highly intelligent, intellectually curious girl.

SEVEN

GROUP THERAPY

There are some who would consider group therapy to be "adjunctive" to individual work. I consider group work to be as important as and, in some situations, even more important than individual work and so I do not use the word adjunctive when referring to group therapy, whether it be for the adolescent or the adult. Rather, I prefer to use the term "combined therapeutic approach" in which I include individual, group, and family work.

TYPES OF GROUP THERAPY

Some therapists make a sharp differentiation among a variety of different types of group therapy. The most common types described in the literature are psychoanalytic group therapy, behavior group therapy, cognitive group therapy, transactional analysis group therapy, and Gestalt group therapy. Each of these focuses on a particular therapeutic aspect. I do not apply any of these labels to the kind of group therapy I provide. Rather, I see myself as genuinely eclectic and feel free to use any element from these various types (and others) that I consider warranted. My group therapy is certainly psychoanalytic in that I am committed to the belief that unconscious processes operate in bringing about many forms of psychogenic psychopathology and that gaining insight into such processes can play a role (with other factors) in bringing about therapeutic change. Such an orientation does not preclude my utilizing behavior modification techniques as I encourage desensitization and provide various forms of reinforcement (most often of a psychological nature). I am very committed to the notion that cognitive distortions play an important role in bringing about psychopathology and that the correction of these can contribute to the alleviation of problems that result from such distortions. I believe, as well, that many of the "games" that the transactional analyst describes are useful in understanding certain forms of interpersonal psychopathology. Although I believe that transactional analysts do not give proper attention to the unconscious processes operative in bringing about the development of these games, this still does not lessen my enthusiasm for their utilization in treatment. Last, although less committed to Gestalt therapy than other forms, I still use play acting and role modeling to a limited degree (as will be discussed below).

The reader may note that I have made no mention of encounter groups. These came into vogue in the late 1960s and early 1970s and residua of the philosophy still prevail in some circles. Manifestations of these remnants are to be seen in the "let it all hang out" philosophy and the notion that merely releasing thoughts and feelings, often indiscriminately, is in itself therapeutic. One of the aims of such emotional displays was to engender similar emotional reactions in other group participants. The theory here was that this in itself would be therapeutic for the others. I have serious reservations about this approach. Although I am very much in favor of a certain amount of emotional release, the release must be tempered with cognition if it is to be properly channeled into healthy directions. Children typically rant and rave when something bothers them; mature, healthy adults have learned that there are better ways to deal with one's emotions, ways that involve judicious combinations of cognition and emotion.

PRIMARY BENEFITS OF GROUP THERAPY

Of the three age levels–childhood, adolescence, and adulthood–group therapy is probably most useful for the adolescent, next for the adult, and least for children. Adolescents appear to be natural "groupies." They gravitate toward groups in order to compensate for feelings of inadequacy. They recognize, at some level, that the group has far greater strength than the sum of the individuals within it. They learn from the group what are the "in" styles, customs, lingo, etc. of the day. They are slavishly dependent on their peers and this dependency can be utilized in group therapy. The therapist, who like the parents is a member of the adult generation, is likely to be distrusted and such distrust may compromise the treatment. In contrast, the adolescent's peers "know where it's all at" and are viewed as having opinions that are more worthy of respect.

Adolescents, especially younger ones, do not generally relish the notion of sitting in a room alone with a therapist for 45 to 50 minutes while his or her "beady eyes" are staring at the patient asking him or her to "say what's on your mind." In the group the youngster can talk when he or she wishes and sink into the woodwork when silence is desired. Whereas in individual sessions the therapist must rely upon the youngster's renditions of what goes on with peers, in the group therapy session the therapist has the opportunity to observe directly such interactions. And this may be one of the greatest benefits of group psychotherapy. Furthermore, in the group the youngster can directly have therapeutic social experiences. Thus, those youngsters with a paucity of friends can be provided greater opportunity for social experiences as part of the therapeutic program.

There are a wide variety of ways in which the group experience can be useful for adolescents. The group helps adolescents improve their peer relationships, something that cannot but be therapeutic. It enables the examiner to observe firsthand the youngsters' interactions with others, providing the therapist thereby with more accurate data about the patient's problems–especially those that are interpersonal. The group helps adolescents learn better ways of dealing with the fundamental problems of life which, as mentioned so many times previously, are at the foundation of most forms of psychogenic psychopathology. The group provides new models for identification, both the therapist and other group participants. It is hoped that the identifications are healthier ones than those that the youngster has utilized previously when dealing with life's inevitable difficulties. The group forces an introspective stance, which can be useful in working out both intrapsychic and interpersonal problems. However, the group focuses more on interpersonal than intrapsychic problems, in that it is not a place where one conducts individual psychotherapy with six or seven observers. Of course, the issues brought up in the group can serve as points of departure for such inquiries in individual sessions. Accordingly, the analysis of a dream would rarely be conducted in group therapy. The group fosters open expression of pent-up thoughts and feelings with an aim toward their healthier utilization (not just blind expression).

GROUP STRUCTURE AND TECHNICAL CONSIDERATIONS

The treatment of an adolescent may involve individual sessions, group therapy, and sessions in which the youngster is present with one or both parents and other family members, as warranted. Nor does one have to have a fixed program regarding the alternation of these various treatment modalities. If any one of the three is likely to be fixed, it is the group therapy sessions in that the group is generally an ongoing, open-ended arrangement in which youngsters may enter and leave at various times, but the group maintains its continuity. Individual and family sessions, however, may be scheduled on a periodic or aperiodic basis as indicated for the particular child. The main criterion by which the therapist should determine the therapeutic structure is this: Are the sessions being used productively? If there are long silences and/or people have little if anything to say, then it is not likely that such therapeutic sessions are useful. The arrangement most likely to be sterile is the individual session in which the patient is alone with the therapist.

Family sessions and group sessions are much more likely to be productive because with more people in the room, there is much more likely to be an agenda and therapeutic activity.

The Question of Optimum Group Size

The ideal situation in which a group can be formed is the one in which there is a large pool of adolescent patients. Furthermore, I believe that it is preferable to have two groups: one of junior-high-school age and one of senior-high-school age. When one pools youngsters together who span ages 12 through 18, there is the risk that some of the younger ones will have antitherapeutic experiences. The younger ones are not as likely to be as sophisticated as the older and may therefore suffer from the embarrassment of their opinions' not being respected. Also, the younger ones may be prematurely exposed to "heavier" psychopathology involved with sex, antisocial behavior, and drugs.

I believe that the ideal number of youngsters to have registered as group members is eight or nine. However, this is not the ideal number to actually have at any specific session. By having eight or nine registered as ongoing members, it is likely that in any week six or seven will be present and this, I believe, is the optimum number. I know of situations in which people have had 15 or 20 patients in a group at the same time. This is unconscionable. Generally, it is not the therapeutic indications that have warranted this number. In private practice, it generally represents greed on the part of the therapist in that 20 people can provide a sizable income. In clinic settings it often represents an attempt at "efficiency" in a situation where a large number of people are being serviced because the facility is clearly not adequate to handle all the referrals in an effective way. The group therapy then becomes an administrative maneuver to satisfy those who are paying for the treatment and possibly dupe all concerned into believing that adequate treatment is being provided.

Obviously, if one needs about 18 teenagers to form two adolescent groups, it is not likely that one is going to be able to form such groups in most private practices. Only in clinic settings is there generally a large enough pool of patients available to form two groups of this kind. Therapists in private practice, however, may still be able to form adolescent groups if they pool their resources. Specifically, one therapist could run the junior-high-school level group and another the senior-high-school level group, with therapists in the consortium referring patients to the groups. This arrangement is not as effective as one in which the same therapist is seeing patients in both individual and group therapy; however, it is preferable to one in which no group therapy is available at all.

Homogeneous vs. Heterogeneous Groups

I generally prefer that the group be mixed boys and girls. Adolescent youngsters have to learn how to relate to members of the opposite sex and a group therapy experience can provide such opportunities. I also prefer heterogeneous over homogeneous groups. Some prefer homogeneous groups such as those for drug addicts, obese patients, alcoholics, etc. Although there are certainly some good arguments for such homogeneity, I believe that the arguments for heterogeneity are stronger. As mentioned so often throughout this book, all patients, regardless of their psychogenic symptoms, are basically utilizing their symptoms to deal with the fundamental problems of life with which we are all confronted. Because therapy focuses on better ways to deal with these underlying problems, it is not crucial that the other members of the group utilize the same symptomatic solutions to these problems. In fact, when they do, the focus often becomes too great on the external symptoms and this takes the group away from focusing on the more important underlying issues. For example, in a group for adolescent youngsters suffering with anorexia/bulemia, it is likely that an inordinate amount of time will be spent on weight, diet, and exercise. In fact, there are some groups of youngsters with this disorder in which each of the meetings is started with a "weighing in" ceremony. Although the prospect of embarrassment may play a role in bringing about therapeutic change, I believe such focus on symptoms robs the patient of the opportunity to delve into the underlying problems from which the symptoms emerge and the understanding of which is important in the psychotherapeutic process. Similarly, a group consisting of youngsters on drugs is likely to focus significantly on what particular drugs they ingested since the last meeting, what dosage, what reactions they had, etc. Here again, although some therapeutic benefit may be derived from such discussions, I believe a heavy price is paid, namely, the opportunity to discuss in depth the underlying problems at the foundation of the substance-abuse.

Although I consider it preferable to have patients with a variety of problems present in the group, I do not indiscriminately place every single adolescent in a group. Youngsters with severe learning disabilities and/or borderline intelligence will not do well in a group of youngsters with normal and above average intelligence. They are likely to be humiliated, merely tolerated, and not taken seriously. And this must be antitherapeutic. It is preferable for such youngsters to be in groups with others who are of the same intellectual level. Although one could argue that I am now recommending a homogeneous group, there can still be heterogeneity among the youngsters in this intellectual bracket. I also would not put severely sick youngsters in a group of adolescents whose problems are mild. The psychotic and/or autistic youngster is also likely to be humiliated, tolerated, or ignored in such a group and this will definitely be antitherapeutic. It is also important that the antisocial youngsters be outnumbered by those who are not antisocial. If the former are in the majority, then there is the possibility that those who do not have problems in this area may begin to develop such. This becomes a situation of the "bad apples spoiling the whole barrel."

The Optimum Duration of the Group Meeting

I have found meetings of 90 minutes to be optimum. If the group becomes smaller, down to four of five youngsters, then 60 minutes may work well. I usually have only one group meeting a week, but believe that in a residential treatment setting, where the youngsters are obviously more readily available, two and even three group meetings a week of even longer duration could probably be useful.

After-Group Meetings Without the Therapist

In my group work with adults I have generally found it useful for them to meet together alone, without me, in an after-group meeting. Ideally, this takes place in their homes and, if the situation warrants it, they can alternate homes each week. If this is not practical, then they can meet in a restaurant. The purpose here is not socialization but further group work at no additional cost. Although this arrangement serves well for adults, it is generally a bad idea for adolescents. One is setting up a situation for freedom to act out and it can thereby become antitherapeutic. Providing the group members the opportunity to meet alone, without the therapist's supervision, increases the likelihood that youngsters who do not act out may be drawn into such behavior. Accordingly, my adolescents in group therapy are usually dropped off by their parents and picked up after the meeting. I have no objection, however, if the parents set up car pools. In fact, this can often be useful in that it provides more contact among the youngsters, but still under supervision.

A Comparison of the Three Levels of Child and Adolescent Group Therapy

Group Therapy for Latency-Aged Children When discussing adolescent group therapy, it is useful to consider the progression from group therapy with latency-aged children, to the junior-high-school level, to the senior-high-school level. Any therapist who has attempted to conduct group therapy with latency-aged children will agree that formidable obstacles are likely to impede the smooth flow of the group sessions. Children in this age bracket are traditionally poor candidates for group therapy because of their age-appropriate rambunctiousness. Horseplay is the rule rather than the exception. Children at this age level are not famous for their desire to sit around in a circle discussing their problems. Giggling, poking, wrestling, and teasing are much more likely to take place than serious discussion. Passing gas is a common prank in such situations—with each member accusing the other of having performed the despicable act: "You did it!" "You're a liar." "You did it.! "No I didn't, it smells like yours." Of course, the therapist might use this issue as a point of departure for group discussion and thereby transform the prank into a therapeutic experience for all concerned. The disadvantage of this, however, is that it may encourage more farting because of the attention it provokes.

I have sometimes found myself in the position of informing a latency group troublemaker that if the antics don't cease instantly, he or she will be sent out of the room. Although there may be some therapeutic value to such a maneuver, it is hard to justify charging parents money under these circumstances. Accordingly, the therapist often finds him- or herself serving more as a disciplinarian than a therapist. Other disruptive antics involve arguing about where each person should sit and then bickering throughout the course of the "therapy" regarding the desire to change one's seat. Another common maneuver is imitation. While one youngster speaks, the other mouths his or her words and tries to engage a third party in similar antics. One youngster coughs and all the rest then start coughing. If the therapy is interrupted by a telephone call, pandemonium is likely to break out.

The Talking, Feeling, and Doing Game (Gardner, 1973b) provides an organization and a structure that is often so powerful that children in this age group may be diverted from their horseplay. One can use it for this purpose in a number of ways. One way I have found useful is to have the first child respond to a card and then get input from each of the other players on the first player's response. Each of the other participants, of course, receives a chip for his or her contribution. The second child may now answer the same question or choose another. In this way I go around the board, engaging each child in the responses of the other. When utilizing the game in this manner, the therapist can choose whether to participate as a player or merely as the one who keeps the game structured and calls on the various participants to wait their turn, respond at a given point, etc. I generally prefer to play as one who takes the cards him- or herself for the sake of "egalitarianism" as well as the desire to provide the patients with the therapeutic benefits to be derived from my revelations about myself. Although *The Talking, Feeling, and Doing Game* may provide some structure in latency group therapy, it is not always successful in this regard. The main determinant is the percentage of children who are going to engage in horseplay. When the group members' disruptive antics are formidable, such therapy may be a "lost cause"—the utilization of *The Talking, Feeling, and Doing Game* notwithstanding.

Group Therapy at the Junior-High-School Level It is useful to view group therapy at the junior-high-school level to be at a mid-point between group therapy with latency-aged children and those at the senior-high-school level. At the junior-high-school level, the youngsters are more likely to sit around and talk directly about their difficulties. However, their capacity to do this is less than that of older adolescents. It is at this middle level, especially, that *The Talking, Feeling, and Doing Game* may be particularly useful. As is true of the situation when one works with these children individually, they often have difficulty initiating and perpetuating a discussion of their problems. Many have directly told me that they enjoy utilizing the game because it gives them ideas and hints about things to talk about. At the junior-high-school level one must be much more structured regarding the group therapy than when treating older youngsters. Also, at this age level I am more likely to bring in parents on occasion than I am at the senior- high-school level. Their participation can be particularly useful. A youngster may complain bitterly about various indignities he or she has suffered at the hands of the parents. Most often the child's view is a distortion and an exaggeration. By bringing in a parent for "his or her opinion" regarding what had happened, it can often provide useful corrections of these distortions and a more meaningful group discussion. Parents sometimes feel uncomfortable being brought in under these circumstances in that they see themselves as being witnesses in a court of children, but they recognize the value of their participation.

Group Therapy at the Senior-High-School Level Work with the senior-high-school students approaches much more closely that of the traditional adult group. At this level I generally do not have an agenda and I let the youngsters begin the discussion with any issue that might come to mind. I generally do not need *The Talking, Feeling, and Doing Game* to provide ideas and suggestions regarding what to talk about. This is in contrast to the younger groups in which I am much more prone to bring up issues. However, there are still certain differences between the structure of the senior-high-school level group and that of my adult group. For example, if a particular youngster is typically reticent to involve him- or herself in discussions, I feel no hesitation actively drawing that youngster in. I might say, "You know, Jane, we've heard from everyone else on this subject but not you. Let's hear what you have to say." If the child is still hesitant, I might say, "I know that your brain has been working throughout the course of this discussion and that you have thoughts on what has been said. We both know that you need *practice* expressing yourself and the group provides you an opportunity to do so in a way that will not result in any problems for you. This is not the case outside of this office where, on occasion, what you say might get you into trouble. But, as we have said many times before, it generally won't." I ordinarily would not take such an approach in adult treatment in that the patient would thereby be infantalized and I would be involving myself in an antitherapeutic maneuver. One could argue that the adolescent is being infantalized by such overtures. I agree that this might be the case, but I believe that the disadvantages are more than compensated for by the experiences the youngster has after being brought out and involving him- or herself in the group discussions. As in all therapeutic maneuvers, there are advantages and disadvantages. It behooves the therapist to identify what these are and then make decisions regarding whether or not to utilize the particular technique.

Sibling Involvement

On occasion, I have invited a sibling of one of the patients to join us in a group session. This usually comes about after the patient has been complaining bitterly about the sibling and I suspect that the situation might be somewhat different from the way the patient has described it. Just as parental participation in this way can be useful, so can sibling involvement. On a few occasions I have actually had two siblings in the group at the same time. I recognize that some therapists would consider this antitherapeutic because it would deprive each of the patients of the privacy and confidentiality necessary for meaningful therapy. I recognize this risk, but I do not believe that it invariably is the case for all adolescent siblings.

There are strong arguments for considering this option. One relates to my view that the optimum therapeutic arrangement is one in which the therapist is seen as the "family therapist." I am not using the term here to refer to the situation in which the therapist does family therapy (although this is one possible option). Rather, I am using the term here in the sense that each of the family members views the therapist as the person to go to when he or she has psychiatric difficulties. And the therapist will see one or more of the family members, as warranted for each particular situation. This does not preclude "farming out" specific individuals in certain situations. Rather, the basic philosophy is that the best approach is one in which all family members see the same therapist and consider this arrangement to be the preferable option. It is only when there are compelling reasons that warrant a split off of one or more people to another therapist that this alternative should be considered. This approach is the antithesis of the one in which it is automatically assumed that each family member shall have his or her own separate therapist and that any comingling of patients with one another's therapist must be a contaminant to the treatment. Psychiatric problems have both intrapsychic and interpersonal contributing factors, and the therapist does well to be familiar with as many factors as possible in both categories. The best way to accomplish this goal is for the therapist to have contacts with all family members. This does not mean that all family members must be in treatment; rather, it only means that intermittent contacts and familiarization with all family members is important for optimum therapeutic progress.

Seeing both siblings together in the same group is consistent with this general philosophy. Accordingly, when sibling number two is being considered for entrance into the group in which sibling number one is already a member, I approach the issue in a matter of fact manner and operate from the general assumption that there will be no problems. This does not preclude my exploring with each youngster his or her thoughts and feelings about being in the group together. Most often there are no problems. When there is hesitation, I will generally explore the reasons for the reluctance. Sometimes the reluctance is justifiable, and then the second sibling will not be brought into the group. Sometimes the reluctance is a manifestation of pathological processes. In such cases I make every attempt to work these out before the second youngster enters. However, I have had one or two occasions when the pathological attitude has not been resolved. In these circumstances I have still brought in the second sibling, the reluctance of the first notwithstanding. Not to do so would be a manifestation of my complying with a patient's pathological demand and such compliance is generally antitherapeutic. My experience has been that the psychological problems that contributed to the reluctance have then been resolved and the two benefit from the therapy. I am not claiming that this will always prove to be the case; I am only recommending that the second youngster be brought in in spite of the first's protestations. There is an important principle of child rearing that is also applicable to therapy: just as parents do well to do what is in the child's best interests, not merely what the child wants, the therapist does well to do what is in the patient's best interests, not necessarily what the patient wants. What people *want* and what is in their *best interests* are not necessarily one and the same.

THE GROUP THERAPY EXPERIENCE

Preparing Newcomers For the Group

Before a youngster joins the group, I generally spend time in individual sessions providing general background information about the group. I will usually tell the youngster how many are presently in the group and what the sexual breakdown is. I give no specific information regarding the nature of the problems that the youngsters have and will not answer questions to that effect. To do so is asking for trouble. The patient will then enter the group wondering which of the youngsters has X problem and which has Y problem and this inevitably compromises free associations, blank screen fantasies, and projections. I assure the newcomers that they are free to speak when they wish to and free not to do so when disinclined to talk. I impress upon them that group therapy is a unique experience in life because one can be completely honest about one's thoughts and feelings about another person and yet there is no need to fear repercussions or other consequences. It differs, thereby, from all other interpersonal experiences in life in which we generally do not reveal certain thoughts and feelings that we have about another person because of the recognition that a certain amount of such withholding is necessary for civilized interaction and effective living with one another.

I impress upon the youngsters the importance of confidentiality and inform them that they have the same obligations for secrecy that I have. It sometimes happens that the youngsters in the group may learn about friends they have in common. At such times I reenforce the importance of their not revealing to third parties (nongroup members) the fact that a particular person is in the group. I impress upon them that even the divulgence of the *name* of a person in the group is a breach of the confidentiality because the person has the right not to reveal to others that he or she is in therapy. I try to separate this respect for privacy from the notion that there is something to be ashamed of about being in treatment. One can respect privacy without feeling ashamed of the fact that one has problems that warrant therapy.

I advise the newcomers that the more they reveal about themselves the more others will benefit from their presence in the group and the greater the likelihood they will get useful feedback. Conversely, those that say nothing learn nothing about themselves and give nothing to the others. As mentioned, adolescents crave information about themselves and this statement generally enhances their motivation to join the group and participate in it. I then explore with newcomers their thoughts and feelings about the group and what anticipations they have. Often such projections can be useful points of departure for therapeutic interchanges. Having no actual reality experiences on which to base these anticipations, they become more useful therapeutically because they are pure projections. Similarly, I do not provide the group members with any information about people who will soon be joining the group. Rather, I only make a simple statement like, "Next week there'll be a new boy (girl) coming into the group." The group might discuss something about the newcomer and I will try to derive as much therapeutic benefit as I can from the interchanges. However, I will strictly refrain from providing any information about the newcomer—lest the blank screen be contaminated.

The First Meeting

When a youngster comes to the group for the first time, I generally begin by introducing him or her to the other members. Very quickly the other patients will ask the newcomer why he or she is there. If the youngster is tense and anxious and prefers not to answer the question at that point, I do not press the issue—in accordance with my previous promise to the patient that I will not force or pressure anyone to talk. Sometimes the youngster will make a comment along these lines: "There's nothing wrong with me, I'm only here because my parents have made me come. They've told me they'll ground me if I don't keep coming here." The other patients may try to puncture the newcomer's defense with comments such as, "Dr. Gardner doesn't take normal, healthy people in here. There must be something wrong with you if you're here." On other occasions the oldtimers will leave the newcomer alone, recognizing that this is a defense and will not push him or her at that point. As mentioned earlier in this book, many adolescents have great difficulty admitting that they have problems that require treatment and may need the rationalization that they are only in treatment because they are submitting to overwhelming parental pressures. As mentioned also, one does well to leave this defense alone as long as the patient is talking about therapeutic issues anyway.

Most often, however, the youngster will say something about the presenting problems. The other patients then generally introduce themselves and say a few things about their problems. After that, there is no particular sequence of events that usually ensues. If at any point an oldtimer is pushing the newcomer hard to discuss certain things, and it is apparent that the newcomer is reluctant, I will generally protect the new person and advise all of his or her "rights" not to discuss a particular issue. However, I am quick to add that my hope is that the time will come soon that the newcomer will feel more comfortable discussing that particular topic. My hope is that after observing others discussing touchy subjects, the newcomer will be more comfortable to reveal him- or herself. And this is most often the case. Often a youngster will ask where the newcomer lives. When the newcomer answers the question, he or she may be asked about third parties (nongroup members) whom they both may know. At this point I will invariably warn all group members about the importance of the confidentiality, even to the point of divulging that a person is in treatment.

Corrective Emotional Experiences

F. Alexander and T. French (1946) and F. Alexander (1950) introduced the term "corrective emotional experience" to refer to an extremely important aspect of therapy. Specifically, therapy provides the patient with a special kind of *experience,* which may or may not be associated with intellectual insight regarding what is occurring. This experience is associated with emotions (often strong) that increase the likelihood that the patient will remember it. It may or may not be associated with insight. In either case, most important is the fact that the experience brings about behavioral change and is thereby of therapeutic value. By placing the adolescent in an environment with other youngsters– and with proper monitoring by the therapist–there is a great likelihood that youngsters in the group will enjoy the benefits to be derived from corrective emotional experiences.

For example, a newcomer enters the group because of a problem with drug abuse. Consistent with my policy of not providing any up-front disclosure, the youngster enters without any knowledge of the nature of the problems of the patients already in the group. Within about ten minutes, he learns that one of the other members has a similar problem. (It often doesn't take longer than this for two drug users to spot one another.) The two immediately embark on a discussion of the various drugs they have used, the "trips" they have taken, and engage in a wide variety of drug-related interchanges. Subsequently, each time they talk they quickly become enmeshed in a discussion of drugs and nothing else. Finally, after a few sessions of this, it is likely that one or more of the other members will point out to them how limited is their repertoire of topics to talk about and how boring they are becoming to the others. Because they have heretofore surrounded themselves with other drug users, they may not be aware of how limited their lives and conversations have become. Being provided these facts by a therapist in an individual session is not so likely to sink in as having the *living experience* of rejection from peers who are bored, irritated, and otherwise alienated by the narrowness of their obsession. It is hoped that this will play a role in their expanding their horizons into other areas and thereby lessen (admittedly in a small way) their need for drugs.

A 19-year-old boy, Jim, entered treatment because of long-standing problems with academic motivation. Basically, he floated through high school and learned very little. Because of his high intelligence he did manage to get through, but attended a school in which the policy was to promote just about anybody who was willing to attend classes for 12 years. He lived in a dream world that he was getting an education but showed no evidence for genuine academic motivation or intellectual curiosity. He then went to "college." I place the term in quotes because the school he was attending was just another one of those institutions in the business to accommodate parents who believe that it is important that their children go to college, but do not concern themselves with whether or not they are receiving an education. Jim had an "eye opener" during his first meeting. Two group members were highly intellectualized boys who were deeply committed to their educations. They were seniors in high school and then in the throes of applying to colleges. Although they were both somewhat pedantic and exhibitionistic with regard to their knowledge, they provided Jim wiith a new experience. He had never been involved to any significant degree with boys who were turned on by academic learning. Intellectually, he knew of such types, but generally referred to them as "nerds." However, he had never had personal experiences of this kind and had never appreciated that such discussions could be a source of gratification. He felt inadequate as he compared himself to these intellectuals; he felt envious of their knowledge; and he felt that he wanted to be like them as well. A new world had been opened to him by the group and the experience played a role in his ultimately becoming more committed to his academic program.

Mark, a 16-year-old boy, entered treatment because of severe rage outbursts. He was an extremely angry boy, but did not engage in antisocial behavior. Rather, the outbursts occurred over minor frustrations and disappointments. In one group session he was confronted by the others with his lack of sensitivity to their feelings, his frequent and discourteous interruptions, and his bombastic ways in general. The patient became quite angry and then turned to me for my opinion on the criticisms. I agreed that he did exhibit these qualities and advised him to consider the possibility that the criticisms were valid. I suggested also that he then try to do something about them. As I was talking to the patient, it became quite clear that he was becoming increasingly enraged. He suddenly got up from his seat and came toward me menacingly. While waving his fist, he screamed, "You God damned fucking liar!" Mark was a big boy, bigger than I, and quite strong. Furthermore, I have twice been hospitalized because of herniated cervical disks and cervical osteoarthritis. A blow in the head or the neck could literally cause me lifelong disability and even paralysis. As Mark approached me, I pointed toward three buttons protruding from the wall near my seat. Putting my finger close to the police button I said, "If you move one step closer I will press the police button. Believe me, these aren't decorations." Fortunately, the patient stopped, was temporarily immobilized, and then returned to his seat.

I then told Mark that therapy was for people who had enough self-control to talk about their thoughts and feelings, rather than act them out against me or other members of the group. I informed him that people who could not do this were not candidates for office treatment and might be considered for hospital or residential treatment—where there would be more external controls for their behavior. I informed him that there were three buttons on that panel, one for medical emergencies, one for fire, and one for police. I spoke determinedly but calmly. I informed him that I was definitely frightened because of my neck condition and was not going to place myself in any position where I would jeopardize my health.

I then used the experience as a point of departure for group discussion. Some considered my response an "act of cowardice" in that I was too "chicken" to handle the situation myself and was so weak that I had to bring in more powerful forces. In the ensuing discussion, they ultimately came to see that there are situations in which it is more judicious to ask for help than to fight alone, especially when the likelihood is that you will lose and even suffer terribly. The flight reaction and/or calling for help are not options that many adolescents consider seriously because of their need to maintain a "macho" image of themselves. We then discussed in detail fight/flight reactions and I expressed my opinion that in our society (especially among men), the flight reaction is not given the respect it deserves. I told them: "When a wolf chases a rabbit, the other animals in the forest who are observing don't call the fleeing rabbit 'chicken shit.' " I tried to help them respect more the flight reaction in certain situations and explained how it is part of our biological repertoire and can be life-saving. I then spoke about situations in which it is perfectly respectable to ask for the help of those who are more powerful and how that too is not necessarily demeaning. Last, I believe that all group members had the experience that their therapist is not omnipotent, that he too has his weaknesses. This too is therapeutic in that it contributes to a lessening of the idealization of the therapist that I consider to be a common antitherapeutic experience.

Peer Influences

Mention has already been made of the slavish dependence of adolescents on their peers. I.D. Yalom (1975) considers the member to member comments to be the most important in the exchanges that adolescents experience in group therapy. The therapist, as an adult, is viewed to be of the parents' generation and is thereby to be distrusted. Adolescent peers, in contrast, are viewed to be the final authorities on what is the "latest" and what is "in," and are thereby viewed as more trusted authorities. This phenomenon is compounded by the fact that many adolescents in group therapy do not "practice what they preach." For example, youngsters who are antisocial must know what is "social" in order to know how to be "antisocial." Interestingly, such youngsters may sermonize to others about being "good" and define very specifically the guidelines for their more desirable behavior. Although not engaging in such behavior themselves, their wisdom is still respected and contributes to therapeutic change. Of course, one must discuss with the preacher the fact that he or she is not subscribing to the guidelines of his or her sermons.

Cigarette companies capitalize significantly on the adolescent's dependence on peer pressure and delusions of invulnerability. More than any others, these two factors contribute to the widespread addiction to tobacco that we have been experiencing for many years. The companies know that an adolescent can be made to believe that he or she will never develop any of the dreaded diseases that the world knows are caused by cigarette smoking. They can also rely upon the adolescent's gullibility, in that he or she can be easily made to believe that smoking makes one more sexually attractive and helps one appear more mature. They also know that the best people to market their weeds are other adolescents in that the nonsmokers are likely to follow the smokers via their slavish need to go along with the group.

Group therapy can be an effective vehicle for counterbalancing these nefarious influences. The same process can be used to help smokers "kick the habit." They can be helped to appreciate that they can indeed die of the terrible diseases that cigarette smoking causes. They can be helped to appreciate that smoking does not necessarily make one look sexy or mature. Many youngsters can be brought to the point of admitting that they initially hated smoking but overcame their disgust because of their strong need for acceptance by their peers. And they can be helped to stop smoking by taking the advice of their nonsmoking peers in the group. Sometimes, in a discussion about dependency, I will sarcastically make comments such as: "That's the kind of person I am. I respect those people who live by the principle: If it's good enough for them, it's good enough for me. I'm a rubber stamp. I'm the kind of person who goes along with the crowd. If the crowd says it's all right, then I'll say it's all right." Generally, the youngsters get my message. This is another example of how the selective use of sarcasm can be used therapeutically. I believe that when my messages are provided in this vehicle, they have more clout than when stated directly.

Frank entered treatment at the age of 14 because of obsessive-compulsive rituals. These involved his having to perform acts twice that would generally be performed only once by others. If he closed the door behind him, he would have to return and open it, and then close it once again. When he turned off the television set, he would have to go back, put it on, and then turn it off again. The compulsion extended to a wide variety of everyday activities—resulting in severe tension, discomfort, and even depression. The symptoms were of six-months duration when he came for therapy.

After the first month of treatment I had absolutely no idea why Frank was having these symptoms. During the fifth week of treatment, his mother mentioned that when he was seven years old he had had sexual encounters with two girls, ages eight and nine. The girls initiated the game and involved him in an activity that closely approximated sexual intercourse. It wasn't until one year prior to the onset of treatment that Frank's mother learned about these two encounters (each time with the two girls) and they had been a source of guilt and embarrassment for him during the intervening years. Unfortunately, the mother's responses did not assuage his guilt. Rather, she made comments such as, "I'm really sorry you did such a thing," "I hope you won't do that again until you're married," and "If you'd only told me then, I would have told their mothers." I then concluded that an important element in Frank's compulsion was his attempt to assuage the guilt he felt over his sexual encounters. The onset of the symptoms at the time of puberty related to the enhanced sexual urges he was experiencing as well as the intensified guilt that he now felt after disclosing the experiences to his mother. He had hoped that she would help ease his guilt; unfortunately, she did the opposite.

Part of the therapeutic program involved helping Frank become more comfortable with his sexual urges. In one group meeting, Frank mentioned how "disgusting" girlie magazines were and, fortunately, the other members of the group disagreed with him. With some encouragement on my part, the group members admitted that they experienced sexual urges when looking at the pictures in such magazines and even masturbated while looking at them. The discussions with the group, as well as my own lengthy discussions with him (alone and/or with his parents), resulted in a diminution of Frank's guilt over his sexual urges and a concomitant diminution of his symptoms. His therapy ended after four months, at which time he was free of his compulsions.

Self-Esteem Enhancement

I have described elsewhere (Gardner, 1973a) the multiplicity of factors that contribute to the development of a high sense of self-worth. Low self-esteem is at the base of many (if not most) forms of psychogenic psychopathology and symptoms are well understood to serve in part to provide compensation for feelings of low self-worth. Accordingly, anything the therapist can do to bring about a genuine enhancement of self-esteem is likely to be therapeutic. The reader should note that I use the word genuine because artificial esteem-enhancing maneuvers, such as gratuitous praises, platitudes, etc., are likely to work in the opposite way. And there are certain elements in the group therapy process that are likely to enhance self-esteem and thereby serve the goals of therapy. Most patients who enter treatment, regardless of age, generally consider themselves to be unique with regard to their symptoms. They often anticipate that the therapist will be revolted when he or she hears about their problems. Simply reassuring a patient that his or her problems are common may be useful. However, when a group of one's peers provide such reassurances, they are likely to be accepted with greater conviction. Helping other youngsters with their problems is also likely to be esteem-enhancing. Similarly, gaining the respect of one's peers for one's advice regarding *their* problems is likely to contribute to the enhancement of a youngster's feeling of self-worth.

As discussed in detail in Chapter One, one of the purposes of treatment is to help patients deal better with the fundamental problems and conflicts of life with which we are all confronted. Getting information that enhances one's repertoire for dealing with these problems is esteem-enhancing. Knowledge is power and knowledge also enhances one's feelings of self-worth. After all, one is then more worthy because one is more capable of dealing with life's problems.

One area in which many patients can have useful, esteem-enhancing therapeutic experiences is in the realm of self-assertion. Such patients may avoid or remove themselves from a frustrating situation in which they are being taken advantage of rather than speak up and demand their rights. In the group, such avoidance is less possible. Others may make comments such as "Why do you sit there and let him talk that way to you?" and "How come you're not saying anything when she does that to you?" The therapist, as well, can encourage self-assertion with comments such as "You're saying nothing while he's screaming at you. Come on, tell me what thoughts are on your mind. What feelings are you having?" The patient is encouraged to talk about what he or she anticipates would happen if these thoughts and feelings are expressed. Although an intellectual discussion on how the anticipated repercussions will not be forthcoming might be useful, it is far more useful for the youngster to have the living experience that such expression does not result in these reactions. Of course, one must then go beyond the group and discuss the possibilities of such anticipated responses in the world outside the consultation room. The similarities and differences are delineated. The likelihood is that after a series of self-assertive experiences in the group, the youngster will be more comfortable expressing him- or herself beyond it.

One situation in which group role playing of this kind can be useful is the one in which a boy is hesitant to call up a girl for a date. He feels awkward regarding his knowledge of what to do and say and is quite fearful of rejection because of his ineptitude. A make-believe telephone call to one of the girls in the group can be particularly useful here. The boy is invited to make his initial statement. One girl is asked to respond. This interchange then serves as a point of departure for group discussion. In the course of such discussions the youngster learns the various ways to initiate the conversation and the various responses that the girl may make. These are roughly divided into those that indicate receptivity and those that indicate the opposite. Although such information can generally be provided in individual sessions, it is much more effective if the provider is an adolescent girl. She is generally viewed as a far greater expert on such matters than an adult therapist, even a female therapist.

Many youngsters in group therapy are shy about entering the dating scene. Here advice, pressure, and urging to desensitize can be useful for such youngsters. I recall one group's focusing on a forthcoming senior prom. At that time three boys in the group were quite inhibited regarding asking girls to the prom. Reassurances to them that there were certainly girls in their schools who would be most desirous of attending the prom did not help them overcome their reluctance and fears. During the same meeting there was a discussion of SAT scores. This group was particularly bright and many were applying to excellent schools. They were well versed with the format of examinations such as the SAT. In the ensuing discussion I told the group members that I was going to give them a multiple choice question, such as the kind one sees on the SATs. It was presented as a question to see how smart they were. The question:

> Which of the following courses of action would be the preferable one for a senior-high-school boy regarding attendance at his forthcoming prom?:
>
> a) Push through his fears. Ask a girl to go with him. Take her to the prom and have a good time dancing, feeling the closeness of her warm body against his, and possibly having a great time—both in and out of bed;
>
> b) Sitting at home alone, depressed, envying all the others at the prom because of the good time they're having and then ending up the evening by jerking off and going to sleep;
>
> c) Spending the evening with some other lonely, horny guys, all making believe that they're having a good time and trying to forget the fact that the others at the prom are probably enjoying themselves immensely;
>
> d) Going to the dance with another guy, one of you dressed as a girl;
>
> e) If you do not consider any of the above to be an appropriate answer, then state what you would consider to be a preferable way to spend the night—when all the others in your class are enjoying themselves immensely at the prom.

Last, as the group evolves into a cohesive unit (its openendedness notwithstanding, there are still some ongoing members at any given point) they develop a sense of camaraderie which can also be ego-enhancing. One develops an attachment to the group and a sense of loyalty to it and this makes one feel better about oneself by being a member of such a unit.

Encouraging Desensitization

Behavior modification can be viewed as nature's natural form of treatment. Long before psychiatry came on the scene, people were alleviating their untoward reactions to various traumas and stresses by reiteration and the associated desensitization that accompanies it. My main complaint about those who are deeply committed to behavior modification as the primary treatment modality is that they do not give proper attention to unconscious psychodynamic factors that are operative in bringing about symptoms. There are some behavior therapists who recognize that unconscious factors are operative but pay little if any attention to them in their therapeutic approach. And there are others who deny their existence entirely.

I believe that an optimum psychotherapeutic program gives serious attention to behavior modification as a therapeutic modality. However, it incorporates such techniques into the natural course of the treatment, without artificiality and without contrivance. In such a program one attempts to provide the patient with a desensitization process that goes naturally with the course of the treatment and the therapeutic experiences. It does not involve clip boards, score keeping, artificial and childlike rewards, or magic reinforcements. There is a place for conscious control and forcing oneself into anxiety-provoking situations in treatment. Whatever understanding one may have of underlying processes that are operative in bringing about one's symptoms, there is no question that the therapeutic approach must involve, as well, forcing oneself to tolerate painful and stressful situations and providing oneself with living experiences that work against the perpetuation of the pathological processes.

There is an overlap between behavior modification and role play. The overlap exists at the point where the role playing attempts to help desensitize an individual to an anxiety-provoking experience. My primary criticism of role play is its artificiality. There are therapists who will ask patients in a group to sit in different chairs as they make believe they are performing the part of various individuals. I find such play-acting contrived. I believe that one does better by merely asking questions like: "Imagine now that you are in your mother's position. What would she say to you if you just said that to her?" "I would like you now to imagine yourself in conversation with your father and he has just said to you what you told me. I'd like you to get some practice now and tell me what would be a good response to him under these circumstances." No body movements are requested; no artificial movements are advised; only a natural and somewhat spontaneous entry into the imagined conversation.

Dealing with a Breach of Confidentiality

As mentioned earlier, I generally make every attempt to respect the patient's confidentiality. In life and death matters and other serious situations, breach of confidentiality may be warranted. However, in such situations I generally follow a fixed sequence. First, I discuss with the patient alone the potential breach, which generally involves reporting selected information to the parents. I do everything possible to get the patient to discuss these issues directly with them. When that fails, we then turn to the group. Here, again, I try to enlist their aid in getting the patient to discuss the problem with his or her parents. If this fails, I then decide what information to provide the parents and what information not to.

I recall one situation in which a teenage girl became pregnant and was not going to tell her parents. She refused to discuss what she planned to do and I suspected she just wanted to deny the pregnancy entirely and hold off worrying about it until some future point. She was already two-months pregnant when I learned of her condition. I knew that the parents' religious beliefs would not have precluded an abortion. It was obvious, also, that the longer she held off telling them, the less the likelihood that this option would be available to her. After two weeks of group discussion, she still refused to tell her parents. At that point, I informed her that I would be telling them. Although she reacted with rage, I suspected that at some level she wanted me to divulge the pregnancy. I invited the parents into a session and gave the patient the choice of joining us or not. Whereas initially she said that she would not participate, she subsequently changed her mind and joined with them in the session. I knew the parents well enough to know that, although distressed by the news, they would not react with inappropriate or punitive measures. The girl was convinced that the "shit would hit the fan" (which it did) and that "they would flip out" (which they partially did) and that "horrendous things" would happen to her. Only the latter prediction did not prove true. Although the abortion was a psychologically stressful experience, her parents were sympathetic and understanding and did not add to her burdens (which is exactly what I had anticipated). By breach of the confidence I not only helped this girl deal with the pregnancy in a more judicious way but provided her with the living experience that her parents would not be so punitive as she had anticipated. In addition, the whole experience brought the family closer together, the nature of it notwithstanding. The girl did continue in treatment with me. Had she really not wanted her parents to know and had she genuinely felt that my divulging her pregnancy was a breach of her confidentiality, she probably would have discontinued treatment. This vignette provides another example of my view stated many times previously that adolescents often want to be coerced.

The reader who is interested in further information about group therapy in adolescents does well to refer to the articles by I.H. Berkovitz (1972), The American Psychiatric Association Task Force Report (1973), I.H. Berkovitz and M. Sugar (1975), I.D. Yalom (1975), I.A. Kraft (1979), and M.A. Riddle and L.A. Vitulano (1986).

EIGHT

WORK WITH PARENTS

As mentioned frequently throughout the course of this book, I work closely with the parents of my adolescent patients. On the one hand, adolescents do need individual work—especially because of their need for independence, autonomy, and relationships outside the home. On the other hand, therapists need ongoing contact with the patient's parents if they are to provide adolescents with a proper therapeutic program. In this chapter I elaborate on the ways in which the parental contribution enhances one's therapeutic efficiency. Therapists who allow adolescents to prohibit parental involvement in their therapeutic work are seriously compromising their treatment. Such involvement with the parents does not have to inhibit the adolescent's opportunity to develop autonomy within the stucture of the therapeutic program. Individual and group work with the adolescent is still certainly possible as the primary therapeutic modalities and these can contribute to the development of the youngster's growth toward independence.

THE VALUE OF THE THERAPIST-PARENT BOND IN ENHANCING AN ADOLESCENT'S TREATMENT

Parental participation can strengthen the therapist's relationship with the parents in many ways. And the stronger the parent's relationship with the therapist, the stronger is the patient's bond with the therapist likely to be. Seeing the therapist "in action" enables the parents to know firsthand exactly what is going on in the sessions. They are not left in the dark about the therapeutic procedure. In the traditional approach to treatment, in which parents are excluded from the therapy to a significant degree, parents are ignorant of what is going on, and this can be a source of irritation and alienation. This is especially the case when the parents are communicated with only to pay for the treatment. When they know exactly what they are spending their money for, they are less likely to harbor negative distortions and criticisms.

The effects of parental participation on the treatment are important and may be even more important than the specific way in which a parent can be useful to treatment. Whereas originally I was taught that such participation would compromise my relationship with the patient, my experience has been just the opposite. It is difficult to have a good relationship with someone who is a stranger, and whose only or primary contact is the monthly bill. Not only is such a situation likely to produce some alienation, but the paucity of contact increases the likelihood that negative distortions and misinterpretations about the therapist will not be corrected. Direct work with the parents provides them with opportunities to air their grievances, express their resentments and disappointments, ask questions, etc. This is the best way to prevent or resolve such problems. Both parents' feelings toward the therapist are extremely important in determining what the patient's feelings will be. A parent's animosity toward the therapist frequently, if not invariably, will be picked up by the patient. A dispute between the therapist and the parents will produce a loyalty conflict in the patient. Most often he or she will side with the parent. After all, the parents are providing the food, clothing, and shelter; they are the ones who are with the youngster the remaining hours of the week. The patient knows where his or her "bread is buttered," and it is extremely unlikely that the patient will, over time, basically support the therapist's position when it is in conflict with the parents'. Accordingly, anything that can improve the relationship between the therapist and the parents is likely to strengthen the tie between the therapist and the patient.

Most parents feel some guilt that their children require treatment. In fact, I would go further and say that parents who do not feel guilt about bringing their youngster to therapy probably have some deficiency in parenting capacity. Traditionally, therapists will try to assuage such guilt by reassuring the parents that they did their best at all points and that, in spite of their benevolent intentions, things went wrong. Such efforts of guilt mollification are not likely to prove useful, especially if the therapist then goes on to ask questions about child-rearing practices. These usually evoke even more guilt as the parents' deficiencies become exposed. When, however, the parent becomes involved directly in the therapeutic process, the guilt associated with the child's involvement in treatment is likely to be lessened. After all, the parents are now working actively in turning around and reducing the problems over which they feel guilty. Therapists who deprive parents of this opportunity deprive them, as well, of a mechanism for reducing their guilt.

PARENTAL COUNSELING REGARDING THE PATIENT

The work with parents that I will be describing in this chapter is most appropriately called *parental counseling*. Such counseling is offered at the outset as part of "the therapeutic package." Most often this is done at the same time that the youngster is present. In this way the patients are given the opportunity for active input into the parental decisions being made about them. If such counseling is done without the patient's participation, there is the risk that the treatment will be seriously compromised. The adolescent's awareness that meetings are taking place behind his or her back—meetings which are secret from the patient—inevitably produces distrust of both therapist and parents and this will compromise treatment. The vast majority of parents welcome such counseling because they invariably have questions regarding how they should deal with their adolescents. Parents who come to me from other therapists, who have excluded them to a significant degree from the therapeutic process, are even more pleased with the opportunity to meet with me regarding their youngster. Although I believe that many therapists exclude the parents because of their firm belief that their involvement will compromise the adolescent's autonomy and thereby be antitherapeutic, I believe that there are therapists who exclude parents because of their own ineptitude and fear of being observed in their work.

Counseling Parents of the Adolescent Who Tries to Preclude Their Involvement in Treatment

There are adolescents who will tell their parents that a proviso of their entering into treatment is that the parents will have absolutely no contact at all with the therapist. I will have no part of such an arrangement. I cannot think of a healthy reason for such a restriction. Invariably it represents an attempt on the youngster's part to prevent the parents' input into the treatment, input that might "smoke out" the adolescent's fabrications or otherwise expose schemes which the adolescent would like to perpetrate with the therapist. On one occasion, many years ago, when I was young and naive in these things, I did agree to see a 15-year-old girl who I was told by the referring physician would see me with the understanding that I would have no contacts at all with the parents. Earlier in this book I described what occurred during this girl's "therapy." In short, she was completely silent and I discontinued the treatment after a few sessions. I subsequently learned that, after refusing to go to treatment, her father had stupidly bribed her with $15 for every session she attended. I only learned this from the referring doctor after I had discontinued treatment because of my conclusion that it was a total waste of time and her father's money.

On occasion, I have received telephone calls from parents who recognize that their youngster needs therapy and state that the adolescent absolutely refuses to come, even for a consultation. After hearing something about the problem, I will generally make one of two recommendations. Sometimes I will tell the parents that they should insist upon the youngster's coming for the consultation with the threat that if he or she does not, certain restrictions and disciplinary measures will be imposed. I make this recommendation in those situations in which I think that the youngster needs some kind of coercion as a face-saving device for coming to the session. At other times I may decide that such a threat is unwarranted or it has proven not to work. In those cases I will advise the parents to set up the appointment and advise the youngster that they themselves will attend and he or she is invited to do so as well. In addition, I advise them to inform the youngster that decisions will be made that will affect him or her and it therefore behooves the youngster to attend if he or she is to have any input into those decisions. When even this doesn't work, I will see the parents alone and give them advice. I provide whatever advice I can and set up another session at which the adolescent is again invited to attend. Sometimes the parental feedback motivates the youngster to participate and thereby protect his or her rights. Generally, after two or three such sessions, if the adolescent still does not attend, we reach a point of diminishing returns and then I may see them again only on a request basis.

Parental Ambivalence About the Adolescent's Treatment

Parental involvement in a child's treatment is, at best, tenuous. Although parents may profess commitment to the therapeutic process, they are generally quite ambivalent and their mixed feelings about the treatment may interfere significantly with its progress and even result in their prematurely terminating therapy. In this section I discuss some of the more common reasons for impaired parental commitment to the therapeutic process. An understanding of these factors can be useful in increasing the likelihood that the therapist will be able to engage the parents more successfully and thereby increase the likelihood of the youngster's involvement in treatment. Some of the more common ways in which parental resistance exhibits itself: lateness to the sessions, canceling sessions for frivolous or weak reasons, forgetting to follow through with the therapist's recommendations, complaining to the patient about treatment (its cost, time consumption, etc.), and withholding payment (ultimately one of the most predictable ways to bring about a cessation of therapy).

The Cost of Treatment Compromised parental commitment to therapy is often caused by the financial privation that it may involve. This is especially the case when the youngster is in private treatment. Whereas initially the parents may agree to commit themselves to the cost involved, when the bills start coming they often have a change of heart and remove the child prematurely from therapy or support the patient's resistances, which are inevitably present. Because the services the therapist provides are not tangible, the parents are likely to consider it a waste of money much earlier than they would after receiving other medical services.

The Expenditure of Time The parent who brings the patient (more often the mother) can generally think of better ways of spending her time. If she has other children and cannot afford housekeepers, then bringing the patient to treatment may become an additional burden. Here again, these extra pressures compromise her commitment to the therapeutic process. I have had a number of parents who were initially enthusiastic about treatment, even though travel to my office involved a significant expenditure of time. Initial enthusiasm, however, waned when they actually experienced the drainage on their time and energy that such trips involved. Accordingly, I will generally see people who come from great distances for consultation only and discourage strongly their committing themselves to an extended therapeutic program. The patient also is likely to be drained of energy by a long trip and will thereby not be a good candidate for therapeutic sessions.

Parental Guilt Most parents experience guilt when the therapist advises them that their child needs treatment. They consider it proof that they somehow failed in the child's upbringing (H.S. Lippman, 1962). A common way that parents assuage such guilt is to rationalize withdrawal of the child from treatment. This is done either overtly or covertly. After all, if they can justify removing the youngster from treatment, especially if they can believe that he or she does not need it, they thereby absolve and even obviate their guilt. Therapists should tell such parents that they appreciate that at every point in the child's development the parents did what they considered to be in the child's best interests (usually the case) and that through misguidance and/or unfortunate circumstances, and/or the unavoidable effects of their own difficulties, their child developed psychiatric problems. Furthermore, the therapist does well to advise such parents that, at the present state of our knowledge, we do not understand all the factors that contribute to a child's psychiatric difficulties. Thus, even if they themselves had no psychiatric problems, and even if there had been no detrimental circumstances, and even if they had assiduously followed the best available advice, their child might still have developed difficulties (J.W. Kessler, 1966). Moreover, they must be helped to appreciate that innate temperamental factors may be contributing significantly to the patient's problems (A. Thomas, S. Chess et al., 1963). My experience has been that a discussion of these factors can often be useful in reducing parental guilt and thereby increasing the likelihood that they will support the patient's therapy.

One of the most effective ways of reducing parental guilt and the resistances that emerge from it is to have the parents participate actively in the patient's treatment. They are thereby helping "undo" what they have "done." By working closely with the parents, the therapist is more likely to develop a good relationship with them. The patient will sense the parents' feelings about the therapist and will then be more likely to develop such involvement him or herself. When parents have a good relationship with the therapist, they are more comfortable expressing resentments and disagreements. The failure to express such differences and complaints is one of the most common sources of parental resistance to the youngster's treatment and removal of the patient from it.

The Therapist's Alienation of the Parent as a Contribution to Parental Ambivalence Therapists who believe that it is their role to protect adolescent patients from the indignities suffered at the hands of their parents are likely to alienate parents. The preferable position should be one of impartiality. The therapist should be viewed by all family members as someone who criticizes the parents when such criticism is warranted and, similarly, criticizes the youngster, again when warranted. The therapist's criticisms, however, should be benevolent and he or she should not "keep score" regarding who is getting more or less. The therapist neither takes the side of parent or child; rather, he or she supports the side of healthy behavior regardless of who exhibits it. Therapists who distance themselves from the parents, who view the parents' involvement as a compromise of the youngster's treatment, and whose only contact with the parents is the monthly bill are also likely to alienate them. Such distance-making operations deprive them of the opportunity for asking questions, expressing disappointments, and voicing resentments. Problems between the parents and the therapist then become unresolved and this can ultimately result in their removing the child from treatment.

Therapy as a Potential Disruption of a Pathological Parent-Child Bond Another common source of parental resistance to treatment derives from the situation in which the parent may not genuinely want the patient to be relieved of his or her presenting symptoms, despite claims to the contrary. The patient's problems may play an important role in the family equilibrium. For example, the overprotective mother may want her child with separation anxiety disorder to stay at home and may undermine the therapist's efforts to get the child back to school (R.A. Gardner, 1984). Parents of delinquent youngsters often gain vicarious gratification from their adolescents's antisocial acting out (A.M. Johnson, 1949, 1959; R.L. Stubblefield, 1967). Ostensibly parents may want their youngster to do better academically but, unconsciously, may undermine the treatment because they fear that the child will surpass them educationally and socioeconomically. I once had a patient, the child of such parents, who came into treatment because of a severe block in achieving academic success. He had a recurrent dream in which he was walking up a mountain on a treadmill. He kept trying to move ahead but got nowhere. The dream was a symbolic statement of a neurotic compromise, both for himself and his parents. On the one hand, he could tell his parents that he was trying harder (something they allegedly wanted him to do). On the other hand, he could point out that he was getting nowhere (in compliance with their unconscious wishes).

Parental Jealousy of the Therapist Many parents become jealous of the patient's intimate relationship with the therapist and may act out such feelings by undermining the treatment. They may consider themselves to have been the ones to have done all the "dirty work": changed the diapers, taken the child to the pediatrician at all hours of the night, and made the hundreds of other sacrifices necesssary for successful child rearing. Yet the therapist is "the good guy" who is viewed by the youngster as benevolent, kind, and sympathetic. Often the parents are threatened by the anxiety-provoking revelations about themselves that inevitably emerge in the patient's treatment, and the desire to avoid these can contribute to their impaired commitment to the process.

It behooves therapists to appreciate these and the multiplicity of other factors that may contribute to the parental undercommitment to the therapeutic process and even removal of a youngster from treatment. The therapist should try to detect these compromising factors during the initial evaluation and deal with them at the outset. Otherwise, they may cause a compromise and even a cessation of the therapy.

COMMON ADVICE GIVEN PARENTS OF ADOLESCENT PATIENTS

Differentiating Between the Controllable and the Uncontrollable

I, like most psychiatrists, have at times had the thought of putting on my walls some important proverbs, maxims, and old sayings that are likely to prove useful to my patients. Most of us recognize that it is unwise to do this because such statements might serve as contaminants to the therapeutic process, especially to free associations in psychoanalytic therapy. There is, however, one quotation on my wall. I place it there because it is probably the most common advice I give to my adult patients and the parents of my adolescent patients. Rather than merely repeat it each time, I take the plaque off the wall and show it to the parents. Most often they are familiar with it. The advice is in the form of a little prayer attributed to the theologian, Reinhold Niebuhr:

> Give me the serenity
> to accept the things I cannot change,
> the courage to change the things I can;
> and the wisdom to know the difference.

Actually, this is an ancient wisdom and its antecedents are to be found in the Bible. The parents of adolescents, especially, have to become strong adherents to this dictum. Otherwise, they are doomed to lead very frustrating lives. The implementation of this philosophy is expressed well in the statement a parent might make to a daughter with antisocial problems after being counseled by me on a number of occasions:

> Dr. Gardner's right. One of my problems has been that I haven't differentiated between the things that I can control and the things that I can't control. And I've got them straight now. And you'd better get them straight also. I can control what happens in this house, but I can't control what happens outside it. First, *I decide* who comes into this house. Those new friends of yours are *bad news*. I refuse to let them in my house. You state often that this is your house, but it's not. It's my house and we permit you to live here. I decide who comes into this house and those low-life characters are not entering this home. What you do with them outside I can't control. But I can tell you this: they spell *trouble*. The more you hang around with them, the more difficulty you're going to have in your life.
>
> Next, with regard to your hiding illegal substances in this house, you have no privacy. As long as I think that you're hiding drugs here, I have every right to search through your drawers and do whatever I want with any illegal substances I find. Your claims for privacy are merely a way of hiding the drugs you've been using. And when I find them, I'll flush them down the toilet. I don't care how expensive they are. When I no longer think you're hiding drugs, then I'll respect your privacy. Respecting your privacy now is just contributing to your drug problem.

Your father and I have been making idiots of ourselves by trying to find out where you go at night. You told us last week that you were staying over Joan's house. We called Joan and she told us that she hadn't seen you in a week. Once again, you lied to us. Then, like idiots, we started calling other homes and even woke up people at one and two in the morning. They have every right to be furious with us and we're not going to do that any more. We are also not going to run around town like crazy people looking for you in parks and parking lots. That was insane. We're cutting that out. We know that you're screwing around and we're petrified that you're going to get some disease or get pregnant. Know this, though, if you do get a disease you're the one who's going to suffer much more than we. And if you do get pregnant, you too will have a much greater burden than we. If you get an abortion, you'll have to live with the knowledge that you scraped out your own kid. And if you keep the baby, then you're going to screw up your life with your new dependent. And if you give it away, you'll live with the knowledge that somewhere, someplace, there's a child of yours–a child you gave away to a stranger. You'll have to live with your guilt. What way do you win on that one?

We don't know what you're so angry about. We know that what you've been doing the last couple of years relates to anger at us, more than anyone else. Sure we've made mistakes; but we certainly don't deserve this. Let's say that you get the extreme vengeance you want. You'll have your father and I rolling around on the floor, tearing our hair out, crying out eyes out, and beating ourselves. So what, then, will you have accomplished? Yes, you will have gotten vengeance, but what you are *not* considering is what you have to do to yourself in order to get it. What you are blind to is the fact that you're fouling up your own life in order to hurt us. All you see is the vengeful gratification, and you don't see the *self*-destructive aspect of what you're doing.

And there's one more thing for you to think about, and that is Dr. Gardner's *kidney transplant principle.* Of the five billion people on earth, who do you think will be on line at the hospital if you ever needed a kidney transplant? Give that some thought when you shit on us!

Of course, a parent is not going to make this speech after the first counseling session. However, a number have been able to make it following a series of sessions that prove that they have conviction for what was said therein. Not only does it contain the message of differentiation between what can be controlled and not controlled by a parent but it provides a youngster with some important insights about what he or she is doing as well.

Differentiating Between Normal and Abnormal Behavior and Dealing with Noxious Normal Behavior

A common problem for parents of adolescent patients, especially for the first youngster to achieve that status, is that of differentiating between normal and abnormal behavior. Although many parents may have read books on the subject and heard about the fact that adolescents often become rebellious during this phase of their life, they often forget what they have learned when it comes to their own youngsters. Accordingly, parents have to be helped to appreciate that a certain amount of rebellious behavior is normal (and even desirable) and they must not take too seriously many of their youngster's criticisms and denigratory comments. I often tell parents that "you've got to thicken your skin." Furthermore, I may also say, "Every parent expects to have to change diapers for a new baby. This is an expected part of the child-rearing process. Similarly, you have to accept the fact that your adolescent is going to shit on you and that too is an expected part of the child-rearing process." Many of the problems that the parents have to deal with result form their difficulties in making these differentiations.

An example is the parents' attitude toward the adolescent's room. Typically, these youngsters are comfortable living in pigsties. I generally advise parents to accept that it is normal for adolescents to be comfortable living as pigs. They should allow the youngster to assume this lifestyle *in his or her own room only*. This does not, however, mean that adolescents should be allowed to create health hazards. They can leave their books, clothing, etc. on the floor or wherever else in their room they decide to leave their "droppings." However, they cannot allow food to decay in their rooms because of the obvious attraction to vermin and the creation of other health hazards. Under those circumstances there must be certain restrictions imposed as well as disciplinary measures utilized (see below).

With regard to leaving clothing in other parts of the house, I advise parents that it is normal for adolescent youngsters to leave a trail of garments as they race through the house. The best solution to this problem is for the parent to pick these up in a bundle and dump them on the floor of the adolescent's room. Of course, clothing on the floor of the room is not then picked up and cleaned by the parents. Rather, the rule of the house is that the only clothing that is cleaned by the parents is that which is placed in the hamper or other designated spot. At some point the youngster will run out of clothes and then have the choice of wearing dirty ones, going out naked, or placing all clothing in the proper receptacle.

It is also normal for adolescents in our society to want to play their stereos at ear-splitting levels. Most communities have ordinances prohibiting such noise (I have no hesitation using that term to refer to much of their so-called "music") after 11:00 p.m. However, this may not be enforced. But even if it is, this does not protect the family throughout the earlier evening from the devastating effects of the cacophony. Telling adolescents that listening to music at such levels is likely to bring about hearing loss and ultimately (in many cases) tinnitus (ringing in the ears) is not likely to prove useful. Because of their delusions of invulnerability, they are not likely to believe that this will happen to them. Telling them that those who play in rock bands already have hearing loss and they keep playing the music louder because they cannot hear it at lower levels, also does not help. One partial solution is to have the youngster listen only with earphones. Although this may provide the family with some peace, it increases markedly the likelihood that the youngster will damage his or her own ears. Warnings that this is likely to occur will generally not be "heard." Some youngsters, however, who insist that earphones compromise their musical enjoyment, will insist nevertheless on blasting their music. A simple solution to this problem is for the parents to take the stereo player and lock it in the trunk of his or her car. After two or three weeks of such privation, the youngster is likely to "remember" to play the music lower.

Discipline and Punishment

The word discipline is derived from the Latin *discipulus*, which means a disciple or a student. The word emphasizes the educative value of the disciplinary measure to the wrongdoer. The word punishment is derived from the Latin word *punire* which means to punish, but which has the connotation of the infliction of pain on the wrongdoer. The emphasis is on penalty and retribution. D.J. Holmes, in his excellent book on adolescent psychotherapy (1964) states: "Discipline, though aggressively energized, denotes a complex of attitudes and actions which is consciously intended to help people live more effectively and, in the long run, more happily. Punishment, in contrast with discipline, denotes a type of action which is primarily motivated by the wish to hurt, cause pain, retaliate in the spirit of vengeance. It is much closer to the acting out of primitive, infantile wishes to destroy and cause pain....No reliable decision can be made about whether a given act is disciplinary or punitive by knowing only the nature of the action. This decision turns instead upon knowing something of the individual's predominant motives for behaving as he does....This distinction between discipline and punishment in no way diminishes the ease with which one may rationalize flagrantly sadistic, destructive actions as being for the victim's 'own good.' "

Obviously, it is preferable that the parents use disciplinary measures when dealing with their adolescents. However, we are all human and the provocations of the adolescent are such that, at times, it is reasonable to expect that parents will be implementing measures that can more appropriately be called punishments. One of the important differentiating criteria between these two is the degree of anger and rage exhibited by the parent when implementing the restriction. The more the rage, the more likely the term punishment is applicable.

It is important for parents to appreciate that all children and adolescents need limits. They are not born with some inner knowledge as to what is right, wrong, good, or bad. (The reader will note that I have no hesitation using such words, even though they are considered to be injudicious by many people in our field. I generally do not like euphemisms. Those who abhor the word *bad* believe that its use lowers the child's self-esteem and may easily be interpreted to indicate that the child is intrinsically and perenially defective. I do not believe this. A loving person who uses the word and who does not basically feel that it has the aforementioned implications will not produce the kinds of ego-debasing responses that are anticipated by those who strictly avoid the word's utilization.) One way of learning what the limits are is to do something bad and then see what the parental reaction will be. In this way the child "learns" what he or she can get away with. It is the far more common procedure than that of asking the simple question of whether or not a certain thing can be done. It appears that the child knows him- or herself that experience teaches much better than an intellectual statement. Not only do children need limits but they generally need strong limits. I often say: "Benevolent despotism is the best system of government for children and other primitive peoples." (Please give me credit for this.) Parents must be somewhat despotic with their children, they must be hardnosed at times, and they must be firm. Parents who "respect" their children to the degree that they do not learn the rules of society are not creating a healthy atmosphere for them. More important, they are not helping them adjust to a world that will not be indulgent and tolerant of their alienating behavior.

It is extremely important that parents avoid using empty threats. If a parent is going to use a statement such as "I won't tolerate that," the parent does well to have some backup action behind it. Otherwise, the threat is meaningless, and the youngster soon learns that it is not to be taken seriously. A related phenomenon is threatening punishments that are so Draconian that they will never be implemented in their entirety. For example, the parent may threaten a youngster with no television for a month for a certain transgression. The youngster knows that there is no way the parent is going to be monitoring the television for a month, especially because there are three sets in the house. Knowing that it cannot or will not be implemented makes the threat empty and contributes to the youngster's ignoring it. Of course, if there is one television set in the house, this can be conveniently locked in the trunk of the car (with the aforementioned stereo set). Even then the parent does well to keep it there for a month or else make more reasonable threats. But, if this threat deprives the parent him- or herself of television viewing, then the parent must suffer along with the youngster (unless the parent has a way of watching television inside the trunk of the car).

I am a very strong proponent of the demerit system as a

disciplinary measure. The system allows one to get significant mileage from the disciplinary plan. Specifically, a particular desired activity is set up as a goal. An example might be a boy's attending a special football game on Sunday. On the evening of the previous Sunday the youngster can be told that he will not be permitted to attend the game if he gets three demerits a day, or 21 demerits over the course of the week. If the youngster gets more than three on Monday, then the parent starts working on Tuesday. And, once 21 demerits are received, the child will be told that he will definitely not be attending the game on the weekend. The ticket may then be either sold or given to another party. It is best that such demerits be non-negotiable, i.e., one should not be able to work them off by good behavior. Otherwise the parent gets into a game of manipulations that may make the whole system inoperative. One of the beauties of the system is that it enables the parent to get a lot of mileage out of it and utilize it for a whole series of transgressions. If one simply deprives the child of the football game after one transgression, then one may have to come up with 20 more deprivations to get the same effect.

There are many youngsters, especially those with severe antisocial behavior, for whom "nothing works." In Vol. III (1999b) I will discuss in detail the approaches to such youngsters.

The College Disease

Earlier in this book I have commented on what I refer to as the *college disease* that many parents suffer from and the plethora of so-called educational institutions that have sprung up in order to provide an educational product for these purchasers. The "students" who attend these so-called educational institutions generally view their sojourns there as just a winter camp experience which alternates with summer recreational programs. What they most often learn there are some new sexual techniques, what their tolerance for alcohol is, and perhaps some new drugs that they haven't tried before. They also learn how easy it is to get a college diploma.

Some parents in this category bring their adolescents for treatment because of poor academic motivation. These youngsters often attend schools where the educational standards are quite low and they are automatically moved ahead every year and then dropped off the edge of the system when they complete the twelfth grade. Some, however, are in more demanding high schools, but they still have little commitment to the educational process. Sometimes the youngster's lack of motivation is indeed related to intrafamilial and intrapsychic problems. At other times, the youngster is merely one of a stream of hundreds of thousands who are moving along an educational system track that demands little and provides even less. Their teachers are uncommitted and unmotivated, watch the clock, do not give homework (homework for the student is homework for the teacher), and so do not provide models for their students – models of people who are "turned on" by learning.

Whatever the cause of the youngster's impaired academic motivation, I often tell such parents that my treatment is not likely to work as long as the youngster knows that, whatever happens, he or she will still go on to college. I ask them if they have the guts to make a bona fide threat, a threat that will under no circumstances be withdrawn. I ask them if they will say to the youngster that if he or she does not show significant improvement in academic motivation that under no circumstances will he or she go to college for four years of nonlearning and self-indulgence. I advise them to warn the youngster that grades themselves will not be the only criterion to ascertain whether or not the youngster is deserving of college. This is important because of the grade inflation that exists in our school systems as well as the capacity of youngsters to manipulate their teachers into giving them higher grades. Rather, the criteria that will be used will be SAT scores and the parents' own observations of the youngster's commitment to learning and the educational process. It is best to leave this vague. To use as a criterion a certain number of hours of homework per night is not useful because the youngster may easily satisfy this requirement with feigned commitment to homework. I warn the parents that they should not make this threat unless they intend to follow it through. I generally advise them to think about it for a week of two and discuss it in detail before making it. I tell them also that they do well to have a plan of operation if the youngster does not indeed go to college.

My experience has been that most parents do not make this threat. They just don't have the "balls" to do it. The notion that their youngster should not go to college is one that is painful, if not impossible, for them to behold. They would consider it humiliating if their child did not have a so-called "higher education." They don't know how they could face their friends. They point out other youngsters who entered college with the same lack of motivation and then turned around at some point along the program. I agree that such youngsters exist, but my experience has been that they are a relative minority.

Some parents of unmotivated adolescents believe that the problem lies in the school and the solution is to transfer to another school. This rarely works. I try to emphasize to such parents that the problem lies in the youngster's head and not in the building in which the learning is taking place. Although stories about people such as Abraham Lincoln and others who learned significantly under conditions of privation may seem cliché, they should still be told. Again, many parents do not follow my advice, spend a lot of money in a special private school, and still find that the youngster is not particularly motivated. When I see an adolescent who is already in the first year of one of these "colleges," is getting low marks (even with grade inflation and limited standards), I generally advise the parents to tell the youngster they are no longer going to "piss away" their money on him or her. I advise them to remove the youngster from school and have him or her go out into the workplace for six months or a year and then rethink the whole college decision. Out in the "real world" the youngster is in a better position to make decisions regarding education vs. other options. In addition, if the youngster is really motivated to go to school, then he or she should be willing to work to contribute toward tuition. Regardless of the affluence of the parents, such youngsters do well to contribute a reasonable fraction of their educational expenses. Such requirement helps separate the truly motivated from the jokers. Unfortunately, most parents with the college disease do not accept this advice.

On occasion, I will see a youngster who is a high school or even college dropout who stays at home and does nothing. The parents are not complaining so much about the fact that the youngster is not getting an education (they are long past that point); they are now complaining about the fact that they have a "parasite" on their hands. And indeed, they do. The kid sits around the house all day, watches television, listens to music, and bullshits with friends. Although in his or her late teens, the youngster is functioning at the three-year-old level. Most often (but not always) there has been a longstanding past history of significant indulgence. And this indulgence must be dealt with at the present time. The parents have to be advised to make life tough for such youngsters. No services should be provided. Such youngsters should be required to cook their own meals, purchase their food, do their own laundry, and be made uncomfortable in many other ways. If possible, television sets should be removed and certainly stereo players. Rather the youngster should be provided, as much as possible, with an atmosphere of sensory deprivation. Even telephone services should be restricted and cut off when possible. Otherwise, the youngster is going to sink into a chronic state of morbid dependency on the parents. Again, many of these parents are not capable of following through with these recommendations, so deeply entrenched is their overprotectiveness.

WAYS IN WHICH PARENTS (USUALLY THE MOTHER) CAN BE USEFUL IN AN ADOLESCENT'S INDIVIDUAL SESSIONS

I generally advise the parent who brings the patient (usually the mother) to sit in the waiting room during the course of the session. I discourage her from leaving, taking a walk, or shopping because I may want her at a moment's notice to participate in the session. Although fathers are most often not available to join the sessions, I invite them to feel free to attend, without prior notification, any session that they might be available. My experience has been that this occurs from five to ten percent of the time. As I do with children, I generally refer to the parents as my "therapeutic assistants."

When an adolescent is talkative, I generally start the session with him or her alone. If the adolescent is not likely to "start the ball rolling" so quickly, I will often bring the mother in at the beginning of the session. I still start with the open-ended question to the youngster to say what's on his or her mind. However, if nothing is forthcoming, I then turn to the mother and invite her to bring up some issue. Most often, she has something to tell me. If she also has nothing to say, I then ask the two of them to try to refresh their memories regarding why the youngster was brought to treatment in the first place. Generally, this question will result in useful material on which the patient, mother, and I can focus. However, if even then both have nothing to say I will suggest that we review the presenting symptoms and discuss the youngster's progress at that point. Usually, residual symptoms are present and we then use their manifestations as a point of departure for discussion.

On occasion there will have been signficant alleviation of the presenting symptoms. In such cases, the question of reducing the frequency of sessions and even discontinuing treatment is discussed. The therapist must appreciate that there are some parents who continue to bring their youngster to treatment even after the patient is asymptomatic or almost so. Bringing the youngster to therapy becomes routinized and the parents may believe that, even though symptom free, the therapist is seeing things that they don't which warrant further treatment. There are therapists, of course, who believe that one should continue seeing asymptomatic patients. This is especially true of classical psychoanalysts who will treat on the basis of their decision that underlying psychodynamic factors, even though unconcscious, warrant treatment until they too become normal. The fact that such human beings do not exist does not deter these individuals from recommending ongoing treatment. In some cases the therapists have genuine conviction for what they are doing; in other cases they are simply exploiting gullible people. I am not claiming that I immediately discontinue treatment as soon as the patient is relatively free of symptoms. I will still recommend some ongoing contact in order to be sure that the changes brought about by the treatment are becoming entrenched into the psychic structure. But even then I will generally cut down on the frequency of sessions.

The presence of the mother in the room enables the therapist to observe mother-child interactions that would not have otherwise been seen. The modes of interaction that we utilize in our relationships with other people are derived from the types of involvements we have established with our parents in earliest childhood. The reproduction of these in psychoanalytic treatment is often referred to as *the development of the transference neurosis*. By bringing in a parent one can observe firsthand the original modes of interaction of which the transference neurosis is a derivative. Observing it in its "pure form" puts the therapist in a better position to understand it. In addition, one can learn directly from the parent—the individual who initiated the particular mode of interaction—exactly what factors were operative in bringing about the particular pattern.

The presence of the parent in the room increases the likelihood that more experiences will take place that will be therapeutically useful. For example, a youngster may fear that a parent's reaction to a particular divulgence will be extremely punitive. The therapist may believe that the adolescent's anticipation of dire consequences is an exaggeration and unnecessarily pessimistic. Verbal reassurances are not likely to work very well. Encouraging the youngster to provide the divulgences between sessions is certainly a better idea, but if the youngster's resistences are strong, he or she will "forget" or claim that he or she was "too busy" to follow up on the homework assignment. By bringing the parent in immediately, after minimal discussion, the youngster can have a firsthand experience regarding the anticipation of formidable parental retaliation. Although we may discuss the pros and cons of the parent's joining us for a few minutes, I generally do not prolong the discussion. My experience has been that the longer one talks about it the more difficult it may be for the youngster to avail him- or herself of the experience. Rather, I discuss it briefly and then, unless the adolescent argues vehemently against the parent's participation, I bring the parent in and proceed quickly with the issues at hand. Before the youngster knows what has happened to him or her, an experience is provided which proves, better than anything I could say, that the anticipated repercussions were not forthcoming. But this is only one example. Any possible type of interpersonal interaction can be useful in the treatment, provide grist for the therapeutic mill, and, when properly monitored, provide corrective emotional experiences.

The mother's observations of the ways in which I handle the youngster, especially when the patient is being difficult, can be useful to her because it provides a model for dealing with these situations herself. (I am not claiming that I always handle every situation in the most judicious fashion. However, I believe that I do so more frequently than most of my patients' parents.)

Sometimes, a mother can be useful in helping analyze a patient's dream. This is more often true with prepubertal patients, but she can also be useful in the analysis of an adolescent's dream, especially a younger adolescent. The therapist should certainly obtain as many associations as possible from the patient. This, of course, is the best way of determining exactly what a dream figure symbolizes for the youngster. However, when the patient provides only a paucity of associations to the dream symbols, the mother's input may be valuable. She can ask the youngster questions about the figure and she can often be a better interrogator than the therapist because she may have some hunches about what is important. And, when this fails, her specific and direct comments about the dream figure(s) can often provide the therapist with useful information for understanding the dream.

One of the important roles of a parent in an adolescent's session relates to keeping the youngster honest. The main reason why adolescents are reluctant to have their parents participate in their sessions is that they fear that the parent will confront them with their fabrications and bring them to the attention of their therapist. Adolescents would much prefer to "sell their therapists a bill of goods" in which the therapist is duped into believing every one of the youngster's distortions and complaints about the parents. The therapist is generally not witness to the events the youngster describes; the parent often is. Accordingly, the parent is in a far better position to "smoke out" the youngster's lies. I wish to emphasize again that the presence and participation of the parents does not usually compromise the therapist-patient relationshp with the youngster—although this is what I had been taught, and this is what many still believe. The basic determinant of the relationship between the therapist and the child is their own personalities. A healthy mother does not believe that her relationship with her first child will be significantly compromised by the appearance of the second or third. No competent therapist would advise a parent to have only one child, lest the relationship with the first be compromised by the appearance of a second. No healthy mother strictly excludes the father's presence on those occasions when she is with her child, with the argument that it will compromise her relationship with her son or daughter. It is not the presence of one or a few others in the room that is the primary determinant of the relationship between two people. The relationship depends more on qualities that exist within and between the two of them. Therapists who strictly adhere to the traditional view—wherein third party participation in the adolescent session is viewed as therapeutically detrimental—may be providing the patient with an antitherapeutic experience. This view expresses, both explicitly and implicitly, the notion that exclusivity is crucial for a good relationship. This can only engender possessiveness, egocentricity, intolerance for sharing, excessive dependency, and other untoward reactions.

SITUATIONS IN WHICH THE PARENT'S INVOLVEMENT IN THE TREATMENT IS CONTRAINDICATED

Excessively Punitive and Sadistic Parents

There are certain situations in which parental involvement in the adolescent's treatment may be contraindicated. These are relatively uncommon but still worthy of mention. Most parents can be relied upon not to punish the youngster for revelations made during the joint session with them. However, some parents are so disturbed that they will use such revelations as an excuse for sadistic and brutal retaliation. It is preferable that such parents not be involved in the therapy, except possibly at the most superficial level. There are also parents who will react with Draconian measures to an adolescent's sexual involvement, no matter how superficial. They are so fanatic in their reactions that it is probably best not to involve them in any discussions directly or even indirectly related to the youngster's sexual activities.

Psychologically Fragile Parents

Some parents are so psychologically fragile that they cannot tolerate the criticisms and other forms of negative feedback that would come their way during the joint therapeutic sessions. This is especially the case for parents who are psychotic or borderline. Such a parent may be so defensive that he or she would not be able to handle many of the therapeutic revelations, even though expressed symbolically. Were the parent to sense the underlying meaning of a hostile symbol, it could be ego-debasing and precipitate psychological deterioration. Involvement of such a parent in the youngster's therapy could be considered cruel and would be likely to alienate significantly both the parent and the patient. Any benefits that the youngster might derive from the parent's presence might be more than offset by the possible compromise of the therapist-patient relationship caused by such exposure. In addition, such benefits might also be obviated by the parental psychiatric deterioration and its resultant compromise of parenting capacity. This is not a common situation, but I mention it because it does occur..

Parents Who Exhibit Formidable Hostility Toward the Therapist

There are parents who are extremely hostile, and such hostility might be exhibited toward the therapist. All therapists must accept the fact that they must tolerate a certain amount of parental hostility. I am discussing here those who exhibit more than the usual amount of hostility that is often directed toward therapists. No matter how hard the therapist tries, such parents never seem to be satisfied. No amount of explanation or discussion seems to reduce their hostility. Yet, such parents may bring their children for therapy. When they are invited to participate actively in the youngster's treatment, they may use the opportunity for the collection of ammunition, for example, "Is this what I'm spending all my money on?—to have you tell him exactly what I tell him?" "How is answering questions about whether or not he gets along with other kids going to help him obey me at home?" and "My husband is right: psychiatry is just a lot of bullshit!" Such parents tend to "cramp my style" when I am working under their observation and scrutiny. I have the feeling that everything I say is going to be used as ammunition against me. Attempts to discuss their negative attitudes often prove futile. Accordingly, I have found it in the patient's best interests to have such parents sit in the waiting room or go out shopping. Although I am deprived of their input, such loss is more than counterbalanced by the enhanced efficiency of the individual therapeutic process with the patient. It is the lesser of the two detrimental alternatives. Therapy, like life, often boils down to such a choice. If there were a better option, I would utilize it. So I work under these compromsied circumstances.

Overbearing, Intrusive Parents

One might ask the question: "What about the overbearing mother who is always intruding in the youngster's therapy? Shouldn't she be kept out of the room?" My answer to this question is: "Not so quickly." Let us take, for example, the following situation. I am in session with Jimmy and his mother. I ask Jimmy a question; his mother answers. At that point I consider myself to have a golden opportunity for a meaningful therapeutic interchange—an opportunity that would not have been possible had the mother been out of the room. At that point I will say to Jimmy, "What just happened?" Jimmy may respond, "You asked me a question." And I will respond, "And what happened then?" My hope is that he will respond, "My mother answered you." To which I will respond, "Right! And what did you do?" Jimmy may answer, "I didn't do anything." To this I will respond, "Yes, Jimmy, that's right. You didn't do anything. But I believe that you had certain thoughts and feelings when your mother answered my question and didn't give you a chance to answer it yourself. What exactly did you think at the very moment she answered? Exactly what were your feelings at that time?"

Here, of course, I will try to get the patient to express the thoughts and feelings that he probably had about his mother's intrusiveness. It is generally easier for the youngster to do this in the therapist's presence. The patient may recognize that the therapeutic situation reduces the likelihood that the mother will react with severe punitive measures while the therapist is there. The youngster may fear, however, that there will be "hell to pay" when he or she gets home, but the patient also knows that there will be at least some protection in the consultation room. This is exactly what happened to Little Hans, Sigmund Freud's famous patient (1909). As I have discussed elsewhere (1972a), I believe that Little Hans was comfortable expressing hostility toward his father in Freud's presence that he was not comfortable expressing elsewhere. I suspect that he felt that his father would not retaliate for such hostile expression in Freud's presence. Unfortunately, Freud did not direct his attention to this important experience that Little Hans had in his consultation. If the therapist is successful in bringing about such expression during the session, and use it as a point of departure for a therapeutic approach to the mother's intrusiveness, it will have served a very useful purpose in the child's treatment.

As mentioned, the richest therapy is that which provides experiences. When the parent is in the room, there is a much greater likelihood that significant experiences will take place. The therapist should view such experiences as golden opportunities, to be grabbed onto and milked to their utmost. They are the most meaningful aspects of the therapeutic process and they should be cherished. Accordingly, I do not quickly remove intrusive parents from the room. I can conceive of the possibility of a parent being so compulsively intrusive that I would not have the opportunity for such interchanges, and that no living space would be provided the patient. However, this has not yet occurred, and I have been successful in utilizing the situations in which intrusiveness was exhibited as a step toward a reduction of the problem.

The Parent with an Incurable Illness

A rarer, but nevertheless very important situation in which the parent's presence is generally contraindicated, is the one in which the parent is suffering with an incurable disease. If the parent is openly discussing the disease, then the parental involvement can be salutary for both the patient and the parent. However, if the parent is using denial and other related defense mechanisms as a way of dealing with his or her reactions to the illness, then parental participation in the youngster's therapy can be detrimental to the parent. One would not want to have such a parent exposed to the patient's working through his or her reactions to the inevitable death of the parent. Such exposure can be cruel and inhumane. Having the parent present would probably lessen the likelihood that the patient will reveal his or her true feelings because of the appreciation (depending upon the patient's age, sophistication, and intelligence) that his or her revelations may be painful and psychologically detrimental to the parent.

CLINICAL EXAMPLE OF PARENTAL AND STEPPARENTAL INVOLVEMENT IN AN ADOLESCENT'S TREATMENT

Bob and Sally were five and three years old respectively when their parents separated. The family lived in a large Eastern city. Their mother remained in the apartment with the children, and the father took an apartment in a nearby neighborhood. He was reliable, attentive, and provided the children with meaningful parental input. About a year later the father met another woman and a year after that moved to a suburban community. He still remained loyal and dutiful to the children and would take them to his suburban home during his weekend visitations. One day, when the children were about eight and six, the mother appeared at the father's doorstep with the children and announced that she had met a man who lived 200 miles away, was going to live with him, and he could now have permanent and complete custody of the children. The mother explained that the father now had a full family with a suburban home and that he could provide the children with a much better life than she. She said she thought it would be in the children's best interests that she have limited if any contact with them again. And so the children moved in with their father and stepmother. The father's new wife had not previously been married, had married the children's father during her mid-thirties, and welcomed the opportunity to have a "whole family" at this relatively late period in her life.

During the next five years the children did not see their mother at all, but did occasionally receive a Christmas present. Then, she suddenly appeared at the father's home and announced that she wished to visit with the children once again on an ongoing basis.

The father's response was to permit the mother to visit the children, but he absolutely refused to finance their air transportation (which he could well afford) or even involve himself in any transportation to airports if the mother were to pay for flights (which he knew she was ill-equipped to do). Rather, he insisted that if the mother wished to see the children she would have to pick them up herself and return them to his home. Accordingly, for each weekend visitation she would have to leave her home early Saturday morning, drive four to five hours, pick the children up, and then drive home with them. Because she no longer had any friends or relatives in the area where the father lived, most often she returned back to her own home 200 miles away. The stepmother had settled in with this tailor-made family and had absolutely no desire for the natural mother to disrupt her now deeply entrenched lifestyle. She basically saw no place for the natural mother in her or the children's lives and viewed her as a noxious intruder. She had no appreciation that the natural mother could still provide valuable input to the children, her abandonment notwithstanding. If the mother was lucky with regard to the traffic, the trip took all day. She would spend Saturday evening and Sunday morning with the children. Then, on Sunday afternoon, she would drive them back (usually hitting Sunday evening traffic), and then drive back to her home. Thus, a weekend of visitation would generally involve 16 to 18 hours of driving. The father was so intent on punishing his former wife for abandoning their children for five years that he had blinded himself to the discomforts of such unnecessary travel that he was causing his children to suffer.

There had never been anything but an extremely strained relationship between the mother and stepmother. When the mother would call the home to arrange for visitations, the stepmother would not even engage in innocuous amenities, but would immediately turn the phone over to her husband, cooly saying, "It's her." When the mother would arrive to pick up the children, she was not permitted in the home; rather, she was required to honk the horn outside and the children would be sent out. And this situation prevailed during the seven-year period of *rapprochement* at the end of which my services were enlisted. At that point the mother was planning to litigate for more money in order to get some relief from this oppressive visitation program. However, all had decided to try to avoid litigation and seek a consultation outside of the legal process.

During my initial evaluation it became apparent that the children were contributing significantly to the polarization of the mother from her former husband and his wife. Although now in their teens, they were still saying to each parent what they believed that parent wanted to hear. They were exhibiting thereby an extremely common maneuver used by children of divorce. I cannot emphasize this point strongly enough. The vast majority (if not all) children of divorce have a loyalty conflict and utilize this maneuver in order to ingratiate themselves to each of their parents. Examiners do well to make the assumption that it is always taking place, because of the rare situation in which it is absent. And the process does not stop in childhood; it generally extends well into the teens and even beyond.

As a result of these maneuvers by Bob and Sally, each parent was brought to believe that the other was the incarnation of all the evil that existed on earth. After a visit with their mother, the children would tell their stepmother and father what a terrible time they had and how many indignities they suffered at her hands. Similarly, when with their mother they would describe the terrible conditions under which they lived in their father's home. Having no direct communication with one another, the parents were in no position to appreciate that they were being "buttered up" in order to gain affection. This is one of the important ways in which the litigious process enhances and perpetuates alienation. Without having the opportunity for direct contact with the other side, the worst distortions became entrenched and delusions of malevolence are likely to persist. And this is especially the case when the children, from the fear of rejection, feed into the process by their fabrications.

After seeing the suburban family in varying combinations, and after seeing the mother alone (she traveled the 200 miles to my office for the purpose of the interview), I recommended an interview in which the three adults, the two children, and myself would be present. The father and stepmother were horrified at this suggestion and initially refused to discuss it further. The mother, although reluctant, was more receptive. Finally, I was able to prevail upon the father and stepmother to try one such interview and to use experience rather than speculation to make their decision regarding whether or not they wished to participate further. Accordingly, an open-ended interview was set up.

When the interview began it was clear that all the parties were quite tense. I believe that the parents were tense because they anticipated the worst kinds of treatment from each other. And the children were tense, I suspected, because they realized that their lying would be disclosed. My experience has been that the best way to "smoke out" these polarizing maneuvers by the children is to conduct a family interview. In fact, it is extremely difficult to get the parents to see how they are being manipulated without such a meeting. Within about a half hour everyone became more relaxed and the adults began to appreciate that they were not indeed the ogres that they had viewed one another to be. In the ten years that the stepmother and mother knew one another, they had never really had one civil conversation. The actual experience for each one of being in the same room and seeing that the other was a human being, without horns, without fire or poison spitting from her mouth, was successful in correcting their distortions. Years of separate psychotherapy would not have accomplished this. I would go further and state that each of these parties could have been in psychoanalysis five times a week and not have accomplished as much on this particular problem as they did in the first hour of this meeting. Next they came to appreciate that they had been "buttered up" by the children. Interestingly, as is often the case, the children showed little regret over the troubles their fabrications had caused.

In the ensuing discussion the father came to understand that he was so enraged at his former wife that he had blinded himself to the distress he was causing his children by insisting that the mother assume all the travel obligations of visitation. Accordingly, he agreed to drop the children off at the airport close to his home and to pick them up there on their return and the mother would pick the children up at the airport on their arrival to her home and drop them off at the airport in order for them to return back to their father. The father decided as well to contribute to the financing of the air travel. As the meeting drew to a close the father stated that he thought it had been quite useful and invited his former wife to join him, his wife, and the children at his home for further discussion. All agreed that this could prove useful, but the stepmother (as was expected) was somewhat reluctant for this meeting in her home. The result was a resolution of the primary problems without resorting to adversary litigation. I am convinced that had this family not chosen this more judicious course, they would have involved themselves in extremely expensive and psychologically draining litigation—which would have been far less likely to have solved their difficulties.

There is another important principle demonstrated here. It relates to a phenomenon that may initially appear to the reader to be totally unrelated to the issue of parental involvement in an adolescent's treatment, but is very much applicable. I am referring to the appreciation by airport officials that when hijackers have seized a plane and threaten destruction of the passengers if their demands are not complied with, it behooves the airport officials to stall the hijackers as much as possible. They recognize that the longer they are successful in keeping the hijackers on the ground, the less the likelihood they will murder the hostages. They know that, at the time that the plane is seized, the passengers are generally viewed as subhuman creatures—as people of a different race, religion, or creed—whose lives are not worth very much. If the hijackers and the passengers are required to remain together for long periods, it is likely that they will get to speak with one another—language barriers notwithstanding.

Gradually the hijackers will recognize similarities between the hostages and their loved ones at home. They are likely to compare the passengers with relatives and friends at home. One woman reminds the hijacker of his sister, another of his grandmother. Some children remind him or his nieces and nephews. And another gentleman reminds him of his grandfather. Ultimately, the hijackers may come to appreciate that all human beings, all over the world—regardless of race, religion, or creed—basically want very similar things for themselves and their families. Specifically, they want their children to grow up physically healthy, reasonably educated, with the opportunity to become self-sufficient, independent human beings capable of supporting themselves and their families with a reasonable degree of comfort and freedom from fear and disease. They come to appreciate that everyone has aspirations and disappointments, hopes realized and hopes dashed. Once such familiarity has been experienced, the hostages are no longer viewed as vile and worthless creatures, and it becomes far less probable that they will be slaughtered. The same phenomenon was operative in the group family session described above and is one of the ways in which joint interviews with a youngster's family can achieve results that may be difficult—if not impossible—to obtain in individual treatment.

DIRECT TREATMENT OF PARENTS

On occasion, parents ask me about marital counseling and even individual therapy for one or both of them. When I was in training, I was taught that such an arrangement *must* compromise the adolescent's treatment. The theory was that it was only via an *exclusive* relationship with the patient, one in which other parties had no significant involvement with the therapist, that therapy could possibly hope to succeed. I consider this position to be one of the great myths of psychotherapy. I believe that just the opposite is true. Therapeutic work with the parents entrenches more deeply the therapist's relationship with them and enables him or her to be in better touch with factors going on in the home that are contributing to and perpetuating the patient's illness. In addition, therapeutic work with the parents is a statement of their commitment to the therapist and this will increase the likelihood that they will be genuinely supportive of their youngster's work in treatment. The ideal relationship that the therapist should have with the family is that he or she be viewed as the "family therapist." I am not using the term here to refer to the situation in which the therapist only does traditional family therapy in which the whole family is seen together on an ongoing basis. Rather, I can use the term to refer to a situation in which the therapist sees one or more of the family members, in any combination whatsoever, as long as treatment is warranted. When an individual no longer considers therapy to be warranted, the person can discontinue the treatment. However, this does not preclude reinvolvement in treatment if warranted. Life is such that new stresses will inevitably occur, stresses that might warrant reentrance into therapy. Last, working directly with parents provides the therapist with even more information about the adolescent's environment than the therapist would have without such intensive involvement. And this cannot but be immensely beneficial to the adolescent patient's therapy.

REFERENCES

Aichorn, A. (1925). *Wayward Youth.* New York: The World Publishing Co., 1954.

Alexander, F. (1950). Analysis of the therapeutic factors in psychoanalytic treatment. *Psychoanalytic Quarterly* 19:482–500.

Alexander, F., and French, T. (1946). The principle of corrective emotional experience. In *Psychoanalytic Therapy: Principles and Application*, pp. 66–70. New York: Ronald Press.

American Handbook of Psychiatry (1974). New York: Basic Books.

American Psychiatric Association Task Force Report (1973). *Behavior Therapy in Psychiatry,* Report No. 5. Washington, DC: American Psychiatric Association.

Axline, V. M. (1947). *Play Therapy.* Boston: Houghton Mifflin.

——— (1964). *Dibs in Search of Self.* Boston: Houghton Mifflin.

Basic Handbook of Child Psychiatry (1979). New York: Basic Books.

Berkovitz, I. H. (1972). *Adolescents Grow in Groups.* New York: Brunner/Mazel.

Berkovitz, I. H., and Sugar, M. (1975). Indications and contraindications for adolescent group psychotherapy. In *The Adolescent in Group and Family Therapy,* ed. M. Sugar, pp. 3–26. New York: Brunner/Mazel.

Ellis, A. (1963). *Reason and Emotion in Psychotherapy.* New York: Lyle Stuart.

Freud, A. (1965). *Normality and Pathology in Childhood.* New York: International Universities Press.

Freud, S. (1900). The Interpretation of Dreams. In *The Basic Writings of Sigmund Freud,* ed. A. A. Brill, pp. 183–549. New York: Random House, 1938.

——— (1909). A phobia in a five-year-old boy. In *Collected Papers,* vol. 3, pp. 149–209. New York: Basic Books, 1959.

Freud, S., and Breuer, J. (1895). *Studies in Hysteria.* New York: Basic Books, 1957.

Gardner, R. A. (1968). Book review, Ginott, H. G. (1965). In *Between Parent and Child.* New York: Macmillan. Reviewed in *Psychology Today* 1(12):15–17.

——— (1971). *Therapeutic Communication with Children: The Mutual Storytelling Technique.* Northvale, NJ: Jason Aronson.

——— (1972a). Little Hans--the most famous boy in the child psychotherapy literature. *International Journal of Child Psychotherapy* 1(4):24–50.

——— (1972b). *Dr. Gardner's Stories About the Real World, Vol. I.* Cresskill, NJ: Creative Therapeutics.

——— (1973a). *Understanding Children: A Parents' Guide to Child Rearing.* Cresskill, NJ: Creative Therapeutics.

——— (1973b). *The Talking, Feeling, and Doing Game.* Cresskill, NJ: Creative Therapeutics.

——— (1973c). Treatment of the projected self. *International Journal of Child Psychotherapy* 2(1):7–12.

——— (1976). *Psychotherapy with Children of Divorce.* Northvale, NJ: Jason Aronson.

——— (1977). *The Parents Book About Divorce.* New York: Doubleday.

——— (1979). *The Parents Book About Divorce.* New York: Bantam.

——— (1984). *Separation Anxiety Disorder: Psychodynamics and Psychotherapy.* Cresskill, NJ: Creative Therapeutics.

——— (1989). The use of the home video cassette recorder in psychotherapy. In *The Psychotherapeutic Techniques of Richard A. Gardner, Rev. Ed.* Cresskill, NJ: Creative Therapeutics, 1992.

——— (1999a). *Developmental Conflicts and Diagnostic Evaluation in Adolescent Psychotherapy.* Northvale, NJ: Jason Aronson.

——— (1999b). *Psychotherapy of Antisocial Behavior and Depression in Adolescence.* Northvale, NJ: Jason Aronson.

Haley, J. (1973). *Uncommon Therapy: The Psychiatric Techniques of Milton H. Erikson, M.D.* New York: Norton.

Holmes, D. J. (1964). *The Adolescent in Psychotherapy.* Boston: Little, Brown.

Johnson, A. M. (1949). Sanctions for superego lacunae of adolescents. In *Searchlights on Delinquency,* ed. K. R. Eissler, pp. 225–245. New York: International Universities Press.

——— (1959). Juvenile delinquency. In *American Handbook of Psychiatry, Vol. I,* ed. S. Arieti, pp. 844–849. New York: Basic Books.

Kessler, J. W. (1966). *Psychopathology of Childhood.* Englewood Cliffs, NJ: Prentice-Hall.

Klein, M. (1932). *The Psychoanalysis of Children.* London: Hogarth.

Kraft, I. A. (1979). Group Therapy. In *Basic Handbook of Child Psychiatry,* ed. S. I. Harrison, vol. III, pp. 159–180. New York: Basic Books.

Lippman, H. S. (1962). *Treatment of the Child in Emotional Conflict.* New York: McGraw-Hill.

Mullahy, P. (1970). *Psychoanalysis and Interpersonal Psychiatry.* Northvale, NJ: Jason Aronson.

Psychiatry (1986). New York: Basic Books.

Riddle, M. A., and Vitulano, L. A. (1986). Group psychotherapy for children and adolescents. In *Psychiatry, Vol. VI: Child Psychotherapy,* ed. A. J. Solnit, D. J. Cohen, and J. E. Schowalter, pp. 469–475. New York: Basic Books.

Strupp, H. H. (1975). Psychoanalysis, "Focal psychotherapy," and the nature of the therapeutic influence. *Archives of General Psychiatry* 32:127–135.

Stubblefield, R. L. (1967). Sociopathic personality disorders I: Antisocial and dyssocial reactions. In *Comprehensive Textbook of Psychiatry,* ed. A. M. Freedman and H. I. Kaplan, pp. 1420–1424. Baltimore: Williams & Wilkins.

Sullivan, H. S. (1953). *The Interpersonal Theory of Psychiatry.* New York: Norton.

Thomas, A., Chess, S., et al. (1963). *Behavioral Individuality in Early Childhood.* New York: New York University Press.

Yalom, I. D. (1975). *The Theory and Practice of Group Psychotherapy.* New York: Basic Books.

AUTHOR INDEX

Aichorn, A., 65
Alexander, F., 71, 246
Allen, W., 20
Aristotle, 30
Axline, V. M., 60

Berkovitz, I. H., 257
Breuer, J., 77
Burns, R., 29

Chess, S., 265

Dosney, W., 34, 40

Ellis, A., 76–77
Erikson, M., 31

French, T., 71, 246
Freud, A., 68, 75
Freud, S., 77, 94–95, 100, 186, 187, 188, 189, 190, 284

Gardner, R. A., 50, 74, 79, 81, 102, 183, 216, 251, 266, 284

Haley, J., 31
Holmes, D. J., 45, 47, 137, 272

Johnson, A. M., 77, 266
Jung, C., 189

Kessler, J. W., 265
Klein, M., 68
Kraft, I. A., 257

Lippman, H. S., 264
Lorenzini, C., 34

Mullahy, P., 81

Niebuhr, R., 268

Piaget, J., 49

Riddle, M. A., 257
Rogers, C., 60

Shakespeare, W., 20, 30–31

Strupp, H. H., 28, 75
Stubblefield, R. L., 266
Sugar, M., 257
Sullivan, H. S., 80

Thomas, A., 265

Vitulano, L. A., 257

Yalom, I. D., 249, 257

SUBJECT INDEX

Abortion, 124–125, 256–257
Abstractions, conceptualizations, 31
Academic inhibition, 274–275
Acquired immune deficiency syndrome (AIDS), 124
Alcohol abuse, 17, 87–89, 91, 120–121, 139–147, 236
Alternative modes of adaptation, 81–82
Anger, acting out of, 47, 53, 96, 164, 248, 256, 269, 272, 282
Anger inhibition, 77, 80, 158, 164, 177, 189, 199–200, 209, 211–212
Anorexia/bulimia, 246
Antidepressants, 141
Antisocial behavior, 111–112, 120–121, 123, 172, 173–178, 183–185, 235, 237, 249, 266, 268, 270
Anxiety, 187, 188, 190, 197, 199, 201
Autism, 237

Behavior modification, 119–120, 231, 232, 254–256
Blame, 107–108
Boasting, 80
"Brainwashing," 19 (*See also* Parental alienation syndrome)
Bribery, 4, 80
Brief psychotherapy (*See* Time-limited psychotherapy)
"Brief therapy" (*See* Time-limited psychotherapy)

Cerebral palsy, 214, 221–222
Cigarettes, cigarette companies, 250
Client-centered therapy, 60–63
Coercion, 45, 46, 102, 126, 130, 132–133, 245, 262–263

Cognitive therapy (*See* Correction of distortions)
Colleges, 24–26, 117, 174, 176, 229–230, 247, 274–276
Competition, 81
Condensation, 188, 201, 205 (*See also* Dreams, dream psychoanalysis)
Confidentiality, 85–97, 244, 246, 256–257
Conscience (*See* Guilt)
Conscious control, 117–119
"Consensual validation," 80
Contracts, 111–112
Correction of distortions, 76–77, 78–81, 231, 232, 216–219, 280–281
Corrective emotional experience, 71–72
Curiosity, 182, 184–186, 167–168

Delusions of invulnerability, 103, 108, 122
Denial, 81, 183–184, 284–291
Dependency, 104, 114–115, 143, 157–158, 176–177, 133, 276–277
Depression, 17, 18, 61–62, 87–89
Deprivation of parental affection, 56–60, 112, 139, 199
Desensitization, 197, 232, 254–256 (*See also* Behavior modification)
Discipline and punishment, 119, 132–133, 270–274
Divorce, 128, 138
Door-to-door salesman principle, the, 128
Dreams, dream psychoanalysis, 106, 126, 186–230, 234, 266, 280
Drug abuse, 91, 139–147, 235, 236, 237, 246–247, 268, 274

Educational aspects of therapy, 28–34, 74–82
Encounter groups, 241
Experiences in treatment, 32–34, 69, 71, 94, 96, 112, 220–221, 233, 247, 279, 284 (*See also* Corrective emotional experience)

Fantasy, fantasizing, 223–230, 247
Fear, panic, 76–77, 128–135, 200–202
Fees, 264
Fight vs. flight, 254–265
Food, 112, 188
Foreign boy question, the, 212–213
Free association and the "blank screen," 72–73, 82, 102–103, 154, 189, 212–213
Frustration tolerance, 402–402, 406

Gestalt therapy, 231, 232
Grandparents, 58
Group therapy, 91, 99, 121, 130, 231–257
Guilt, guilt-evoking mechanisms, 34–40, 77–78, 80, 108, 126, 132, 133–135, 160, 169–170, 173–175, 187, 190, 197, 199, 201, 206, 209, 210, 212, 228–229, 251, 261, 264–265

Hallucinogens, 141, 146
Homicide, 86, 87–90, 91, 96, 115, 164, 171–172, 193
Homosexuality, 18, 136, 192–197
Honesty, 159–160, 162–163, 280–281
Hospitals, hospitalization, 118, 197, 248
Humor, 133–135, 172–173

Idealization of the therapist, 14–15, 154
Identification: with peers, 234; with the therapist, 15–21, 43, 72–74, 158–159, 160, 172–173, 184–186

Identity, identity confusion, 92, 101
Idolization of the therapist, 14–15
Insight, 33–34, 44–46, 54, 69, 71, 117
Intellectual impairment, 237
Intimacy, 82–84, 116

Jail, 118, 191

Kidney transplant principle, the, 107–108

Ladies first principle, the, 135–136
Learning disabilities (*See* Neurologically based learning disabilities
Lesbianism (*See* Homosexuality)
"Lessons in constructive living," 75–76, 233–234, 252
Little Hans, 94–95, 284
Loyalty conflicts, 285–290
Lying, 8, 18–19, 93, 126, 134, 160, 190–192, 280–281

Malpractice, 88, 90
Masturbation, 94, 124, 127, 134, 168–169
Metaphor, 30–31, 116
Military services and combat, 26–28, 110, 174, 197, 207
Motivation for treatment, 44–46, 100–102, 165–168, 170–171, 182–186

Neuroleptics, 141
Neurologically based learning disabilities, 81, 237
Nightmares, 188, 198–200
Nondirective therapy, 60–63

Obsessive-compulsive behavior, 260–261
Oedipus complex, 17–18, 100, 187

Panic (*See* Fear)
Parental overprotection, 266
Peers, 4, 7–8, 233–234, 249–251
Pinocchio, 34–40
Praise of patients, 71
Pregnancy, 91, 124, 127, 256–257
Projection, 49–50, 63–65, 72, 154, 199, 201, 205, 222–223, 224
Promiscuity, 6–7, 91, 120, 138–139
Psychopathy, sociopathy, 38, 48, 190–192
Psychosis, 118, 119, 139–147, 171–172, 237, 282 (*See also* Schizophrenia, Autism)
Punishment (*See* Discipline and punishment)

Rational-emotive psychotherapy, 76–77
Rationalization, 46, 102, 118, 128, 244
Reaction formation, 196
Rebellion, 101, 120–121
Reflected appraisals, 81
Repression, 73, 93–94, 100, 111 (*See also* Dreams, dream psychoanalysis)
Resistance, 45, 46, 106, 113, 126, 202, 216–220, 262–263
Respect, 14 15, 155
Revelation of the therapist's deficiencies, 82–84, 117, 156–157, 160–163
Role playing, role models, 232, 253, 255–256
Romantic love, 192–197
Rorschach test, 21

Sadism, 24–26, 281
Sarcasm, use of in therapy, 128, 133–135, 250
Schizoid personality disorder, 211
Schizophrenia, 211

Scholastic Aptitude Test (SAT), 229, 253–254, 275
Schools, 16–17, 118–119, 157–158, 166–168, 170–171, 183, 184, 185–186, 276 (*See also* Colleges)
Secondary elaboration, 188 (*See also* Dreams, dream psychoanalysis
Secrets, 93
"Self-actualization," 60–61, 73
Self-assertion, 7, 74, 94, 157–159, 162–163, 175, 177, 227–230, 253–254
Self-esteem, self-worth, 45, 47, 49, 58, 78, 80, 81, 84–86, 111–113, 125, 135, 166–167, 170–171, 176–177, 227, 247, 251–254, 273
Separation anxiety disorder, 266
Sexual abuse, 250–251
Sexual behavior and disorders, 91, 122–139, 145, 168–170, 172–173, 189, 201–202, 206, 213–230, 235, 250–251 (*See also* Homosexuality, Masturbation, Pregnancy, Sexual abuse, Sexually transmitted diseases)
Sexually transmitted diseases, 134 (*See also* Acquired immune deficiency syndrome)
Shame stage, shame, 37
Shyness, 131–133, 213–230, 241, 253
Sibling rivalry, siblings, 241–243
Silence, 93, 104–108, 234, 262
Sleep disorders, 188
Smoking (*See* Cigarettes)
Socioeconomic deprivation, 266
Sports, 4–35
Statue of Liberty syndrome, the, 22–23, 26, 54
Stealing, 93
Stepfamily, stepparents, 285–290
Sublimation, 120, 172–173
Suicide, 86, 89, 90, 91, 96, 172, 228
Superego, 77, 100, 178, 209
Suppression, 92, 111, 209
Symbolization, 188, 189, 198–200, 210, 205–212 (*See also* Dreams, dream psychoanalysis)
Sympathy, empathy, 21–22, 33, 48–49, 50, 102, 108, 130–131, 160, 162, 171, 172, 173–175, 177–178

Talking, Feeling, and Doing Game, The, 83, 102, 149–179, 182–186, 240
Teachers, 275
Termination, 288
Time-limited psychotherapy, 10–12
Transactional analysis, 232, 233
Transference, transference neurosis, 67–71, 72, 278–279
Truancy, 93

"Unconditional positive regard," 58, 60–63

Values, 16–21, 72–74, 113–114, 123–128
Vicarious gratification, 266
Videotapes, 9–10, 182, 216–230

Work, work ethic, 7, 157, 158–159, 167–168, 173–175